ROUTLEDGE LIBRARY EDITIONS: JEWISH HISTORY AND IDENTITY

Volume 2

JEWISH LIFE IN MODERN BRITAIN

JEWISH LIFE IN MODERN BRITAIN

Edited by
JULIUS GOULD AND SHAUL ESH

LONDON AND NEW YORK

First published in 1964 by Routledge & Kegan Paul

This edition first published in 2020
by Routledge
2 Park Square, Milton Park, Abingdon, Oxon OX14 4RN

and by Routledge
52 Vanderbilt Avenue, New York, NY 10017

Routledge is an imprint of the Taylor & Francis Group, an informa business

© 1964 Board of Deputies of British Jews

All rights reserved. No part of this book may be reprinted or reproduced or utilised in any form or by any electronic, mechanical, or other means, now known or hereafter invented, including photocopying and recording, or in any information storage or retrieval system, without permission in writing from the publishers.

Trademark notice: Product or corporate names may be trademarks or registered trademarks, and are used only for identification and explanation without intent to infringe.

British Library Cataloguing in Publication Data
A catalogue record for this book is available from the British Library

ISBN: 978-0-367-44247-7 (Set)
ISBN: 978-1-00-300850-7 (Set) (ebk)
ISBN: 978-0-367-46472-1 (Volume 2) (hbk)
ISBN: 978-0-367-46478-3 (Volume 2) (pbk)
ISBN: 978-1-00-302896-3 (Volume 2) (ebk)

Publisher's Note
The publisher has gone to great lengths to ensure the quality of this reprint but points out that some imperfections in the original copies may be apparent.

Disclaimer
The publisher has made every effort to trace copyright holders and would welcome correspondence from those they have been unable to trace.

JEWISH LIFE
IN MODERN BRITAIN

*Papers and Proceedings of a Conference
held at University College London on
1st and 2nd April, 1962, by the Institute
of Contemporary Jewry of the Hebrew University,
Jerusalem, under the auspices of the
Board of Deputies of British Jews*

Edited by
JULIUS GOULD *and* SHAUL ESH

ROUTLEDGE & KEGAN PAUL
LONDON

*First published 1964
by Routledge & Kegan Paul Limited
Broadway House, 68–74, Carter Lane
London, E.C.4*

*Printed in Great Britain
by Cox & Wyman Limited
London, Fakenham and Reading*

© *Board of Deputies of British Jews 1964*

*No part of this book may be reproduced
in any form without permission from
the publisher, except for the quotation
of brief passages in criticism*

Foreword

SIR BARNETT JANNER, M.P.

IT gives me great pleasure to introduce this volume on behalf of the Board of Deputies of British Jews. The Board was proud to be one of the two bodies which sponsored the two-day conference out of which the book has come.

It was Professor Moshe Davis who made the first approaches from our co-sponsors, the Institute of Contemporary Jewry at the Hebrew University, Jerusalem. He came to see me about arranging a conference under the auspices of the Board and discussed the project with my wife as Chairman of the Education Committee and myself. I told him that I was sure the Hon. Officers and the Board as a whole would readily fall in with the proposal, and so it was.

Professor Davis, as all who know him will agree, has many admirable characteristics and particularly the dynamic energy and speed of operation which is typical of his American origin. He also shows a fertility of ideas which is characteristic of the Israelis among whom he is now exercising his talents as the Head of the Institute of Contemporary Jewry. In two or three short stays in this country he managed to see a number of distinguished scholars in sociology and history and bring them to share his enthusiasm.

In my days as a student, history was more a record of the distant past than knowledge of the happenings which were shaping my life or the lives of my contemporaries. I have since got used to the idea of history as an approach to events of the day; and to methods of social research designed to make available a full and accurate record of the present.

I often feel what a pity it is that the growing generation in Israel is often unacquainted with developments and situations among Jews in countries outside Israel. This, to some extent, is matched by a corresponding lack of knowledge on the part of the Jews in the Diaspora about social developments in Israel. To remedy this situation is one of the tasks of the Institute of Contemporary Jewry.

Foreword

In addition to the traditional forms of academic study, there is the modern method of seeking information and facts by also being on the spot. If you want to learn about the Jewish community in Israel and its ways of life, your best plan is to go and stay there for a sufficient time. If you want to learn about the Jewish community, its situation and the trends of its developments, in any other country, it is equally a good plan to go there and learn directly from the Jews of that country and from those who are engaged academically in the sociological study of that country's affairs.

It was in this spirit that our conference was planned. The conference was the second of its kind—the first having been held in the Argentine a year before. A number of scholars and what for the sake of convenience we termed 'practitioners' in communal work, prepared and presented papers bearing upon the current situation in this country in relation to 'Jewish Communal Organization', 'Social and Economic Structure', 'Trends in Anglo-Jewish Religious Life', 'Jewish Education', 'Topics and Methods of Future Research'—statistical and demographical, historical, and finally one paper on the field of 'Oral History'.

About sixty specially invited scholars and persons of practical competence in the fields covered by the papers joined in the discussion —the discussion itself being as important a part of the conference as the papers upon which it was based. The proceedings of the conference—papers and discussion—are now embodied in a volume to serve as a permanent record to stimulate plans whereby specialists in the appropriate fields may be enabled to extend our knowledge.

Finally, it gives us very great pleasure to acknowledge the characteristic generosity of Dr. Alec Lerner whose ready support helped largely to make the Conference and this book possible.

Contents

FOREWORD by Sir Barnett Janner, M.P.	*page* v
INTRODUCTION: THE THEME OF THE CONFERENCE by Moshe Davis	ix
EDITORS' PREFACE	xiii
JEWISH COMMUNAL ORGANIZATION by Adolph G. Brotman, *followed by discussion*	1
THE ECONOMIC AND SOCIAL STRUCTURE OF ANGLO-JEWRY by Ernest Krausz, *followed by discussion*	27
TRENDS IN ANGLO-JEWISH RELIGIOUS LIFE by Norman Cohen, *followed by discussion*	41
JEWISH EDUCATION IN GREAT BRITAIN by Isidor Fishman and Harold Levy, *followed by discussion*	67
THE ANGLO-JEWISH COMMUNITY IN THE CONTEXT OF WORLD JEWRY by Cecil Roth	93
STATISTICAL RESEARCH: NEEDS AND PROSPECTS by S. J. Prais, *followed by discussion*	111
TOPICS AND METHODS OF FUTURE RESEARCH: SOCIOLOGICAL by Maurice Freedman and Julius Gould, *followed by discussion*	137
ORAL HISTORY AND ITS POTENTIAL APPLICATION by Shaul Esh and Geoffrey Wigoder	155
TOPICS AND METHODS OF FUTURE RESEARCH IN CONTEMPORARY ANGLO-JEWISH HISTORY by Vivian D. Lipman, *followed by discussion*	165
Discussion on *Future Research Studies*	187
PROGRESS AND PROSPECTS: A POSTSCRIPT by Julius Gould	195
LIST OF PARTICIPANTS	201
GLOSSARY	205
INDEX	209

Introduction: The Theme of the Conference

MOSHE DAVIS

Head of the Institute of Contemporary Jewry, Hebrew University, Jerusalem

THIS volume, which records the proceedings of the Conference on Jewish Life in Modern Britain, is the first in the series of conference reports initiated by the Institute of Contemporary Jewry in various centres of the Diaspora as well as in Israel. Like all the other undertakings of the Institute, this effort derives from the profound need to gain world perspectives on the contemporary Jewish situation.

Into the last three decades of Jewish history, centuries of the odyssey, the travail, and the grandeur of the Jewish experience were compressed. But if the happenings of these events loom large in our minds, their implications are unfortunately not profoundly understood. Professor Morris Ginsberg formulated them succinctly in an article in 'Agenda'[1] two decades ago. 'The problem with which the Jews are confronted today,' he wrote, 'is of a magnitude unparalleled in the long history of the Jewish people, for never before has it been world-wide in its significance, never before have the Jews been threatened with destruction or disintegration in so many parts of the world at the same time . . . In short, the Jewish problem . . . is world-wide in scope and deeply entangled in the major issues with which the world is now confronted . . .'

This world-view of the Jewish people is basic to an understanding of the social, cultural and spiritual trends in Jewish life today, even in the context of specific Jewish communities. It applies particularly to the Jewish communities in Western lands, where they live in a variety of democratic societies. Cutting across all these communities

[1] *The Jewish Problem in Agenda*: October, 1942.

are such phenomena as the relocation of centres of Jewish settlement, the physical proximity and resulting inter-relatedness of Jewish communities in the air-age, diversity rather than uniformity as the developing pattern of organized Jewry, the changing role of traditional values in the majority of Jewish communities, the wider acceptance of religion as a matter of legitimate difference between citizens within their respective countries, and the reality of the State of Israel as the living embodiment of Hebraic culture and creativity.

To explore these forces which have been transforming the contemporary Jewish world and to attempt to create a systematic and scientific approach to their study, are the tasks to which the Institute of Contemporary Jewry is directed. The work proceeds carefully and with much meditation and planning, for the architecture of research, like structural architecture, must be based on order and logical sequence. Moreover, such study and planning requires the proper utilization of one of the great gifts of contemporary research —the inter-disciplinary approach, wherein the disciplines of demography, social psychology, sociology, literature and history must all find their proper and co-ordinated place.

There are many serious obstacles to the attainment of the desired standard of research in contemporary Jewish life and institutions. Among them are: (1) the problems of perspective and balance in a field in which we are simultaneously the object and the subject; i.e. the problem of producing a self-portrait of our times in relation to the perspectives of history; (2) the very newness of research in contemporary civilization generally in most universities and the consequent lack of scientific tradition in the subject as in the case of several of the social sciences which have developed in recent decades; (3) the methodological paradox wherein abundant primary source material exists, but is scattered and unsorted, and, for the most part, has not passed the basic stages of scientific assessment; (4) above all, the great changes and fluidity in contemporary society generally and also in the world Jewish community which compel continuous re-ordering and reorganization of scientific data and analysis.

These difficulties are not unique to the Jewish specialist. They are inherent on the very problem facing all contemporary, sociological and historical research. The question Alan Bullock poses so effectively in the Leonard G. Montefiore *Festschrift*,[1] 'Is it possible to write Contemporary History?' and which he answers with equal effectiveness, is being dealt with in ever increasing measure by various schools of *Zeitgeschichte* now being established in many centres of research. It is encouraging to note that social scientists and

[1] See M. Beloff (ed.) *On the Track of Tyranny*. London: 1960, p. 6

Introduction: The Theme of the Conference

historians are learning to work on an inter-disciplinary plane. The success of such enterprise in the social sciences is bound to stimulate a scholar specializing in the study of Jewish life.

Regrettably, these advances cannot be reported as yet for the studies in contemporary Jewry. Thus far, as many of the contributors to this book attest forthrightly, we are caught in the proverbial cultural lag between developments in general and Jewish society. The lag is evident both in the substantive and methodological aspects of contemporary Jewish studies, in the collection of materials as well as in their analysis and interpretation. Regrettably, there is an astonishing lack of basic studies in the field, and the studies are of an extremely parochial nature, that is to say they examine the subject either without adequate reference to the total environment, or to the varying Jewish experience outside the immediate local framework. Moreover, some of the most profound problems affecting the inner structure of Jewish life (e.g. inter-marriage, alienation, cultural assimilation) are virtually untouched scientifically, almost as if we were frightened of the consequences of accurate knowledge.

All this emphasizes the importance of the Institute's global research programme wherein the prime objectives are to establish norms of research in this new and developing field, and to stimulate students to pursue studies in this sphere. However this work should not and indeed cannot be attempted in Jerusalem alone. The scope of the Institute's study is the character of Jewish communities throughout the world, as well as in Israel. Thus it is indispensable to devise a method not only to seek out the fullest co-operation with these communities and their scholars, but also to engage in collaborative scholarly projects which alone can guarantee a balanced and sound basis to the scholarly undertaking.

Towards that end, and, it must be underscored, only as an initial probing into the problem, the Institute initiated a series of conferences in various Diaspora centres. The first of these conferences was held in the Argentine and considered the position, organization and communal life of Argentine Jewry. As a result of the stimulus of this conference, the Buenos Aires *Kehilla* has founded a department for research into the Argentinian Jewish community and several scholarly projects are under way. The second conference was the meeting in London, the proceedings of which are published in this book. The third, dealing with Continental Europe, was held in Brussels under the joint auspices of the Institute and Centre des Hautes Etudes Juives of the Institut de Sociologie at the University of Brussels. Co-operative efforts have also been undertaken on the North American Communities in other areas of the Institute's research programme.

Moshe Davis

The conference, which was so hopefully received by British Jewry, owes its success to many people. Among them in particular I am very happy, on behalf of the Institute of Contemporary Jewry, to express thanks to the Board of Deputies of British Jews, to Sir Barnett Janner, its President, and to Lady Janner, Chairman of the Board's Education Committee, who helped greatly in the realization of the conference. To them, to Professor Morris Ginsberg and to Jacob Braude, Julius Gould, Maurice Freedman, Vivian Lipman and J. G. Weiss we are deeply indebted for their able and effective role in the creation and implementation of the conference programme.

I would also like to express full measure of gratitude to A. G. Brotman, Secretary of the Board, for the work he did as Conference Secretary and co-ordinator of the Scholars groups in London and Jerusalem.

To Professor Norman Bentwich, Dr. Alec Lerner and Sir Ifor Evans, Provost of University College London, we express our deepest gratitude for their advice and assistance in the preparation of the Conference and for the co-operation we received from University College and the British Friends of the Hebrew University. It was with the generous support of Dr. Lerner that the conference came to fruition.

As one studies the records of European communities today, the British Jewish community stands out, by the will of God—as a brand maintained whole after its plucking from the fire, the only community in their part of the world in which the continuity of its centuries has not been destroyed and which continues today into tomorrow on the strength of its own past.

This truth imposes a moral imperative upon us. Those of us whose chosen vocation is scholarship must find a way to explain to ourselves and others the meaning of this historic truth. In this manner scholarship transcends the academic pursuit: it can also serve the needs of the hour. This book is a declaration of trust in the role of scholarship in the clarification of the contemporary Jewish situation and in the assessment of the paths we can pursue for the enlargement of Jewish life.

Editors' Preface

THE nine chapters of this volume contain the papers which were presented at the Conference on Jewish Life in Modern Britain: to these has been added a short attempt to relate the theme of the Conference to some subsequent work and developments. The contributors approach their common subject matter from varying perspectives. We believe that the approaches of the historian and the social scientist are supplemented in a most useful way by contributions from those who are actively concerned with, e.g. Jewish communal organization or education in Great Britain.

When the papers were delivered at the Conference they were followed by very full and informative discussions. What was said at these discussions has been edited and is presented in this book. Many prominent figures both from academic life and from the many fields of Jewish activity in Great Britain took part in these discussions. We feel that their contributions took up and explored many of the issues raised by the Conference speakers. We are grateful to those participating for allowing us to include this material. We would like also to express our thanks to Sir Barnett and Lady Janner, Professor Morris Ginsberg, Professor Moshe Davis and Dr. J. G. Weiss who took the chair at the various sessions of the Conference.

This book is intended as an introduction to the study of Jewish Life in Modern Britain. The subject matter is diverse and, as was emphasized by many of those who spoke at the conference—in many respects—unstudied. It is our hope, as it is of all those associated with this volume, that it will stimulate much further and more detailed work on the fields upon which it touches. Happily, at a time of rapid development of the social sciences in Great Britain, the Jewish community has become aware of the potential value of research in the Jewish social structure and social problems. It may be that this awareness, in part at least, arises out of the growing concern about the future shape and character of British Jewry. It can surely be canalized into very fruitful endeavour, both scientific and practical.

We have prepared (p. 205 et seq.) a short Glossary of the principal Hebrew and Yiddish terms that are used in the book.

Editors' Preface

The views expressed by the contributors—either in the main papers or in the discussions—are their own individual views and should not be taken to be those of the editors or of the Board of Deputies or of the Institute of Contemporary Jewry.

JULIUS GOULD
SHAUL ESH

London–Jerusalem
1964
5724

Jewish Communal Organization

ADOLPH G. BROTMAN

IN the case of the British Jewish Community it is probably more appropriate to deal with the subject of this chapter in terms of 'organizations', rather than 'organization', as the latter word implies some central and controlling body for every phase of Jewish communal life, as was, and to a certain extent is, the position in the *Gemeinden* in some Central European countries. The nucleus of the Community, in this, as in other countries, is the congregation and its synagogue, but the traditional requirements for Jewish life in a community do not end there. Provision must be made for the teaching of children; for the carrying out of Shechita; for Jewish burial; and for the care of the poor and unfortunate. The respective cultural, social and similar organizations and institutions all developed in accordance with the expanding needs of the Community. The increase in number and variety of such organizations and institutions is a reflection both of the increasing security of the particular community in the Diaspora and of the fact that the struggle for religious freedom and civic equality is past and won.

This chapter accordingly deals in sequence with the present position of synagogal organization; the organizations connected with religious life; with charitable organizations; and lastly with a number of institutions of a significant or typical nature.

SYNAGOGUES AND SYNAGOGAL BODIES

General: After the 're-settlement' of the Jews in Britain in 1656, the earliest congregation to establish a synagogue was the Spanish and Portuguese congregation—their first house of prayer being opened in Creechurch Lane in the City of London in 1657, and their existing synagogue in 1701. The Ashkenazim in 1690 established their first synagogue—the Great Synagogue in Duke Street (later Dukes Place), also in the City of London. The Great Synagogue was unfortunately destroyed by bombing during the last war, but was re-established at Adler House, E.1. in 1958.

The earlier synagogues in the provinces were in such places as Birmingham, Chatham, Edinburgh, Exeter, Falmouth, Hull, Liverpool, Manchester, Penzance, Plymouth, Swansea—most of them ports, and all of them providing opportunities for small traders. In many of these the Jewish community has grown considerably as shown by the number of synagogues. In others, such as Penzance and Falmouth, the previous existence of a congregation is evident only in the name given to streets, e.g. Market Jew Street in Penzance, or the location of disused Jewish cemeteries. In the country as a whole new synagogues are established almost every year. They are indicative not only of the natural growth of the Jewish population, but also of a shifting population from small communities in the provinces to the larger towns, and, to a certain extent also, of the movement of the Jewish population from the poorer to the more affluent sections of the town, or to new townships established to relieve overpopulated and congested urban centres such as London and other big cities.

It is estimated that there are about 450,000 Jews in Britain, most of them British born and more than half of them living in London. There are over 200 synagogues in the Metropolis, though some of these might be better described as 'houses of prayer' as they range in size from imposing edifices, with a membership of well over a thousand, to small prayer rooms which satisfy the requirements of two or three Minyanim.

London: The majority of the synagogues in London are grouped together in synagogal bodies of which the largest is the *United Synagogue* (Ashkenazi) established under an Act of Parliament in July 1870. The United Synagogue has twenty-five constituent synagogues; twenty-one district synagogues; and thirty-one affiliated synagogues—these three categories representing gradations of control by the United Synagogue central administration.

Next in size among the orthodox (Ashkenazi) synagogal bodies is the *Federation of Synagogues* formed in 1887, comprising fourteen federated synagogues and forty which are affiliated. The Federation was established to meet the requirements of a section of the immigrant population towards the end of the last century, who did not find the United Synagogue in accord with their own forms and traditions of worship.

A third orthodox Ashkenazi body is the *Union of Orthodox Hebrew Congregations,* established in 1926, representing in the main the orthodoxy of Central Europe rather than that of Eastern Europe and having a number of synagogues mainly located round the

Jewish Communal Organization

parent synagogue of the group—the Adath Yisroel, in the North-East London area.

There are also about twelve independent orthodox Ashkenazi synagogues in London, although some of them are associated with one or other synagogal grouping for burial purposes and other religious concerns.

The *Spanish and Portuguese Congregation of Jews*—the oldest in Britain—still has a place of worship at the Bevis Marks Synagogue, erected in 1701 and two others in West London. Within the last few years an influx of Sephardi Jews from Moslem countries in the Near East and North Africa has made it necessary to increase provision for congregational worship in respect of such immigrants, and a number of synagogues have been established in North and North-West London to meet these needs.

The *Reform Congregation* was established in 1840 as the West London Synagogue of British Jews. There are now six other Reform synagogues in London.

The *Liberal Congregation*, of which the principal synagogue is in St. John's Wood Road, was established in 1910, and there are now in London altogether nine Liberal synagogues.

Provinces: Reform Synagogues have been established in Bournemouth, Bradford, Brighton, Cardiff, Glasgow, Leeds, Maidenhead, Southport, and these, with the London Reform Synagogues are associated in the body known as 'The Reform Synagogues of Great Britain'.

The Union of Liberal and Progressive Synagogues (Jewish Religious Union) has also associated synagogues in Bournemouth, Brighton, Crawley (Sussex), Leicester, Liverpool, Southend.

The Union of Orthodox Hebrew Congregations, the majority of whose constituents are in the London area, have also affiliates in Gateshead, Glasgow, Leeds, Manchester and Sunderland.

There are three Sephardi synagogues in Manchester and one in Ramsgate.

The grouping of synagogues with central administrative control is found to any large extent only in London. In the Provinces, generally speaking, synagogues are, with such exceptions as the United Hebrew Congregation in Leeds, independent synagogues co-operating for such specific purposes as Shechita and cemeteries.

In the larger provincial centres of Jewish population there are 116 synagogues, ranging from two synagogues in Bradford (with a Jewish population of 700) to thirty-eight synagogues in Manchester and Salford (with a Jewish population of 28,000); the great majority of these synagogues being Ashkenazi orthodox. In the smaller centres throughout the country there are altogether seventy-nine synagogues, with Jewish populations varying from a mere handful to about 600 (Portsmouth). A number of these small communities have no ministers or teachers and their survival as entities remains an anxious and continuing problem for the general community.

Although there has been a tendency, sometimes very marked, for the small provincial communities to decrease in number because of migration to larger urban centres, there has also been a small movement in the opposite direction due to war-time conditions. The general evacuation from large urban centres to the country during the war naturally involved the migration of Jewish communities to country places where Jews had not lived before and in some of these evacuation areas small communities have established themselves and are still in existence. Similarly, a number of previously settled communities in such evacuation areas have even grown (Oxford).

The influx of immigrants from Central and Eastern Europe before and after the last war has to some extent reproduced a situation which was more in evidence when the very much larger wave of Jewish immigration took place towards the end of the last and the beginning of the present century. It was then quite usual for immigrants from the same townships or districts abroad to form themselves into congregations because of similar religious background and form of worship, and even to name their synagogues after their original homes, as e.g. the Roumanian; the Vilna; the Warsaw Synagogue, etc. With the more recent influx of refugees there has been a similar but not so marked trend for Jewish organizations from the same countries in Europe to form synagogues for worshippers with the same background. A notable difference, however, lies in the fact that one or two of these newly formed 'reconstituted' synagogues are of the Liberal or Reform type. It is appropriate here to point out that the terms 'Liberal' and 'Reform' in Britain have a connotation different from that in the U.S.A. and other parts in the world.

ECCLESIASTICAL JURISDICTION

The Chief Rabbinate is an office that derives from the original Great Synagogue in London and a few associated synagogues. The Rabbi of these London synagogues gradually became recognized by the provincial synagogues as an authority and a guide on religious matters, and this recognition was progressively extended to include the congregations in the countries of the British Empire—now the Commonwealth. The Chief Rabbi is now referred to as the Chief Rabbi of the United Hebrew Congregations of the Commonwealth. His authority extends not only to the synagogues of the United

Synagogue, which provides the major portion of the funds for the upkeep of the Chief Rabbinate, but also to many of the other Ashkenazi synagogues in London and the provinces who accept his jurisdiction in religious matters and acknowledge him as their ecclesiastical head as well as spokesman of the British Jewish community on public occasions. The Chief Rabbi presides over the London Beth Din which is also maintained by the United Synagogue. The larger centres of Jewish population, Glasgow, Leeds, Manchester, have their own Batei Din for decisions on ecclesiastical matters arising locally. On matters of major religious importance, the Chief Rabbi and the Beth Din are available for consultation.

The ecclesiastical head of the Sephardi community in this country is the *Haham*, who with the Sephardi Beth Din exercises over his community the authority and jurisdiction corresponding to that of the Chief Rabbi over the Ashkenazim.

INITIATION SOCIETY

The Initiation Society, established in 1745, trains Mohelim under medical supervision and maintains a register available for use where the services of Mohalim are required.

SHECHITA AND KASHRUTH

Shechita, the Jewish method of slaying animals for food, is legally permitted in Britain under the Slaughter of Animals Act, 1933, which includes provisions exempting the Jewish method from the general requirement of the Act that all animals should be stunned prior to slaughter. The administration of Shechita, the training of Shochetim and other purposes connected with Shechita are dealt with by the relevant Boards of Shechita which have been set up in all the large centres of Jewish population. On the *London Board of Shechita* there are represented the United Synagogue, the Federation of Synagogues, the Spanish and Portuguese Synagogue, and other orthodox synagogues. The Chief Rabbi and the Haham are *ex-officio* members. The Shechita Boards in the provinces consist of representatives of the orthodox synagogues—both Ashkenazi and Sephardi. Licences to Shochetim are granted by the 'Rabbinical Commission' set up under the Slaughter of Animals Act.

The work of the Shechita Boards throughout the country is co-ordinated by the *National Council of Shechita Boards*, which meets periodically to discuss technical problems that arise in connection with the practice and administration of Shechita.

The *Kashrus Commission* which has the general purpose of supervising the observances of Kashruth at festive gatherings and celebrations in the Greater London area supplies Shomerim for such functions, and also for Jewish hotels at certain seaside and holiday resorts. The Shechita Boards derive an income from a tax levied on kosher meat which covers the expenses of administration of the Shechita Boards, salaries to Shochetim, training of Shochetim, etc.; and any surplus is used for Jewish religious education.

The Union of Orthodox Hebrew Congregations maintain their own Shechita and Kashruth Committee (Kedassia).

BURIAL GROUNDS

In London the big synagogal groups and one or two of the independent synagogues have their own burial grounds and in the large provincial centres there are Burial Societies which carry out funeral arrangements in co-operation with synagogues which are affiliated or have in other ways arrangements for the purpose of interment. No Jewish interments take place except through the Burial Societies. The small provincial centres have often arrangements with the local municipal cemeteries for the use of a portion consecrated for Jewish burial.

JEWISH RELIGIOUS EDUCATION

Primary and to a certain extent secondary education is given in religion classes attached to synagogues or in Talmud Torahs. In London and in the Provinces this form of Jewish education is supervised by Boards of Education. *The London Board for Jewish Religious Education* is responsible for the administration and supervision of by far the largest number of Jewish classes. The Central Council for Jewish Religious Education established in 1946, provides inspection of classes in Jewish education in the Provinces and arranges also for correspondence courses in Hebrew and elementary Jewish religious knowledge for children in isolated places where classes do not exist.

The Reform and Liberal Synagogues have classes in religion and Hebrew, and where such classes cannot be provided, they also make arrangements for correspondence courses.

Advanced religious education is provided in a number of yeshivoth in Gateshead, Glasgow, Liverpool, London, Manchester and Sunderland. At these yeshivoth the instruction provided is probably of as high a standard as anywhere in Europe now that the Nazi holocaust has destroyed the scholars and scholarship of Central and Eastern Europe.

Jews' College which was founded in 1855 has been the training ground for Ministers of Religion who have served not only the religious life of synagogues in this country, but of many throughout the British Commonwealth, and indeed other countries throughout the world. Whilst its primary aim is to attain the highest standards in Jewish religious studies, it provides also secular education of university standard.

Within recent years there has been a marked development in the establishment of Jewish Day Schools—primary and secondary. There have always existed a number of Jewish private boarding schools. An important innovation in this category is Carmel College, established in 1948, which was founded as a Jewish 'Public School' run on the lines of the numerous Christian Public Schools which are a notable feature of English educational life.

CHARITABLE ORGANIZATIONS

Looking after the poor and sick is of course a traditional task of every Jewish community and one of the primary matters of communal attention. Thus in the very early history of the resettlement of the Jewish community in Britain we find records of charitable endowments, not only for the relief of poverty and sickness, but for such benefits as dowries for brides. In the great cities of London, Manchester, Leeds, Glasgow and others these tasks are carried out by 'Boards of Guardians'. The term 'Board of Guardian' was adopted by the Jewish organizations providing relief, from the bodies doing that task among the general public, and although the term has now been dropped from the relief and welfare work of the country as a whole, the Jewish Boards of Guardians still retain that term.[1]

The *Jewish Board of Guardians* in London has developed in the course of its over one hundred years' existence a very wide scope in relief work, and although it has a large income, this, as in the case of most charitable bodies, is never sufficient for its needs. It has erected and maintains homes for the aged; it protects and guides women and young people in need of care; it aids small traders by way of loans to establish themselves in business; it has a boys' industrial department to help and guide them in taking up employment; it has a Health and Convalescent Department, and an Advice Bureau which deals with the numerous personal problems of those who cannot from their own resources materially and otherwise cope with the vicissitudes of life. On a small scale similar work is carried on by provincial Boards of Guardians, and in a still smaller but more intimate way, by the various Ladies' Guilds and Funds attached to many synagogues.

[1] Changed as from January 1964 to Jewish Welfare Board (Eds.).

Adolph G. Brotman

Within the last two decades Britain has become what is popularly known as a Welfare State in which the care of the poor, formerly met by a mixture of voluntary and state effort, has now been largely superseded by State assistance, and the extremes of poverty, and, certainly, destitution, have largely disappeared from British life.

There remains however the need for Jewish Boards of Guardians because Jewish religious requirements make it necessary for Jews to have facilities for kosher food, Sabbath and Holy Day observance and a congenial Jewish environment. Some Jewish institutions, particularly Jewish hospitals which now come under general state administration, still maintain Jewish associations; as for example the London Jewish and the Bearsted (Maternity) Hospitals, where kosher food requirements can be more easily met than in other hospitals under State control. Jewish institutions for the blind and for the deaf continue to exist as such mainly for the reasons already given—the importance of a Jewish environment and facilities for religious observance. The Jewish Orphanage in London established many years ago is still in existence and continues to carry out its beneficial work. Other long established institutions are the Home for Aged Jews, Nightingale Lane, Wandsworth Common and the Home for Jews suffering from incurable diseases where they can spend the last period of their lives under suitable supervision and care.

The influx of refugees from Nazi oppression before the war and in the immediate post-war years have added their own particular aspects to problems of relief, especially for the elderly who were generally too advanced in age to establish themselves economically in this country and for whom provision of old age homes is a crying need still only partially met. An interesting aspect of this particular problem is that a congenial environment requires not only that these old age homes should have facilities for Jewish observance, but that these should also be congenial in respect of common language and common cultural background.

RELIEF ORGANIZATIONS

The Central British Fund for Relief and Rehabilitation continues the relief work first begun in 1933 on the advent of Hitler and carried on for the relief of the various streams of refugees from other countries before and during the war and in the post-war period. Alone or in co-operation with such bodies as the American Joint Jewish Distribution Committee it contributes funds for relief in a number of countries in North Africa, the Middle East and in Europe where Jewish needs exist and where the conditions of the country concerned make it possible for relief work to be carried out.

The Federation of Jewish Relief Organizations, established in 1919, was set up to collect funds for the impoverished Jews in Poland and other East European countries, and as far as possible is still carrying on work in this and other areas.

The international relief organizations O.R.T. and O.S.E. have affiliates in Britain.

The Jews' Temporary Shelter established in 1885 was brought into being to meet the needs for temporary asylum of the tide of immigrants who came to this country, some of them to seek a home in this country and many to go on farther afield to the United States and other overseas countries where they could settle. The work of the 'Shelter' declined gradually after the First World War, and whilst at one time after the Second World War it appeared that as a result of the virtual destruction by the Nazis of European Jewry there seemed to be small likelihood of further East European immigration or need for the services of the 'Shelter', subsequent events and developments, especially in Moslem countries, have again shown the necessity for the continuance of the Shelter, which is in fact in constant use at the present time.

REPRESENTATIVE AND SOCIAL INSTITUTIONS

Institutions and organizations in this category came into existence at a comparatively late stage following the resettlement of Jews in this country. The first and essential requirement of the settled community was to have security in the worship and practice of their religion. When the situation was thus secure the Jewish community was able to turn to other problems; in particular the acquisition of civic and political rights.

For this purpose an instrument was developed known originally, at the date of its foundation in 1760, as 'The London Committee of Deputies of British Jews' and now known as 'The Board of Deputies of British Jews'. This is the representative body of the community which embraces practically every facet of Judaism and Jewish interests in this country. The overwhelming number of established synagogues—Orthodox, Reform and Liberal—elect Deputies to represent them on the Board, such Deputies being elected by democratic procedure for a three years term.

From its earliest years the Board's constituencies electing Deputies were the synagogues, and this, in the main, is the situation at present. Since the beginning of this century the Board has admitted to representation a number of lay institutions having specified Jewish interests, as for example the Jewish Friendly Societies, the Union of Jewish Women, Jewish Youth, and Jewish Student bodies, and the Association of Jewish Ex-Servicemen and Women.

The Board is a deliberative assembly conducting its proceedings on Parliamentary patterns and it meets every month in plenary session to discuss and decide upon the various reports and recommendations of its committees which are charged with specific fields of the Board's work. The Chief Rabbi of the Ashkenazi Community and the Haham are, by the Board's Constitution, its 'ecclesiastical authorities' who have to be consulted when religious matters arise for the Board's consideration.

BOARD COMMITTEES

The oldest committee of the Board, the Law, Parliamentary and General Purposes Committee, keeps a careful watch on Bills in Parliament and proposals for municipal enactments in order to see that Jews are not adversely affected by reason of their Faith. The Foreign Affairs Committee on behalf of the Board deals, either alone or in co-operation with similar bodies, with the problem of assistance to Jewish communities abroad who are subject to oppression or persecution. The Defence Committee was brought into being in 1936 when fascist movements in this country, in sympathy or collaboration with nazi and fascist movements abroad, made anti-semitism a prominent part of their campaign for political power. The present work of the Defence Committee is, in the main, to exercise constant vigilance and take suitable action in respect of anti-semitic manifestations and activities. The Central Lecture Committee has since 1933 developed an expanding educational and cultural programme designed to promote harmonious inter-group relations in the United Kingdom. The Education and Youth Committee seeks as a primary object to promote and further Jewish education and work for Jewish youth. The Erets Israel Committee is particularly interested in matters relating to Israel and in the means whereby—without political involvement—it can further the interests of the people and State of Israel. The Shechita Committee is concerned with the defence of Shechita against attacks and aspersions on its humaneness. The Aliens Committee advises and assists aliens in respect of the laws and regulations which affect them.

The Board is essentially a voluntary association with constituencies embracing the entire Community, and as a voluntary association it has no legislative or compulsory powers. Its representative and authoritative character is recognized by the Government, which in several statutes—the Marriage Acts, the Shops Act and one or two

Jewish Communal Organization

others—calls upon the President of the Board, or the Board as a body, to carry out special tasks in implementation of Parliamentary legislation. There are no Jewish charities represented on the Board, although it has a Charities Registration Committee to register charities which are properly administered, and whose accounts are duly audited. The Board has no party political associations or commitments. All religious trends and Jewish causes are either represented on the Board or have means of giving expression to their views at the Board, which can thus be considered as a forum for the ventilation and discussion of every matter which has Jewish relevance, whether of a domestic or external nature. Apart from its normal functions, the Board has shown that in times of emergency, as for example during the last war, when urban populations—among them many Jews—were evacuated, it could accept special responsibilities. It then arranged in co-operation with a number of functional organizations to ensure that the essential services of the Jewish community, i.e. facilities for worship, teaching of children, arrangements for kashruth, etc., were carried out as far as the emergency situation permitted and to the greatest possible extent.

At the end of 1961 the Board had represented on it:

122 London Synagogues	— represented by	192 Deputies
99 Provincial Congregations	— ,,	139 ,,
7 Commonwealth Synagogues	— ,,	7 ,,
46 Institutions	— ,,	51 ,,
	Total:	389

ASSOCIATIONS, ORGANIZATIONS, INSTITUTIONS, ETC.

The task of co-ordinating the activities of the growing Jewish communities in the big cities has, within the last twenty years, shown the need for some kind of local and representative bodies. Representative Councils have thus been established in Birmingham, Glasgow, Hull, Leeds, Liverpool, Manchester, Newcastle, Nottingham and Sheffield. These Councils not only deal with the local matters of Jewish concern, but meet with other representative Councils two or three times a year at different centres in order to discuss matters of common interest, and where these appear to have community-wide implications they are referred to the Board of Deputies for consideration and suitable action. Some Representative Councils are constituents of the Board and appoint Deputies.

Over the years a number of bodies have been established which are in the main societies of individual members, although sometimes branches and affiliated groups of the societies have been formed.

The first to be established was the Anglo-Jewish Association in 1871, the original purpose of which was to take over the work of the Alliance Israélite Universelle during the period of the Franco-Prussian war when the Alliance was prevented from carrying on its educational and other activities on behalf of Jewish communities in the Middle East and Eastern Europe. From 1878 until 1943 there was an agreement between the Board of Deputies and the A.J.A. for the conduct of 'foreign affairs' by a Joint Committee, but the agreement for joint activities was not renewed by the Board in 1943. The A.J.A. has widened its original objects, which were mainly concerned with endeavours to ameliorate the position of Jews abroad, and is now also engaged in cultural and social activities in the domestic field.

Several organizations in this country, such as the British Sections of the World Jewish Congress, the Agudath Israel and the World Union of Progressive Judaism, have come into existence as branches of central international bodies. The District Grand Lodge of B'nai B'rith in this country is of course linked with the world-wide Order of B'nai B'rith. International co-operation among Jewish organizations is not limited to the British branches of international organizations mentioned. It also extends to the Board of Deputies of British Jews and to the Anglo-Jewish Association, both of which are member organizations of international groupings which have received recognition as consultative bodies at the Economic and Social Council of the U.N.

FRIENDLY SOCIETIES

The Friendly Societies, which were established during the past seventy years, were formed on the model of the non-Jewish Friendly Societies designed, in addition to their social activities, to enable their members to receive monetary benefits during illness or other adverse circumstances; and in the case of Jewish Friendly Societies during Shiva. The Societies have now much less importance and influence than in their earlier years since help in case of need and unemployment, etc., is given by the State under National Insurance, and also because the kind of membership which formerly provided the bulk of the members has now greatly decreased with the improvement of the general economic situation and increasing possibilities of entering middle-class and professional employment. The Association of Jewish Friendly Societies was established in 1915 to promote co-operation among affiliated societies. The total Jewish Friendly Society membership is estimated at 30,000.

Refugees and immigrants who have come to this country during the last three decades have to a certain extent established societies to concern themselves with their particular interests—e.g. the Association of Jewish Refugees, which is almost entirely composed of refugees from Germany and also from Austria, and similar associations and welfare groups of Jewish immigrants from the Baltic, Poland, Hungary, Czechoslovakia and other countries.

ZIONIST MOVEMENT

British Jews have from the earliest years of the Zionist movement played a very prominent part in its progress, especially after the Balfour Declaration and the Mandate for Palestine, when the chief centre for the work of the Zionist Executive in the Diaspora was in London.

The Zionist Federation of Great Britain and Ireland is the oldest organized body of Zionists and has branches and affiliates in practically every Jewish centre in this country. The main Appeal Organization for Israel is the Joint Palestine Appeal, but practically every ancillary Israel enterprise or institution—religious, educational, charitable, welfare, cultural and social has its aid bodies in this country, as, e.g. Friends of the Hebrew University; Bar Ilan; Magen David Adom; Jerusalem Baby Home; Friends of the Midrashia; Friends of the Art Museums of Israel; 'Bridge' in Britain.

The Mizrachi Movement is active in Zionism and religious education, and participates in the Joint Palestine Appeal. The Federation of Women Zionists is non-party and makes a notable contribution to the advancement of education and social welfare in Israel.

YOUTH MOVEMENTS

Numerous clubs and similar institutions provide for the leisure-time activities of Jewish youth. Facilities are generally available for games, sports, dances and social activities of a cultural nature. Most of the clubs of which several were established more than sixty years ago, come under the 'umbrella' organization of the *Association for Jewish Youth*. The Association itself dates back to 1899, and has as a fundamental aim the development of devotion to Judaism and high standards of citizenship. The Association has a representative Religious Advisory Committee, and its activities include week-end and one-day courses for club managers and members, provision of literature on Judaism and the selection of club prayers and readings.

Among general youth movements are the Federation of Jewish Youth Societies, Jewish Lads' Brigade, Jewish scouts and guides. The Inter-University Jewish Federation arranges week-end schools, study groups and Hebrew classes; and it has been helped by the establishment of the B'nai-B'rith Hillel Foundation, well known in the life of American Jewish students. The Union of Maccabi Associations in addition to its cultural programme maintains the interest of its members in the development of Israel.

There are a number of youth organizations whose activities are orientated towards Israel. These include the Habonim organized on the lines of the Scout movement, and groups which have links with the political parties in Israel. The B'nei Akivah movement's influence is most marked in the religious field. There are also youth organizations which stem from the Reform and Liberal congregations.

WOMEN'S ORGANIZATIONS

The Union of Jewish Women (founded 1902) and the League of Jewish Women (founded 1943) have general aims directed to service in the fields of social, civic, educational and general welfare of Jewish women and children.

The Federation of Women Zionists, the Women's Mizrachi Organization, and the Pioneer Women of Great Britain, are organizations for varied aspects of Zionist endeavour.

CULTURAL ORGANIZATIONS AND INSTITUTIONS

The Jewish Historical Society, established in 1893, is an institution which carries out work at an academic level in furtherance of research in the history of the Jews in Britain and in the Commonwealth. Within recent years other institutions have been established with academic aims, e.g. in 1955 the Leo Baeck Institute—an institute for research and publications on the history of German Jewry; the Institute of Jewish Studies, established in 1953 which promotes research on Judaica and publishes its transactions in the *Journal of Jewish Studies*.

The following Jewish Libraries are available for research work: Jews' College Library; Mocatta Library; the Library of the Jewish Memorial Council; the Wiener Library—which specializes in research and material on the Nazi period of Germany and fascist movements generally; the Parkes Library which contains works

Jewish Communal Organization

and studies on Christian-Jewish relations—historical and contemporary.

The Jewish Museum at Woburn House is under the administration of the Jewish Memorial Council and houses a collection of Jewish ritual antiquities, old manuscripts and books particularly relating to the community in Britain.

The Ben Uri Gallery endeavours to promote interest and achievement in Jewish art; and arranges from time to time exhibitions, concerts and lectures on Jewish art.

PROFESSIONAL AND ECCLESIASTICAL ORGANIZATIONS

A number of such organizations have been established, e.g. the Association of Jewish Journalists; National Union of Hebrew Teachers; Agudath Hashochetim; Association of Ministers (Chazanim) of Great Britain.

COUNCIL OF CHRISTIANS AND JEWS

Arising out of the work of rescue and relief of refugees in which Jews and Christians co-operated particularly before the war, there came the proposal that this co-operation should be established on a permanent and wider basis, so as to counter racial and religious intolerance and promote understanding and co-operation in the general life and activities of the country. From its beginnings in 1942 the Council has had as joint Presidents, the ecclesiastical heads of Christian denominations and the Chief Rabbi, and as members, distinguished representatives of both the Christian and Jewish communities. A number of local Councils have also been formed with the same objects as the parent body. The Council continues to make a significant contribution towards the improvement of relations between Jews and Christians and the promotion of toleration and understanding among all sections of the community.

THE JEWISH PRESS

The oldest Jewish journal in Britain, *The Jewish Chronicle*, celebrated its 120th anniversary in 1961. Although its subtitle is *The Organ of British Jewry*, it is in fact privately owned and not the official mouthpiece of any particular organization or section of the community. Undoubtedly, however, it has a big influence on Jewish public opinion in this country and has a very good reputation abroad.

The Jewish Observer and Middle East Review is the successor of the former *Zionist Review*. *The Jewish Review* which has the subtitle of

National Organ of Religious Jewry expresses the viewpoint of Mizrachi.

Local Jewish papers exist in Manchester (two), Liverpool, Birmingham, Glasgow, and Newcastle.

SOME CONCLUSIONS

An attempt has been made in this Chapter to deal with the subject of 'Communal Organization' qualitatively rather than quantitatively, i.e. to describe typical examples of organizations without full enumeration or presentation of their work in detail. This course—even if advisable—could hardly be taken within the compass of what is intended to be essentially a basis for discussion.

Without donning the mantle of a prophet, it is nevertheless possible to observe trends in communal activity and in organization from which inferences as to the future may be drawn. There is for example little evidence of a greater centralization of control of synagogues, or of greater authority being given to the Chief Rabbinate in ecclesiastical matters, than already exists. Quite apart from the separatism from traditional Judaism represented by the Reform and Liberal Synagogues, there are religious elements often referred to as 'ultra-orthodox' which seem to prefer to remain outside the ecclesiastical jurisdiction of the Chief Rabbinate. Nor is there very much evidence of a tendency to fusion or unification of separate bodies whose functions overlap to a smaller or greater extent in the lay sphere. It would however seem to be against the interest of the community as a whole that these differences should develop into a wider cleavage.

It is generally assumed that the drift in religious adherence is from the 'right' to the 'left', but that is an assumption which can hardly be proved statistically. For every example of a 'lapsed' scion of a rabbinical family can be adduced a son or daughter of unorthodox parents reverting to strict observance of traditional Judaism. One can also point to the considerable change that has come over the appearance of certain districts in North-East London, in which looking at the 'chassidic' dress and comportment of many Jews there, one can easily imagine oneself transported to a typical pre-war Jewish township in Poland.

The strength and the continuity of the Jewish community in this, as in other European countries, was maintained before the war by immigration from the great reservoir of Jewish learning and Jewish culture which overflowed from Central, Eastern and South-Eastern Europe. That great store of spiritual and cultural wealth was annihilated in the tragedy of the Second World War and what assurance of continuity there can be must now be secured from our own inner resources. This has been seen and foreseen by both religious and lay leaders of the community, among whom the importance of giving every Jewish child a sound foundation of Jewish religious knowledge is almost an article of faith. Equally fundamental is the realization in responsible Jewish circles that the survival of Jewish communities outside Israel is bound up with the security and continuance of the Jewish State in Israel.

It is these two factors in the contemporary scene which are likely to have the greatest influence in fashioning and maintaining the British Jewish community in the future.

Discussion

PROFESSOR Morris Ginsberg singled out for comment two points in Mr. Brotman's exposition:
'Firstly, as he explains, it is more correct to speak of 'organizations' rather than 'organization'. We must agree with him, further, that there is no evidence of growing unification, at least in the sense of centralization. Jews have always talked at length of unity, no doubt, mainly because there is so little of it. Unity in any case can be overrated. Diversity, individuality, are necessary to vitality. The important thing is to distinguish between those elements in the common life which call for large scale organization or require universal participation and those which are best left to individual or group initiative.

The second point is the stress he lays on the synagogues as the central institutions round which the rest cluster. Looking towards the future, it is clear that much depends on the vitality and survival power of the synagogues. There is a good deal to be said for the view that, without an active synagogal life, firmly rooted in religious traditions, but adaptable and responsive to modern thought, the Jews cannot survive as a distinctive community. There are, of course, many non-religious or secular groupings in the community, but it is doubtful whether these would survive for long if they were not linked in some way with Jewish traditions fostered by the synagogues.

The vitality of the synagogues within, and their impact on other organizations without, are therefore of the greatest significance for the survival of the Jewish community.

Looking first at the quantitative aspect, Mr. Brotman tells us that new synagogues are built every year, but gives no further analysis. It is estimated that the number of buildings doubled between 1911 and 1952—an increase which roughly parallels the change in population. On the other hand, in the period 1952–7 the increase has fallen by 10 per cent and it may be that this indicates a continuing decline. As to membership, Dr. Neustatter in the book *A Minority in Britain* (edited by Dr. M. Freedman), estimated that for 1950 about one quarter of all Jewish men were members of synagogues. A later estimate puts the figures as between a third and a half of all adult men. With this may be compared the proportion of children receiving religious instruction, which is estimated as between 50 per cent and 60 per cent. There is a general impression that religious apathy or indifference is on the increase. It is to be noted that similar statements are frequently made about Christianity. The late Hensley Henson, Bishop of Durham said in 1946:

Discussion

We see in our land tens of millions of men who acknowledge no connection with religion, and, as a result of this, a large proportion of our children are growing up without religious influence or religious teaching of any kind.
(*Bishoprick Papers:* Oxford, 1946, p. 306).

With this may be compared the estimate of frequency of attendance of religious services summarized for example by Carr-Saunders, Caradoc Jones and Moser in their book on *Social Conditions in England and Wales*[1] where the percentage of the samples attending once a week or more is given as between 13 per cent and 15 per cent. An interesting point they make is that frequent church going becomes markedly less common with decline in the social scale.

In the U.S.A., as is well known, there has been in recent times what has been described as a 'return to the synagogues'. This is seen in the steady increase of synagogue construction, membership and attendance. The increase is in part connected with the movement of the Jewish population from areas of 'first settlement' to the new suburbs and, no doubt, on a smaller scale something similar is happening in the larger cities here. Very interesting questions are raised by what is happening in the U.S.A.:

(1) Has there been a decline here in recent years rather than an increase? This, as we have seen, requires further investigation.
(2) What is the religious significance of synagogue membership and attendance?
(3) To what extent are the synagogues, as they seem to be increasingly in the U.S.A., 'community centres'—catering for a wide range of social activities not distinctively religious in character—and do these centres form the basis of a distinctive group life to a greater extent than they do for example in the Christian communities of the various denominations?

On the religious quality of synagogue attendance and membership it is easy to dogmatize. But in fact we have not the psychological analysis in depth which would be required for a just estimate. For the U.S.A. it has been said that the 'return to the synagogue' does not mean a revival of Judaism, but that it connotes 'a religiousness without religion, a religiousness with almost any kind of content—or none—a way of sociability or "belonging" involving no inner conviction or serious commitment'. But this is too sweeping. It takes no account of individual variations. We must distinguish at least the following groups. Firstly, there are people with firm beliefs who find in the synagogues a way of satisfying their religious needs. There are others who have no definite beliefs, but who consciously or unconsciously, are in search of beliefs, of a faith capable of giving them inner strength and a basis for whatever in life is held to have worth or value. Among these there must be many 'hungry sheep who look up and are not fed'. There are, thirdly, others for whom synagogue membership has little or no significance, but is a way of showing their solidarity with the Jewish people and satisfying their desire for identification with it. This

[1] Oxford: 1958. p. 260.

desire is said to be strongly felt in the U.S.A. by the third generation. It would be interesting to inquire whether this is true here also.

Finally, there is the question whether non-religious or secular activities tend to be organized in connection with the synagogues or community centres to the same extent as they do in the U.S.A., and whether there are many important group activities which have a momentum of their own independently of the synagogues. These questions are particularly relevant in the communities arising in the new suburbs. Upon this depends the answer to the question whether distinctive forms of Jewish group life can survive for long if deprived of the impetus they owe to the religious traditions sustained by the synagogues.'

Mr. Armin Krausz argued that Anglo-Jewry is over-organized with very little, if any, co-ordination or overall direction. 'It can be likened to an orchestra with many great and famous soloists attempting to give classical performances without the leadership of a conductor.'

'These great soloists each appear to lay down their own path upon which to walk. All too often, these paths wind their way in different directions and do not always aim for the identical ultimate goal. In addition:

(1) There are in this orchestra also units which are self-appointed and preclude other organizations from entering the field of their activity no matter how important it has become to the whole community.
(2) There are other units which have deviated from the path originally set for them but they still pursue that same policy without reproof and hold on to office as a sort of ancillary to their real efforts to gain national repute.
(3) To a third category in this orchestra belong those units who while holding no mandate at all from the community nevertheless act on its behalf even in moral and spiritual issues.

'Let me give you a few nameless examples. There are organizations functioning, which have courageously taken upon themselves to solve a grievous problem within Anglo-Jewry—that of Jewish accommodation for University students. That problem has since grown out of all proportions. The Board of Deputies has become alive to it, but is unable to establish an effective co-operation even though the problem is rapidly growing into serious dimensions and has far outgrown the ability of that organization to cope with it. This happens despite a unanimous vote of the Deputies for that co-operation to be established.

'Among those in the second category, you will find an organization established to serve Anglo-Jewry as a whole in a most vital role but which today has dwindled down to a representation of some half-dozen or so in attendance perpetuating the fiasco of electing among themselves a national chairman and other Hon. Officers, as a sort of useful ancillary to efforts at gaining for themselves national importance. Modesty alone should compel such people to relinquish their office if they are unable to muster stronger support in Anglo-Jewry or allow a committee of inquiry to look into their affairs and make suitable recommendations.

'One belonging to the third category has already been named. *The*

Discussion

Jewish Chronicle is a most respected Jewish weekly. It is privately owned, and controlled by a few directors, most of whom are members of the liberal community, but who through the mouthpiece of an eminent editor nevertheless insist on appearing as "The Organ of Anglo-Jewry". How can they project themselves in all honesty, to speak for Anglo-Jewry which has no voice in its conduct?

'These inconsistencies must inevitably and grievously harm Anglo-Jewry. It would be useful if a small but effective "Higher Co-ordinating Committee" would be formed from among our spiritual and lay leadership so that they are able to speak with "the voice of Jacob", and at the same time also possess the authority usually associated with "the hands of Esau". A sort of court of appeal, whose direction would be voluntarily accepted by all communal organizations and where necessary, co-ordinate the activities of these organizations for the common good of Jewry.'

Mr. Jon Kimche followed—stressing 'the lack of reliable material' for those anxious to make serious studies of Anglo-Jewish institutions.

Miss Beatrice Barwell felt that the impression might arise that all the organizations listed in Mr. Brotman's paper have an equality of influence on the community. She urged the conference to recognize that the image projected on the community by many of the organizations listed by Mr. Brotman is very variable. 'I would like to quote three examples to make the point: firstly, there is a mention of the Initiation Society. There is no mention of a small organization called the Kosher School Meals Service. Anyone who knows religious life in this community would recognize that both these organizations are struggling, that they are small, and yet that they are fundamental to the continuity and to the permanence of Orthodox Judaism.

'On the other hand, the Zionist movement has been mentioned and it has a tremendous depth of impact on the community—and has a great influence on the masses of Jewry, even if not indicated in Mr. Brotman's contribution. In this connection, the immense Zionization which has gone on in Anglo-Jewry—particularly since the establishment of the State of Israel—has of course given a great impetus to this as has the fact that the Zionist movement through the National Funds—the J.P.A. the J.N.F. and many others—is responsible for the collection of something like £3 milllion per annum for Israel. I think too that the colour of the community has become predominantly Zionist. I must mention also the Zionist youth movements and the fact that Jewish Agency activity in this country makes a powerful impact in the fields of Modern Hebrew, Aliyah, etc. Nor must one forget the influence of the Israel Embassy, the Israel Government Tourist Office, etc.' Miss Barwell agreed that, very rightly, Mr. Brotman had dealt in some detail with the Board of Deputies as the representative body of Anglo-Jewry and had stressed the importance of its work. 'Nevertheless, I think it true to say that the impact of the Board of Deputies on the mass of the Jewish community in this country is very peripheral. The majority of Jews are unmoved by its work although they may benefit from it. When, for instance, the Board of Deputies wanted to make known its work among youth organizations, particularly in relation to

Jewish Communal Organization

Defence work, it found a lamentable ignorance in all branches of the community.

'In any assessment of Jewish life in modern Britain today, one must take into account this factor, and indeed the Conference may well think that a study of the comparative influence of communal organizations might prove a valuable subject for future research.'

Dr. Levenberg emphasized five major factors which should be investigated so far as Jewish communal life in this country is concerned. 'The first factor was referred to by Miss Barwell—What is the impact of Israel and the Zionist movement on the Anglo-Jewish community? This is a very important factor because the influence of Israel is, perhaps, greater than the influence of the synagogues. Israel has penetrated to various circles of young people.

'The second problem is the question of integration. Anglo-Jewry is becoming more and more integrated into the general population. There are twenty Jews in the House of Commons, which is higher than the proportion of Jews in the general population. There is also a large number of Jewish mayors.

'The third factor is that of emigration. The number of Jews who are going on aliyah is about 500 a year. We know that a number of Jews have left this country for Canada, Australia, the U.S.A.—energetic elements who are lost to the Jewish community here.

'The fourth factor is that there is a trend to move away from political life in the community to social life. The emergence of movements like the B'nai B'rith is very symptomatic of what happens in the community.

'Fifthly, what is the influence of Hebrew and what is the influence of Yiddish? Is Hebrew a growing language? Is Yiddish declining?'

Dr. Levenberg also observed that Mr. Brotman had dealt mainly with London; 'It dealt chiefly with what it calls the Anglo-Jewish Establishment. What about the position in the provincial cities? The position in the provincial cities differs from London and this is a point which requires further investigation.'

He also raised the question of the trend among the younger generation. 'We are apt to lose sight of the fact that a new generation is growing up which shows different trends: there are a large number of young people taking part in the movement for nuclear disarmament; people are interested in all kinds of new ideas. There are new Jewish writers; in other words, in my view there should have been a special paper dealing with trends among the younger generation in Anglo-Jewry.'

Mr. Leonard Stein intervened to say how warmly he agreed with the statements made by Miss Barwell and Dr. Levenberg about the importance to be attached to a study of the impact on Anglo-Jewish life by the establishment of the State of Israel. 'That subject does not seem to have been touched upon at all in the programme. It seems to me that if you are engaged upon serious study of Anglo-Jewish life from the standpoint of contemporary history, that should be the central feature of any such study.

'This is not the occasion to enlarge upon the exact nature and degree of the impact of the establishment of the State of Israel on the relations

Discussion

between British Jews and their fellow-citizens. It is a matter which clearly calls for investigation on the part of those engaged in a serious study of contemporary Anglo-Jewish life. There is also the question of the effect of the establishment of the State of Israel on the internal life and social structure of the Anglo-Jewish community itself—on the tests of communal leadership, on the accepted status-symbols, on the attitude of those Anglo-Jewish circles in which Zionism was, not so long ago, severely frowned upon, but in which an interest in Israel is now not merely respectable but positively fashionable. Generally, one would like to see an enquiry into the effect of the establishment of the State on the whole world of ideas in which the Anglo-Jewish community is moving today, and on the direction it is likely to take in the generation following our own.

'It does seem to me that these matters should be among the main subjects of further research.'

The Reverend I. Livingstone next drew attention to omissions. 'Mention might also have been made of, say, the Conferences of Anglo-Jewish Preachers under the Chief Rabbi's jurisdiction, which have been held since 1902, and also of the Union of Anglo-Jewish Preachers, which has been functioning since 1894. This Union was not restricted to "orthodox" ministers, and it enabled ministers with differing views to find opportunities for united efforts whenever possible.' He also commented on the problem of small communities. Much could be done if there could be more co-ordination and co-operation between bodies and individuals that had been suggesting ways and means of dealing with the problem.

The next speaker was Dr. S. J. Roth. He spoke on the role of the synagogues in Anglo-Jewry. 'The reason why the synagogues, in my view, do not offer enough to those who belong out of a sense of loyalty is that they have not extended their activities as they do in the U.S.A.' He also spoke of the community's weakness in the sphere of cultural affairs—though, to some degree, 'this was compensated by the growing influence, over the last sixty years or so, of the Zionist movement'.

Mr. Kaizer felt that the paper should have included some reference to the Yiddish press. Dr. Cecil Roth then stressed the problems which arise from the difficulty of defining who 'the Jews' are. 'It is very important for us to realize that there are large numbers of persons in this country who are completely outside the focus of our sights. We have left a very large section completely out—the Jew who is not a member of any Jewish organization but considers himself a Jew; the Jew who is not a Jew by religion but who considers himself a Jew. A large proportion of Jews in England are not Jews in one sense but from the point of view of the population at large are Jews. I would like to see an investigation of the membership of a synagogue of forty years ago and see where the descendants have gone. What has happened to the Anglo-Jewry of two or three generations ago?'

Mr. Brotman replying to the morning's discussion said that it had for him served the useful purpose of drawing attention to points which he might have emphasized or elaborated.

With regard to the comment that his contribution neglected to mention

Jewish Communal Organization

those Jews who were not affiliated to the Jewish community through the Synagogue, he pointed out that whilst, of course, in any investigation and research work it was essential to take into account those Jews also who were not members of synagogues or otherwise affiliated to Judaism, nevertheless, such unaffiliated people were not organized. His paper dealt only with communal organization, and he could not very well deal with any section of the population until it was *organized*. He agreed that he had given inadequate attention to the Zionist movement in this country, but to a certain extent this was intentional because in his view Zionist activities among all communities had very much in common in their aims and in their impact on communal life.

The Economic and Social Structure of Anglo-Jewry

ERNEST KRAUSZ

A SERIOUS analysis of the socio-economic structure of any community must be based on reliable statistical data. In the case of Anglo-Jewry, however, such information is very limited, and consequently some of the generalizations will be of a broad nature, serving mainly as indications to: (*a*) major changes that have taken place; (*b*) current trends; and (*c*) the important areas to be studied in the future.

The Jewish *entrepreneurial* role in the British economy has undergone an important change in that the part it plays today in the sphere of finance has become relatively unimportant, as compared with its significance in other spheres. Thus, while 'at the turn of the century Jewish merchant banks and stockbrokers dominated their respective spheres . . . Lyons and Montague Burton were small struggling firms and G.U.S., and Sears had still to be founded'.[1] Jewish influence in the City is far less than is generally assumed. This is shown by the fact that there are no Jews on the Board or among the directors of the Bank of England, and—in recent years—of the 150 directors of the Big Five commercial banks, only four were Jews.[2] And even in the field of merchant banking many establishments have lost their Jewish identity through the complete assimilation or sometimes outright conversion of the descendants of original founders. Again, mergers with and control by non-Jewish firms, as well as the existence of many active non-Jewish directors in what we accept as Jewish establishments, has further lessened Jewish influence in the City.[3]

[1] Henry Spencer, 'Advancing Britain's Standards' (7), 'Merchant Bankers & Stockbrokers' in the *Jewish Chronicle*, London, 11th November, 1960, p. 39.
[2] I. Cohen, *Contemporary Jewry*, London, Methuen & Co. Ltd., 1950, p. 107.
[3] 'London's Merchant Bankers', the *Jewish Chronicle*, London, 5th August, 1960.

Ernest Krausz

The field in which Jewish enterprise expanded most in the twentieth century, and where it introduced modern methods of large-scale production and distribution, has been particularly that of consumer goods. Jewish *entrepreneurs* have imaginatively seized upon 'the new needs of a growing industrial population',[1] and the latter benefited by being enabled to purchase good quality and reasonably-priced clothing, footwear, and other articles.[2] Looking at some of the biggest and best known business enterprises controlled by Jews, such as Marks & Spencer, Great Universal Stores, Montague Burton, J. Lyons, Sears Holdings, and City Centre Properties, we find in fact that they cover mainly the manufacture of clothing, furniture and footwear, the distribution of these and other consumer goods through chain-stores, and property development.[3] Jews are also prominent, on a smaller scale, in the following trades: jewellery, furs, plastics and cosmetics.[4] On the other hand, Jewish participation in the basic and heavy industries, in agriculture, and in many important fields such as the aircraft industry, shipbuilding, or the motor-car industry, is insignificant.[5] Jewish concentration in the spheres mentioned is due mainly to the following factors: (*a*) the forcing of immigrants into peripheral trades; (*b*) the seeking of a livelihood through immigrant trades and crafts, e.g. peddling, tailoring, etc.; (*c*) the lesser need of capital and the greater ease of expansion in light industries; (*d*) foreign connections that have proved an advantage, e.g. in finance or luxury trades.

On present evidence it is difficult to state what the proportion of self-employed is in the Jewish population. The lowest estimate puts it at 15 per cent, which is more than twice as high as the national average.[6] The greater desire for economic independence among Jews is reflected by the popularity of such callings as taxi-driving or hairdressing, where prospects for working on one's own account are

[1] V. D. Lipman, 'Trends in Anglo-Jewish Occupations' in *The Jewish Journal of Sociology*, Vol. II, No. 2, London, November 1960, p. 211. See also: N. Barou, *The Jews in Work and Trade*, Trades Advisory Council, London, 1945, Chap. II.

[2] Paul H. Emden, *Jews of Britain*, London, Sampson Low, Marston & Co. Ltd., 1943, p. 476.

[3] See Henry Spencer, 'Advancing Britain's Standards' a series of seven articles in the *Jewish Chronicle*, London, 30th September, 1960–11th November, 1960. See also Paul H. Emden, op. cit. pp. 473–501.

[4] V. D. Lipman, op. cit. p. 213. See also H. Neustatter in *A Minority in Britain*, ed. by M. Freedman, London, Vallentine, Mitchell & Co. Ltd., 1955, p. 129.

[5] See Bernard Harris, 'The People Who Do Not Worship Today' in the *Sunday Express*, London, 16th November, 1958. See also V. D. Lipman, *Social History of the Jews in England 1850–1950*, Watts & Co., 1954, p. 174.

[6] See N. Barou, op. cit. p. 7. See also V. D. Lipman, 'Trends in Anglo-Jewish Occupations', op. cit. p. 213.

good.¹ Thus, the Jewish Board of Guardians found in recent years that the number of prospective borrowers who wished to become their own masters did not lessen, in spite of the availability of employment offering high wages.² Similarly in the professions the proportions entering, for example, the medical and legal fields are very high—the explanations for this being the scope for independence and high earnings as well as the prestige value of these occupations. The proposed careers of Jewish men students at British universities is a pointer here: of twenty possible careers listed, medicine, law, dentistry, and accountancy made up over forty-six per cent of the choices.³

Although there is some information regarding the number of gainfully occupied persons in the minority—46 per cent as against 58 per cent in the general population, the lower proportion in the case of Jews being due mainly to the much smaller number of women going out to work and the relatively greater number of young people continuing their studies after the age of fifteen⁴—there is a complete lack of verifiable data with regard to the distribution of Jews in various occupations. There is evidence of a general nature, however, suggesting that the 'Jewish trades' are being abandoned—a move that has assumed immense proportions in the post-war period. Thus, the tailoring trade in London is losing thousands of workers annually, the main reasons being: (*a*) that the young are not encouraged by their elders to follow this occupation, which holds for the latter memories of long hours, the evils of seasonal work and of the sweating system, and (*b*) that there is the lure of the more 'glamorous professions'.⁵ Even in Leeds with its strong Jewish concentration in the clothing industry, where its earlier economic pattern has been preserved more closely than is the case in London and other centres, a decline had

¹ Ibid.

² See Jewish Board of Guardians, London, 97th Annual Report, 1955, section on Loan Department.

³ See Raymond V. Baron, 'I.U.J.F. Survey of Jewish University Students, 1954–5,' in *The Jewish Academy*, London, 1955–6, pp. 11, 12. With women students the most popular career was medicine, followed by teaching and social work, p. 11.

⁴ Eleven per cent of Jewish women go out to work as against 34 per cent of the general population. The figures for the Jewish population are based on a sample survey carried out between 1950 and 1952, and the comparative figures for the general population are from the 1 per cent sample census 1951. See H. Neustatter, op. cit. p. 125. In 1954–5 Jewish students at British universities accounted for 2.8 per cent of the total number of students, although Jews account only for about 1 per cent in the general population. See Raymond V. Baron, op. cit. p. 9.

⁵ See 'Jewish Tailors Fading Away', the *Jewish Chronicle*, London, 10th June, 1960—containing an interview with Mr. M. Mindel, London Regional Organizer of the National Union of Tailors and Garment Workers. See also The Jewish Board of Guardians, London, Annual Report, 1959, p. 36.

set in.¹ Another example showing the same trend is readily given by furniture-making, where in 1930 it was estimated that there were 6,000 to 8,000 Jewish workers in this trade in East London alone,² but by 1957 it was thought that 'in London less than a thousand Jewish workers were employed in the industry'.³

Having cast aside the traditional Jewish occupations, what lines of employment do young people seek? The Reports of the Jewish Board of Guardians and the Sabbath Observance Employment Bureau provide us with some information, and although this is based on the placing of only limited numbers of people into occupations, it serves, nevertheless, as a useful guide to recent trends. With the majority of those fifteen- to sixteen-year-old boys seeking craft training the most popular trades seem to be hairdressing, jewellery, electrical engineering, motor engineering, radio and television servicing, and the printing trades.⁴ The proportion entering crafts, however, seems to be low, for there is a tendency to seek white-collar work; hence the number of salesmen, office clerks and managers has been very much on the increase.⁵ With the girls the tendency to give up dressmaking or millinery, for example, and to become salesladies, secretaries or shorthand-typists is even more marked.⁶ There is then the surge to the professions where the greatest popularity is enjoyed by medicine, law, dentistry, and accountancy.⁷ It appears, therefore, that what has taken place in the last few decades has been a diversification in occupations, with a very strong accent, however, either on trades that lend themselves easily to self-employment, or on white-collar occupations and the professions.

The changes that have taken place in the economic structure of the community have had notable effects on its social structure. Thus, the economic advancement has brought about a vast decline in the Jewish working class, auguring the possibility of its virtual elimina-

[1] See V. D. Lipman, *Social History of the Jews in England 1850–1950*, p. 174. See also E. Krausz, *Leeds Jewry*, Cambridge: Heffer, 1964, p. 16.

[2] V. D. Lipman, ibid.

[3] A. R. Rollin, 'Jews in the Industry', the *Jewish Chronicle*, London, Supplement: 'Houses into Homes', 25th January, 1957.

[4] See Jewish Board of Guardians Annual Reports, Boys' Welfare and Industrial Committee, London, 1957, 1958 and 1959.

[5] See Sabbath Observance Employment Bureau, Annual Reports, London, 1952–7. See also V. D. Lipman, *Social History of the Jews of England 1850–1950*, op. cit. p. 174.

[6] Ibid. See also V. D. Lipman, 'Trends in Anglo-Jewish Occupations', op. cit. p. 24.

[7] See Raymond V. Baron, op. cit. pp. 11, 12, and as mentioned above. See also H. Neustatter, op. cit. pp. 130–32.

The Economic and Social Structure of Anglo-Jewry

tion. But while Jewish workers have been abandoning the earlier staple trades, such as clothing and furniture-making, this did not apply to Jewish employers. Not only have the latter sometimes emerged as economic magnates in these same fields,[1] but they also remained in very large numbers as owners of medium or smaller sized workshops or factories. The Leeds and London clothing industries serve as very good examples here.[2] Similarly, in the furniture industry, the Bethnal Green area of London, for example, seems to have a majority of Jewish employers[3] and it has been stated for London in general that 'the proportion of Jewish furniture employers is very high, probably fifty per cent; and the proportion of retailers and distributors may be still higher'.[4]

An interesting development parallel to the decline in the number of Jewish workers has been the disappearance of Jewish trade unions: in the first decade of the twentieth century the average number of London Jewish labour and trade unions in existence was twenty-two;[5] during the ten years before the Second World War the average number fell to four;[6] and in the post-war period only one small Jewish trade union still remained.[7] The profusion of unions in the earlier period was due in some measure to the many splinter groups that were formed. Some of these joined other similar unions or ceased to exist when, as often was the case, their most active members left for America or started on their own as masters. At the same time as Jewish workers began to leave the smaller workshops and joined the large-scale factories, the interests and objects of Jew and Gentile became identical and 'this led to the eventual amalgamation of Jewish and non-Jewish unions into the national organizations of today.[8] The important point to be noted, however, is that some of the branches of these national unions, which a few decades ago consisted almost entirely of Jewish members, now have only small minorities of Jews in their membership.[9]

The move into the middle class has taken place with a remarkable speed and has affected the majority of the community. The most

[1] See above p. 28.
[2] See A. R. Rollin, 'Industry & Commerce' in the *Jewish Chronicle Supplement: Tercentenary of British Jewry*, 27th January, 1956, p. 49.
[3] James H. Robb, *Working-Class Anti-Semite*, London, Tavistock Publications Ltd., 1954, p. 48.
[5] See *Jewish Year Books*, London, 1900–1909.
[4] A. R. Rollin, 'Jews in the Industry', op. cit.
[6] See *Jewish Year Books*, London 1929–38.
[7] This is 'the Small Jewish Bakers' Union with fewer than 100 members'. See A. R. Rollin, 'Industry & Commerce', op. cit. p. 49.
[8] A. R. Rollin, ibid. See also E. Krausz, op. cit. Chap. I. pp. 14, 15.
[9] See A. R. Rollin, 'Jews in the Industry', op. cit.

patent manifestation of the minority's greater affluence has been the tremendous move to the suburbs, both as regards the vast numbers involved and the tempo at which it has taken place. The older areas of settlement, such as the East End of London, Cheetham in Manchester, Chapeltown in Leeds, or the Gorbals district in Glasgow, have been deserted. These 'former "ghetto" quarters have changed their complexion';[1] they are in fact losing completely their Jewish flavour. Although we now have the newer densely Jewish populated areas, such as Hendon (London), Prestwich (Manchester), or Moortown (Leeds), which could be regarded as modern versions of the 'ghetto', as well as large concentrations of Jews in areas immediately adjoining these new centres, Jewish migration is spreading to even more distant places.[2] This continual shifting of the Jewish population, caused in the main, not by a wish to get away from Jewish neighbourhoods, but primarily by the aim to rise further in the social scale,[3] has brought about a number of problems. First, there is the expense and time lag involved in keeping pace with these shifts in the provision of synagogues, Hebrew classes, Jewish day-schools, club facilities, and other amenities to meet specifically Jewish needs. Second, we do not know what effects life in 'suburbia' is having on the Jewish family, religious outlook, attitude to Zionism, and generally on identification with the community.

Another interesting aspect of the attainment of middle-class rank is that of prevailing consumption patterns. Some data are provided by a Readership Survey carried out for the *Jewish Chronicle*, which published some of the findings in 1959.[4] Thus, more than half of the households interviewed had a car in the family and no fewer than 86 per cent had television sets. Eighty-eight per cent of the households owned vacuum cleaners and 86 per cent had refrigerators. Only twenty-seven per cent, however, purchased any book the previous year and of these more than half bought novels. 'Only one-tenth of the twenty-seven per cent, i.e. less than three per cent of the whole sample had purchased books of a religious or Jewish character'.[5] Over half the households possessed a gramophone and in their music preferences more than half were interested in classical music, only

[1] See Harold Soref, 'A Demographic Revolution' in the *Jewish Chronicle*, London, 14th March, 1952, p. 21.

[2] See Harold Soref, ibid.; also I. W. Slotki, 'How Many Jews in Manchester?' in the *Jewish Chronicle*, 31st March, 1961, p. 18; and E. Krausz, op. cit. pp. 28–30.

[3] See E. Krausz, ibid.; See also Howard M. Brotz, 'The Outlines of Jewish Society in London' in *A Minority in Britain*, op. cit. p. 148.

[4] The survey was conducted by Research Services Ltd., under the direction of Dr. Mark Abrams. See two articles published in the *Jewish Chronicle*, London, entitled 'Who Are You?', 6th March, 1959, and 13th March, 1959.

[5] ibid.

twelve per cent in crooners and twenty-two per cent in Jewish music. 'Two-thirds had taken a holiday away from home during the previous year (the proportion for the country as a whole is one half). More striking was the fact that nearly half . . . went abroad, which is six times as high as among the general population.'[1] When considering the figures given in the Readership Survey we must take into account the relatively high proportion of middle-class people among the readers of the *Jewish Chronicle*. Nevertheless it does seem that Jews have taken up the twentieth-century mode of life even more than their Gentile neighbours.

It could in fact be argued that most of the changes in the socio-economic structure of the community have been in line with general trends in the larger society, the difference being that these changes in the minority have been more accentuated and have taken place more rapidly. The development of tycoonism and competitive aggressiveness, the strong drift to white-collar work and the professions, the move to the suburbs and upper- or middle-class consumption patterns, are all the products of Western industrialized society. The greater impact that these have had on Jewish society may be explained by the fact that the Jew has exhibited greater adaptability to the changing and unstable conditions, due to his being more thoroughly urbanized and, also to the necessity to overcome his immigrant or minority status. In the sense discussed here the Jew represents the 'typical' individual who has adjusted himself successfully to the economic and social conditions of modern Western society.

A great deal of research has to be carried out, however, in order that a clearer picture may emerge of the socio-economic structure of Anglo-Jewry.[2] Much is needed in the way of factual information and the accompanying sociological interpretation of the facts. The following are some of the areas where it would be useful and interesting to carry out such work:

(i) The effect of industrial and business 'rationalization' on the number and type of self-employed, particularly the 'small man', in the minority.
(ii) Occupational distribution in the community as a whole, with special attention to occupational selection among youth.

[1] ibid.

[2] Most of the examples adduced in this paper have been drawn from the larger communities and particularly from London. It may be noted that over 60 per cent of the Jewish population live in Greater London and 80 per cent in the six largest cities in the U.K. (See the *Jewish Year Book*, London, 1962). This is not to deny the proper place that the socio-economic structures of the smaller communities ought to take in a comprehensive study.

(iii) The economic and social conditions of the community both as affected by and as an effect on the relationship with the host society.
(iv) Social mobility, the rise of a new *élite*, and problems of leadership.
(v) The effects of suburbanization, especially as regards the individual's identification with the community and the maintenance of a cohesive minority group.

Discussion

PROFESSOR Ginsberg opening the discussion congratulated Mr. Krausz on the skill with which he had handled the rather scanty data available to him and on his choice of the areas upon which future studies should be concentrated.

'A solid beginning has been made by Mr. Krausz himself, by the late Dr. Barou, Dr. Neustatter and, from the historical angle, by Dr. Lipman. It is clear, however, that much remains to be done both for the larger and the smaller communities in this country.

'In discussing those matters it is important to bear in mind that there are, in fact, very few comprehensive studies of the social structure of any large scale modern societies and I feel that in this field Jewish writers have in fact often been pioneers. Already in the early decades of this century Lestschinsky and others made serious efforts to classify Jewish occupations and to trace their historical development in various countries. In our own time the difficulties encountered in studying the distribution of occupation among Jews and its bearing on social structure are in part due to the fact that the study of social structure in general has only recently come to be taken seriously. Even so, the fundamental concepts remain vague and ill defined. Thus, for example, the notion of social class is only now beginning to be analysed afresh and in a manner free from initial commitment to Marxist theories. Consider the difficulty of defining clearly what is meant by the middle class, or the middle classes. All that we can say is that they include all the groups which in some sense lie between the upper classes at one extreme and the working classes at the other. But these in turn are difficult to delimit.

'I take it that by the upper class we mean all those who maintain a relatively high standard of life, largely on incomes from accumulated wealth—large landowners and rentiers, big capitalists, high officers and the higher professional men. But the term also includes the hereditary aristocracy which may be impoverished, parvenu capitalists of mediocre cultural level and professional men whose income may not be at all high. There are similar difficulties in fixing the limits of what are called the working classes. No wonder therefore that the concept of the middle classes eludes definition. They cannot be defined by the source of their incomes or the amount of income nor by cultural level or interest in cultural matters. Thus the "intellectuals" who are usually classed as middle class may have less in common with say, farmers, shopkeepers and small employers than those have with skilled manual workers. There is perhaps still some use in the distinction made between the "new" and the "old"

Discussion

middle class. The former includes all those that have sprung up since the development of large-scale industry and who are intimately linked with and dependent upon it—small middle-scale entrepreneurs, small rentiers, technicians and administrators and the lower and middle levels of the professional classes. The "old" middle class consists of survivors of the older methods of production and trade, shopkeepers, small-scale producers, independent craftsmen and others of more recent growth but using similar methods.

'To determine whether Jews are becoming more "middle class" it would therefore be necessary to sort out the many diverse elements included and to compare them with the corresponding groups in the general population.'

Professor Ginsberg was of the view that, despite the vagueness of the definition, there can be no doubt that there has in fact been an increase in the size of the middle classes. 'But this has to be related to the growth of the middle classes in the general population. Professor Bowley[1] calculated for 1931 that if we take 1881 as the base-year, the middle classes grew in the ratio of 100 to 195, while the ratio for the growth of the working classes was 100 to 163 (all occupied, 100 to 163). The detailed comparison made by G. D. H. Cole between the distribution in 1851 compared with that of 1951 shows an enormous rise in the clerical, financial, administrative and professional occupations. In this the Jews have shared in varying degree.'

Mr. Krausz had drawn attention to the difficulty of determining the proportion of 'self-employed' among Jews. 'The lowest estimate puts it at 15 per cent, which he says is more than twice as high as the national average. According to the figures cited by Carr Saunders, Jones and Moser (in their book on *Social Conditions in England and Wales*) under the rubric of "own account" the proportion of self-employed in England and Wales in 1951 shows a decline as compared with 1931.

1931	1,156,000	61 per 1,000
1951	1,073,000	53 per 1,000 i.e. 1 in 20.

'It is clear however that this is a very mixed group including professionals at high salaries at one extreme and small businessmen, gardeners, and charwomen at the other. No doubt there is a similar difficulty in defining "self employed" or "independents" among Jews.

'I should like to say a few words on the term "*élite*" which, though used widely elsewhere, has not quite taken root in England. Its precise meaning is certainly not clear.

'Perhaps the word should be used despite its vagueness to refer to all those who wield considerable influence within any particular group or layer of society. The problem for the sociologist is then to examine not only the influence of the several elites within their group but also the influence which these groups guided by the several *élites* have over the wider community.

'In its application to the Jewish community we may therefore ask what is the nature of the influential elements within the synagogues or other

[1] A. L. Bowley *Wages and Income In The United Kingdom*, Cambridge, 1937, pp. 128–9

associations, how they are recruited and to what extent they are concentrated in certain families? How extensive is their influence outside their own groups? Is there an *élite* in the sense of the "100 families", a sort of hereditary aristocracy directing the principal communal activities? How are these older *élites* related to the new ones due to the rise of Zionism, the new rich and the rise of new intellectual elements?

'Some of these questions have been referred to by Mr. Krausz but I think all the areas marked out by him for future study are of importance in any scientific treatment of the social structure of Anglo-Jewry.'

Dr. S. Prais commented upon Mr. Krausz's remark that 'economic advancement has brought about a vast decline in the Jewish working class, auguring the possibility of its virtual elimination.' Dr. Prais agreed that the community has in the past generation or two taken on an increasingly middle-class character. This could be because of economic advancement, as Mr. Krausz said; but it could also be because the synagogue has not made much attempt to meet and attract working-class elements at a suitable level. 'As a result assimilation may have been relatively greater among the working class section of the community. I should welcome Mr. Krausz's views on this possibility.'

Dr. Cecil Roth felt that the character of the data presented really meant that the paper should have been entitled 'Economic and Social Structure in *Synagogal* Jewry in Great Britain.'

Dr. J. Highet, speaking as a Gentile and a Scot, expressed his appreciation of the opportunity afforded him to attend the Conference. 'I am a member of a small nation whose people are in many respects similar to your own. My people, like your own, have a strong religious tradition and both share world-wide reputation for stable family life, a capacity for hard work, a high level of native intelligence, and a concern for scholarship. There is one further similarity: like the Jews, the Scots are in a minority situation in a predominantly English context.

'In reading the various papers before us I was particularly struck by the repeated emphasis on the need to obtain more information than at present exists on the Jewish community in Britain. In particular, I can well appreciate the difficulties Mr. Krausz encountered, for I met similar difficulties—on a much smaller scale—when, some years ago, I tried to present a picture of the Jewish community in the city of Glasgow. Even the community's leaders seemed not to be in possession of facts regarding the number of Jews in the city, their occupational distribution, total synagogue membership, and so forth—and indeed confessed that they did not know what source might possess them to which they could refer me.

'Mr Krausz points out that the part played by the Jewish entrepreneurial role in the sphere of finance has become relatively unimportant. I would urge that the widest possible publicity be given to this fact, for it is clearly not widely recognized. If I may say this to the present company without offence, the feeling that Jews are especially prominent in that sphere is one of the elements in Gentile suspicion and coldness where these attitudes exist.

'I was struck also by the reference to "the tremendous move to the

Discussion

suburbs"—a development which I can confirm in regard to my own city of Glasgow. Coloured minorities are now taking over those downtown areas of the city—especially the Gorbals district—which were once the main locus of Glasgow Jewry. (Indeed, it is interesting that more recently coloured people who have gathered some money together are now following the Jews in the emigration from the Gorbals: they are going through the same little cycle of social change but are doing so over a shorter span of time than the Jewish community took to accomplish it.)

'This Jewish emigration to the suburbs is one indication of what Mr. Krausz rightly describes as "the move into the middle class". If, again, I may say so without offence, I am certain that one of the elements, in what resentment is felt by some non-Jews to Jews, is the feeling that the Jewish community in the city is "disproportionately" affluent, and however irrational and erroneous it may be, the sneaking suspicion that Jews are mainly engaged in transactions of a questionable kind, or that they exploit the "gullible" Gentile consumer.

'These later comments may seem more relevant to a discussion of Jewish – non-Jewish relations, but they bear closely on several passages in Mr. Krausz's contribution.'

Dr. Highet went on to take up Mr. Krausz's point that the Jew has adjusted himself successfully to economic and social conditions of modern western society, and asked if we are to conclude from this that there are no Jewish 'casualties' in a socio-psychological sense—in other words, that Jews are hardly at all to be seen on the psychiatrist's couch.

He also took up the observation made by Professor Ginsberg, in his introductory remarks, that surprisingly few socio-economic studies of an entire nation exist. 'A small nation not far from here, however, has accomplished this, not just once but twice and is at present engaged in a third. I refer to *The Statistical Account of Scotland* under the guidance and editorship of Sir John Sinclair, published in the late eighteenth century. *The Second Statistical Account of Scotland* was published in the middle of the nineteenth century and the *Third* is currently in hand. Some of its volumes have, indeed, already appeared, and it was for a chapter in the volume on *The City of Glasgow* (part of this "Third S.A." Series) that I tried, with little success, to obtain for the city's Jewish community information of the kind sketched out for Anglo-Jewry in Mr. Krausz's paper.'

Mr. Kimche referred to the implications of property development under Jewish auspices and of Jewish activity in the retail trades. He urged study 'not merely of the Jewish side of the story but also of the effect of this Jewish position on the British economy and on the non-Jewish population'.

Dr. Levenberg was the next speaker. 'The facts presented by Mr. Krausz are very important but I suggest that we should guard against jumping to conclusions. I have studied his sources. Many of these studies were written years ago; quite a number of the articles mentioned were written for the *Jewish Chronicle* and the *Jewish Year Book*. It is my definite feeling that there is not here a basis for scholarly conclusions. If

The Economic and Social Structure of Anglo-Jewry

my judgement is correct I believe we are just at the very beginning of studying the problem.'

He went on to single out two interesting observations which Mr. Krausz had made: 'The Jews have taken up the twentieth century mode of life even more than their Gentile neighbours.' 'In the sense discussed here the Jews represent the typical individual who has adjusted himself successfully to the economic and social conditions of modern western society.' Dr. Levenberg said that this shows how shaky is the social and economic basis of Anglo-Jewish life, because it is linked with a certain economic structure of society which may be of a transitory character.

'I will now raise two further points:
(1) Suppose, for example that Britain joins the Common Market, what will be the impact on the Anglo-Jewish community?
(2) What will be the change in the present prosperity?

'One should not eliminate altogether the possibility that Jews may be the social and economic victims of any wind of change as far as economic life is concerned.

'Mr. Krausz has argued that Jewish influence in the City is far less than generally assumed. This may be right. But we have to study the phenomenon of the Jewish millionaire. How many Jewish millionaires are there in England? What impact do they make on the position of the Jews in this country?

'Mr. Krausz also commented upon "the vast decline of Jewish working classes." What does it mean? Do we consider as "workers" only people employed in factories? What about the large number of Jews working in small undertakings and in offices? Many of these people are members of trade unions. I believe we need a new definition of "the Jewish working classes".

'What about the occupational trends among the younger people? Do they follow the professions of the older generation? I do not think so. Enormous changes have taken place. What are the younger people doing? In my view this would be an important part of the investigation of the social and economic structure of Anglo-Jewry. We should not rush to conclusions; we may obtain a completely false picture.'

Mr. S. S. Levin raised the question of the future supply of officials to manage the various institutions of Anglo-Jewry.

'Anglo-Jewry has several distinguished civil servants to manage its affairs. It seems to me that we have these people by reason of good fortune rather than by reason of good design. There is, I submit, a proper place in our discussions for the future provision of Jewish Civil Servants.

'In the past we have been fortunate in securing outstanding men who possessed a deep religious background and a Jewish home life which made it essential for them to find a calling which would enable them to keep the Sabbath and the traditions of Judaism. We have now entered a period in which the five-day week will be accepted as the economic norm. It seems certain, therefore, that some who might otherwise have entered the service of the Jewish community may look farther afield for their occupation. The future provision, therefore, of Jewish communal professional

Discussion

administrators, their selection and training, is of vital concern to Anglo-Jewry, and a *sine qua non* is the provision of conditions such as salary, security and pension likely to attract the right men.'

Mr. Henry Shaw raised a topic into which research on the economic structure of the community might enter.

'Would it be possible', he asked, 'for three Jewish youth clubs which cater largely for working youth, say, Victoria, Brady and Stamford Hill, to form the centre of a research study to ascertain what kind of jobs the boys and girls take on leaving school? I think you would be surprised to learn how many working-class Jews there are in lower grade clerical jobs, rising in the income groups through, say, hairdressing, into the working *élite* of the taxi driver.'

The Rev. W. W. Simpson regretted that 'in the list of papers submitted to the Conference there is not a paper reflecting any study or any consultation with members of the non-Jewish community.'

Mr. Krausz replied to the discussion. 'The comments made seem to fall into three main categories. First, as Professor Ginsberg has pointed out, there is the problem of definitions. It is certainly most important to know exactly what is meant by "the middle class" or "the *élite*"; otherwise one can make serious mistakes. Secondly, the paucity of material has been mentioned, especially as regards Jews on the periphery of the community, who Dr. Roth, quite rightly, feels must be included in future studies. But may I just say this: it is difficult enough to get information on the more identified Jews, even on those who are within Jewish organizations; the difficulty of getting material on Jews who are on their way out of the community is almost insurmountable.

'Thirdly, may I comment as regards the decline of the Jewish working class and of Jewish trade unionism, to which Dr. Levenberg has referred? I mention in my paper not only that the Jewish trade unions, except for one, have disappeared, but that the Jewish membership of (general) trade unions has tremendously declined. Again, the number of Jewish trade union leaders has certainly gone down, and if one compares the present situation with the picture given, for example, by Lloyd Gartner (*The Jewish Immigrant in England 1870–1914*) of the tremendous activity by Jewish trade unionists and socialists in the earlier part of this century, the great difference becomes obvious.'

Trends in Anglo-Jewish Religious Life

NORMAN COHEN

The General Situation
'Trends' is a disarming word which has, I understand, been eliminated from the title of most of the other contributions in this volume. This is, of course, only right because it brings an air of imprecision where one would expect to find definite statistics and reliable information. However, in the sphere of religious life it is extremely difficult to reduce the attitudes and observances of individuals to any simple statistical formulae. The figure of children attending Jewish Day Schools gives a reliable indication of their educational programme, but the number of persons attached to a religious organization gives no indication of anything beyond the bare fact of their being affiliated. A family, for instance, may join the Reform Synagogue in order to indicate its complete breach with traditional Judaism, but another family may, by joining the same Synagogue, be returning to a faith from which they have long been estranged. Furthermore, within the various synagogal organizations the widest range of religious outlook is to be found. I personally know of members of the Reform Synagogue whose observance of kashruth is quite adequate, and many members of the United Synagogue who completely ignore the Dietary Laws.

The question of religious trends in Anglo-Jewry cannot be separated from the general picture of religious observance to be found in the non-Jewish world. The attitudes of the outside world have always had an effect on the views of the Jewish community and nowadays the influence is more direct. In this connection, therefore, it is pertinent to point out that, in the non-Jewish world, standards of religious observance and of religious interest are at a low ebb. The picture of a limited number of enthusiastic participants and a great mass of apathetic persons who require religion only on a few occasions in their lifetime is one that is met with in all communities (the Roman Catholics are probably the only group which can show real progress). Were there to be a marked revival of interest in religion—if only for social purposes—(as, I am told, is the case in the U.S.A.), this would, no doubt, be accompanied immediately by an enhanced religious interest on the part of Anglo-Jewry.

Indifference
The basic fact of religious life in Anglo-Jewry is that the great bulk of the community has only the slightest concern with Judaism. The casual observer might not think that such is the case. There is, at first sight, an impressive façade of institutional religion. There are any number of religious organizations; there is a great deal of fund-raising that centres around the Synagogue. But, behind it all, the amount of apathy is not to be underestimated. Reliable information is not easy to obtain, but I was interested to read that the Habonim Movement conducted a little survey among their members (and these are young people who come from a background where there is sufficient interest in Jewish matters for them to join a Youth Movement) which showed that only twenty-three out of forty-seven families lit candles on Friday night, and that ten families out of the forty-seven do not observe Yom Kippur. In my daughter's age-group at her Secondary School, fourteen out of thirty-two Jewish girls eat the school lunches, although kosher lunches are available at a canteen immediately adjoining the school. These figures are not advanced as being in any way definitive, but, from my own knowledge of communal life, I would say that they are not misleading in their implication. Based on such insights, I would hazard that at the present time twenty per cent of the community is recognizably orthodox (using the term rather loosely), ten per cent is avowedly Reform and seventy per cent are largely indifferent, but, nevertheless, retain a synagogal affiliation, usually with an orthodox organization. In addition, however, there are large masses of completely unaffiliated Jews, whose numbers cannot be ascertained with any reliability. These, however, have probably passed the point of no return and they can be ignored in any consideration of communal conditions.

The central feature of Anglo-Jewish religious life has probably become the barmitzvah ceremony, which attracts large numbers of persons who do not otherwise frequent the Synagogue, even during the Penitential Days. Particularly this applies to women, who on these occasions, show a painful inability to take even an unintelligent interest in the proceedings. Second to the barmitzvah ceremony is fund raising, which attracts energies not available for religious observance, and associated with fund raising is the unfailing fear of anti-semitism. In short the force which binds Anglo-Jewry together is not faith but gregariousness.

This binding force may not be of the highest order, but it is not ineffective. Whereas, in previous centuries, the acquisition of great wealth was often the precursor of conversion, today quite a few millionaires are firmly and openly Jews and work (or at any rate, allow themselves to be repeatedly fleeced) on behalf of the community and the State of Israel. Conversionism is not a major problem. Such successes as the missionaries have are usually among those whose contact with Judaism has virtually ceased. More alert interest in the religious welfare of university students would probably reduce the loss of those who, at Oxford or Cambridge, see Christianity at its best, while at home they scarcely saw Judaism even at its worst.

ORTHODOXY

The Chief Rabbinate
In a community that shows every sign of disintegration and drift, the one institution which still has the power to attract loyalty and impose some degree of unity is the Chief Rabbinate. This institution is, without doubt, the most important in the history of the Anglo-Jewish community. Because of this institution, immigrants were able to mix with the older families in a way that was impossible in communities where there was no centrally recognized authority. The fact that standards of observance are, even now, higher in Anglo-Jewry than in most Commonwealth Jewries is largely due to the respect for tradition centred around the Chief Rabbinate. Closely allied to this institution is that of the Beth Din, which was once a rather unimportant body of assessors to the Chief Rabbi, but has now become one of the leading features in orthodox life and is discussed in greater detail at a later stage.

New Trends
There has been a remarkable change in the whole atmosphere of orthodoxy in Anglo-Jewry. In 1931, Jews' College celebrated its seventy-fifth anniversary. Greetings were received from the Liberal Seminary of Berlin, and Rabbi Reinhart, of the Reform West London Synagogue, personally conveyed the congratulations of the Hebrew Union College of Cincinnati. Although Dr. Büchler, the Principal at that time, was a strictly orthodox man, he had to accommodate himself to a milieu where strict orthodoxy was not wanted and to producing clerics of whose religious and intellectual failings he was painfully aware. It is, however, important to recollect that in 1931

Anglo-Jewry—however significant it might have been politically and socially—was of little consequence to the religious life of World Jewry. The giants of Jewish intellectual life were on the continent, at German Universities, or in Lithuanian Yeshivot. Anglo-Jewry's theological standpoint was then of little consequence.

In 1933 there came the great divide. Refugees came to this country, bringing with them standards of culture and observance with which the community had previously been little acquainted. Dayan Abramski, one of the greatest halachic experts in the world, joined the London Beth Din. Another factor was that one of the daughters of the Chief Rabbi married Dr. Schonfeld, the rabbi of the Adath Israel Congregation, and undoubtedly this helped to alter Dr. Hertz's personal attitude to right-wing orthodoxy.

Orthodoxy, until then, had been uninfluential. It had been largely confined to poorer immigrants who were numerous and could be vocal, but who exercised no real control over events or institutions. The important people of the community frequently shed most of their orthodox attitudes. The Honorary Officers of the United Synagogue, for instance, were rarely rigorous in their practice. I might mention, in this connection, a fact told to me by Dr. Bernard Homa, that at one time plans were mooted for a united Beth Din for the whole of London. It was suggested that a clause in the constitution of the proposed Committee of Management should limit membership to those people who were Sabbath-observers. The late Sir Robert Waley-Cohen found the clause completely unacceptable, as it would have meant the exclusion of himself and all his colleagues. In recent years, the position has changed out of recognition; there is now a flourishing Jewish Day-School Movement; large numbers of Anglo-Jewish youth spend at least a short period at the Yeshivot; there are valuable orthodox Youth Movements, such as B'nei Akivah; there is Carmel College—a college run on public-school, but nevertheless orthodox, lines; and, most important of all, there are now considerable numbers of persons who, in districts such as Hampstead Garden Suburb, have found it possible to combine social emergence, and even affluence, with a high standard of observance.

At the same time there has been an important change in the qualifications expected in the Anglo-Jewish minister. The introduction of the Rabbinical Diploma Class at Jews' College after the war marked a new era in the history of that institution. For the first time intensive rabbinical studies were introduced into the curriculum and Jews' College has since provided rabbis for many important posts (even, by one of the ironies of history, for the community of Frankfurt-on-Main). The level of Rabbinical achievement is not staggeringly high (inevitable when all the students have family and congregational commitments), but it is far superior to anything that ordinary ministers ever reached before. Unfortunately the Jews' College rabbis who remain within the United Synagogue have good reason to complain that both the Beth Din and the United Synagogue view them still as mere ministers and give them neither opportunity nor encouragement to exercise halachic authority.

All these factors have continued to produce a change of atmosphere. The persons whose child attends a Jewish school may not alter their own standard of observance, but they have certainly modified their outlook. Instead of competing for a place at a non-Jewish establishment with a Jewish quota, they accept the reality of a Jewish approach to education. The parents, and perhaps even the grandparents, find that they have made contact with a Judaism that reaches beyond the synagogue service. There are quite a few persons who have nowadays reversed the usual Anglo-Jewish claim and boast that they have a 'froom' grandchild.

The popularity of Jewish Day Schools is of particular significance for the future of traditional Judaism, for they are all run on orthodox lines. In the case of some members of the Zionist Federation this meant the sacrifice of certain firmly-held principles and there was some complaint of a 'sell out' to the rabbinate. They soon realized the value of founding schools in association with existing congregations and probably nobody now would contemplate non-religious Jewish schools. The schools will attain greater significance when they are able to cater for a larger number of senior pupils.

THE TWO ORTHODOXIES

Orthodoxy consists of two types. The more rigorous, both in London and in the Provinces, remain apart from the main community. They pay a certain amount of deference to the Chief Rabbi and the various Batei Din, but they prefer to have their own organizations for kashruth, burial and so forth. They range from congregations who carry on, with self-satisfied dignity, the traditions and outlook of the separated communities in Germany, to congregations whose level of observance would have seemed rather exaggerated in the most orthodox centres in Eastern Europe. With what may be unswerving loyalty, but also with some signs of exhibitionism and conceit, the latter maintain the garb, language and outlook of earlier centuries. (As many of them are English-born and have adopted, rather than inherited, this approach to Judaism, there is matter here for psychological as well as sociological investigation.) They have even established, despite the objections of the educational authorities, a couple of schools where English language instruction is reduced to the barest minimum possible.

Nevertheless, with the cessation of immigration, the importance of this group cannot be over-estimated. They guarantee the future of the community better than the most expensive synagogues.

The second type, less fervid, stays within the established community, where they represent a new development. Readers who remember Zangwill's book *The Grandchildren of the Ghetto* will recall the surprise with which Esther Ansell heard that Raphael Leon, English-born and an Oxford graduate, still put on tephillin every morning. As they met at a dinner party, it is clear that Raphael's religiosity had not gone so far as the wearing of koppel over meals. (A sentence or two of Zangwill often gives a vast amount of social history. Raphael represented the *ne plus ultra* of United Synagogue Judaism in the 1880s but he would not seem very striking now.)

One of the aspects of Anglo-Jewish life that marks it off from what was common elsewhere in the recent past is that a good level of Jewish knowledge and of Jewish observance are usually interlinked. A few persons who combine Jewish and secular knowledge and who are observant as well are able to exercise an influence on congregations quite disproportionate to their numbers. This is responsible for much current unrest.

The loyalty offered to the Chief Rabbi in days gone by was often of a somewhat formal type. He was revered as the spokesman of the community to the outside world, he came along to one's synagogue on rare, but important, occasions. But he guided with a very light rein. The Reverend X, whose Jewish studies terminated when he was eighteen, who dressed like an Anglican clergyman, carried his umbrella on the Sabbath and was very broadminded about the dietary laws, was the real religious guide of his congregation. Owing however to changes in the community, the Reverend X has now frequently been replaced by Rabbi Y, who eats with very few of his congregants and generally comports himself in an orthodox fashion. This is not a development which has found universal favour. Discontent has been deliberately fostered by interested parties, and the old easy-going compromises over theology and practice have been ruthlessly probed. We shall return to this later on.

THE BETH DIN

In the light of these developments we can understand the emergence of the London Beth Din to an importance never before achieved by this body. It is deeply conscious of its responsibilities as the most important Beth Din left in Europe. It endeavours to apply the full range of halacha to the problems of the community. But it is an unimaginative and rather negative body of persons, who allowed their relations with some of the lay leaders of the United Synagogue to deteriorate disastrously. Two Hebrew responsa testify to their power to have the original design for the Marble Arch Synagogue altered (the intention was to build flats over the Synagogue). Visitors to London, on the other hand, cannot obtain a supervised meal on the Sabbath, because the Beth Din has found no way to control the restaurateurs or to manage without them. Their capacity to oppose is much greater than their ability to innovate and they have added to their difficulties by their aversion to any form of public relations.[1]

THE MIDDLE OF THE ROAD

Much has been heard of the disappearance of the 'middle of the road' Anglo-Jew. There is no doubt that the large intermediate body of persons has tended to fade from the communal scene. This is easy to understand if it is appreciated that the 'middle of the road' Jew was not—as his apologists like to make out—walking with steadfast gait between the two opposite walls of fanaticism and assimilation. On the contrary, he was crossing a road from immigration to disappearance. The immigrant came poor, observant, and hard-working; as he rose in the social scale, he aped the attitude of the older-established families, including, of course, their religious views. As the older settlers disappeared through drift, intermarriage or sterility, the one-time immigrants took their place and were themselves replaced by a more recent set of arrivals. The 'middle of the road' was accordingly a wide expanse which people crossed at their leisure. While they paused on the way out, they provided the community with most of its lay leaders. Now, however, the numbers crossing the road have dropped in a marked degree. Firstly, there is no immigration; secondly there is no disgrace any longer in being attached to the 'old school'. In fact, partly owing to the influence of the young people on their parents, there is a move back from the middle to the traditional side. Consequently, the middle of the road presents a picture of chaos. Its occupants no longer move in one direction and have no set purpose. It is to this class of reader that the *Jewish Chronicle* appears to address itself when it considers religious

[1] For many years, the Hon. Ewen Montagu, the President of the United Synagogue, was openly and bitterly critical of the *dayyanim*. His resignation in 1962 marked the end of the era of the ascendancy of the 'Old Establishment'. His successor Sir Isaac Wolfson, multi-millionaire son of an immigrant, is himself orthodox and strongly sympathetic to the rabbinate. The struggle for religious paramountcy within the United Synagogue has thus, for the time being, been won by the right wing.

questions. To my mind, the attitude of the Organ of Anglo-Jewry merely makes inevitable the ascendancy of the right-wing which it so frequently deplores. By adding to the bewilderment of the middle of the road, it is made more difficult than ever for them to assert leadership. Especially unlikely is the possibility that any change in the direction of religious movement will be effected by any particular appointment to any particular office.

DRAWBACKS

However, it must be appreciated that all the foregoing applies to a limited number of persons. The inherent weakness of the orthodox position is that it has too little contact with the main bulk of the community; it is utterly devoid of any missionary feeling; it tends to be far too complacent and far too willing to accept the position by which orthodoxy is confined to a limited number of persons residing in a few select areas. It is also too much geared to the requirements of the wealthy and very little interested in the problems that affect the less affluent. It is also impoverished intellectually. The extraordinary reliance placed on the effectiveness of the works of Samson Raphael Hirsch[1] is only an indication of weakness. No present-day writer within the orthodox fold has produced any constructive religious works. Finally, there has been an unbalanced emphasis on kashrut. This has become more of a fetish than a set of laws. Neither the laws of family purity, nor the ethical implications of Judaism, get anything like the same attention. Nevertheless, whatever the failings of this particular brand of orthodoxy, its adherents are articulate and influential. It is likely to continue self-perpetuating and will increasingly provide Anglo-Jewry with a large number of lay leaders.

CONSERVATISM

In view of this state of affairs, it is not unnatural that some persons feel that modifications in the orthodox position are necessary if traditional Judaism is to make any impact on the broad mass of the community. It cannot be doubted that the rather stodgy and unimaginative Judaism offered by many ministers, whose fundamentalism sometimes appears to owe more to intellectual apathy than to religious conviction, makes no appeal to persons who have drifted away from the orthodox position.

The extreme rigidity of some of the attitudes of the Beth Din are also not calculated to appeal to a large number of people. They wish

[1] Distinguished German Rabbi at Frankfurt (born 1808, died 1888).

to have a traditional life with some of the asperities removed, and, in this, they hark back nostalgically to an earlier period in Anglo-Jewish life and would like to make contacts with the conservative movement in America. The number of people who are consciously thinking along these lines is very limited, but the fact that the *Jewish Chronicle* seems to reflect these sentiments makes the movement appear far stronger than it really is. It might possibly make a considerable appeal to the community. This, however, could be successful only if it openly stated its aims and deliberately formed synagogues where these would be realized in practice. The effort which has been made to infiltrate orthodox institutions has succeeded only in arousing very great opposition, and it appears probable that the movement will make no further progress. If, however, these views were to be more honestly presented to the public, many persons who like their orthodoxy without tears would probably find that, in fact, it offered them a traditional way of life which enabled them to feel linked with Jewish observance without being committed to any more extreme position.

Though many of those most deeply involved would deny it strongly, the recent intense effort to appoint Rabbi Dr. Louis Jacobs to the Principalship of Jews' College may properly be dealt with in this section. Dr. Jacobs' theological views, as expressed in his books *We Have Reason to Believe* and *Jewish Values*, and more especially as reported in the *Jewish Chronicle* of 8th June, 1962, clearly show him to be a conservative, rather than an orthodox, rabbi. His views may, in fact, be widely shared, but present tendencies in Anglo-Jewish orthodoxy demand either a public allegiance to fundamentalism, or, at least, complete reticence on the matter.

Dr. Jacobs, however, had for some time rather gratuitously emphasised his modernism, and combined this with a certain indifference to minor matters of ritual, such as keeping his head always covered, which orthodox opinion found unsatisfactory in one who hoped to be the Principal of a rabbinical seminary. The frantic campaign waged on his behalf by the *Jewish Chronicle* was an utter failure. Dr. Brodie refused to sanction the appointment—the inevitable consequence of the deep antipathy both felt and expressed by rabbinical opinion—and those Honorary Officers of Jews' College who had supported Dr. Jacobs resigned and were replaced by others whose views were likely to favour a continuation of the right wing trend evident for some years past.

Norman Cohen

PROGRESSIVE JUDAISM

The year 1933 also provided a turning-point in the development of Progressive Jewry in Great Britain. They, too, reaped the benefit of the presence in this country of scholarly persons who, in the same way as their orthodox counterparts, had managed to reconcile Western culture with Jewish attachments. The Progressive Movement is, in fact, far more dependent on foreign-born ministers than is the orthodox community. They have found it so difficult to recruit sufficient numbers of ministers that short-term contracts have had to be offered to American Rabbis to bring them to these shores as religious leaders for the Progressive Movement. Anybody who reads the *Affirmations of Judaism*, published by the late Chief Rabbi in 1927, will be struck by the fact that the vigorous missionary activity of the Progressives, against which he protested bitterly, are no longer anywhere in evidence. The truth is that these are no longer needed. There is a steady flow of recruits to the Progressive Movement from the semi-orthodox ranks. Some persons genuinely cannot stand what pass for religious services in the orthodox community. There is no doubt that unimaginative Judaism, allied to a feeling that decorum invariably leads to reform, has made many orthodox services unaesthetic as well as unintelligible. Some persons prefer to associate themselves with religious organizations where their standards of observance will be considered proper rather than heterodox. A large number of no firm religious views become tired of remaining on the waiting list of the orthodox synagogues in popular districts and join the Progressives in order to have a seat on the High Holy Days.

Last, but certainly not the least important of the factors, is intermarriage. I have tried to obtain figures of conversions from the Orthodox, Reform and Liberal movements and I have to report a complete blank. The orthodox authorities impose standards of observance on would-be converts which very few indeed can possibly attain. I believe that the Reform Synagogue is far more accommodating and the Liberals more accommodating still. Both are probably exploited for marriage purposes by persons who have no further use for them once the ceremony is over. It appears that no central record is kept in the Progressive Synagogues of marriages where there has been a prior conversion, nor of marriages which would not be considered valid by orthodox authorities. The result of this, however stern it may sound, is that every marriage that takes place under Progressive auspices is presumptively invalid from the point of view of *din*. My own opinion is that both orthodox and progressives, in their different ways, are responsible for heartbreak and communal chaos. Neither side can be proud of the practical results of its policies, no matter how cogent may be the theoretical arguments with which they buttress them. Public opinion is no longer so outraged by intermarriage, now reckoned to amount to perhaps fifteen per cent of all Jewish marriages, a growing proportion of which are celebrated at Register Offices.

Reform and Liberal
Although it is convenient to treat Progressive Judaism as one entity, in practice Reform and Liberal Judaism show many differences. The Reform movement itself has exhibited a tendency to resile from 'Classical Reform' to a more traditional attitude (e.g. barmitzvah at thirteen, instead of sixteen). The new views, coupled with a clash of personalities, led to a bitter controversy at Upper Berkeley Street and the formation of a sort of *austrittsgemeinde* in Knightsbridge. As a sign of their new orientation, the Reformers have given the title of Beth Din Zedek to their Rabbinical Court, a piece of misleading magniloquence which Anglo-Jewry might well have been spared.

The Liberal Synagogue adheres to the more radical line laid down by C. G. Montefiore and Dr. I. Mattuck. The two movements have often discussed closer association, but little of practical significance has been accomplished. At one time they had a gentleman's agreement not to poach on each other's territory, but this seems to have gone by the board. They were unable to agree on a joint Ministers' Training College and they have adopted different standards over proselytization. They are, in fact, affected by the prevailing atmosphere of bourgeois complacency and the steady growth in their numbers without much effort on their part seems to satisfy their ambitions. Their intellectual vigour is not very impressive. They both publish rather dull magazines and contribute little to the cultural life of the community, even in the sphere of Anglo-Jewish history in which they might be expected to take a keen interest. Segregation in education is, of course, unacceptable to reform ideology, but, without it, progress in Jewish studies is apt to be slow and difficult. The growth in the numbers of the progressive movement is accordingly not matched by any equivalent growth in its influence. This could be achieved only by much higher standards of enthusiasm and learning, which would, in turn, produce a native-born ministry.

Toleration
If the two wings of the progressive movement find difficulty in co-operating, it is not surprising that contact between progressives and the orthodox is practically non-existent. As the centre of gravity in the orthodox community has moved to the right and the

progressives feel themselves less of a minority movement, all desire to work together has faded. It is not, however, fair to blame post-1933 conditions exclusively for this state of affairs. The beginning of the Liberal movement at the turn of the century caused the Reform Synagogue to move farther away from traditionalism and, even so, points of contact were always fewer than contemporary latitudinarians like to believe, and owed more to social pressures than to religious idealism. The high-water mark of toleration is usually alleged to be the Montefiore-Loewe *Rabbinic Anthology* of 1938. Yet neither author gave way to the other's viewpoint—the volume is more the record of a debate than a joint venture in authorship—and Loewe's Introduction, with its apologetic overtones and acceptance of orthodox standards in which not even ministers worried about 'shaatnez' is far from the outlook of traditionalism today.

Much of the gap must, however, be attributed to the anti-Zionism which characterized the progressive movement in the mandatory period. The establishment of the State of Israel extinguished anti-Zionism as a live issue, but theological objection to statehood remained innate in the movement. Zionism itself is not much of an influence on the religious life of Anglo-Jewry. Kol Nidrei night has been exploited for its fund-raising potentialities; a prayer for the State of Israel is recited weekly, but no alteration in ritual or pronunciation has been effected. On the other hand, Zionist activity is an umbrella under which orthodox and secularists work together in some degree of unity and the virtual absence of the Progressives greatly weakens, in the eyes of the orthodox, their claim to be part of k'lal Yisrael. In any case, toleration is not merely a question of Orthodoxy's accepting the claims of Reform. There must also be a willingness for Reform to appreciate the viewpoint of Orthodoxy and of this there is little evidence.

RELIGIOUS LEADERSHIP

Communities cannot rise higher than their leaders, and, conversely, it is difficult for religious leaders to rise higher than the communities wish. If the views presented earlier in this chapter are correct, it would suggest that much Anglo-Jewish religious leadership is of no high calibre, and I do not think that the issue can be shirked, however much, on personal grounds, one would prefer to pass it over.

The unfortunate truth is that the ministry is not an attractive profession for Anglo-Jewish Youth. Its financial rewards are much lower than those which may be obtained elsewhere, and possibilities of religious observance are now much higher in many outside professions and trades than they were, say, at the beginning of the century. This, combined with the general lack of religious interest, has made few people keen on taking up a ministerial career. Young persons in the Reform Camp have not the basic Hebraic knowledge which would enable them to take up theological studies without a complete break with their previous scholastic background. In the orthodox fold, the more intensive the Jewish religious training that a young man has received, the less inclined he feels for the inevitable compromises that accompany a minister throughout his career. Ill-paid ministers in an affluent community are subjected to temptations which must, all too often, affect the way in which their tasks are discharged. Routine duties, such as pastoral work and preaching, are given the minimum thought and attention, because salaries are unaffected by the manner in which these duties are performed. Flattering toasts or insincere memorial addresses, however, bring their own financial reward. This is a state of affairs which is not conducive to religious enthusiasm; many ministers themselves feel intensely frustrated and no clear or inspiring leadership is given to their congregants. (Adult education, for which there is real need, was started two years ago with great publicity and dropped, after one year, with no good reason. The cessation was more in character than the commencement.) Some ministers quite openly batten on their congregations and most adopt the undignified pose of being the loudly suffering servants of the Lord.

There is quite definitely a shortage of ministers. It is questionable whether it is any greater than the shortages found in many other professions and consequently too much reliance should not be placed on the reasons advanced by the ministers to account for this. Thus they complain about the lack of advancement within the ministry, but as, in a mobile community like Anglo-Jewry, today's fashionable synagogue is often tomorrow's white elephant, a plan of advancement is difficult to prepare. And in truth, if a minister stays with a congregation for thirty years and more, it is the congregation which suffers more than the minister.

THE END OF THE MATTER

Solomon Schechter pin-pointed both the strength and weakness of S. R. Hirsch together with his place in the history of religion, when he wrote of him: 'Whose defiance of reason and criticism even a Ward might have envied, and whose saintliness and sublimity even a Keble might have admired.'[1] Hirsch is the tutelary deity of neo-orthodoxy and a detailed comparison of Anglo-Judaism today with the Anglican Church after the rise of the Oxford Movement would be

[1] S. Schechter. *Studies in Judaism* First Series page XX. J.P.S.A. (1945 edition.)

instructive. (Ward and Keble were respectively its lunatic and exalted fringes.) The Anglican Church at the beginning of the 1830s may be compared with the Chief Rabbinate of a century later, in being in virtually complete charge of the religious scene. To the Oxford Reformers this ascendancy was accompanied by a dangerous, possibly fatal, compromise over religious principles. Doctrines whose real significance had remained in obscurity under the dust of decades of indifference were elevated into dogmas and turned into rallying cries. The rites and beliefs of Roman Catholicism were copied until many left the Church of England altogether. The Evangelical wing of the Church reacted by affirming its own views with fresh vigour and were regarded by their opponents as little better than Nonconformists. The essential unity of the Anglican Church has never been recovered and the alleged British willingness to compromise is not too evident in ecclesiastical history.

The lesson to be derived from this is that while individuals or organizations may be criticized or praised for the way in which they discharge their work, they are also the agents of historical forces which cannot be checked and which are untouched by censure. Anglo-Jewish religious life might be improved or worsened by alterations in its leadership, but the underlying situation would remain unchanged.

Discussion

THE discussion on Mr. Cohen's paper was opened by Dr. Shaul Esh.

'It seems that Mr. Cohen had some misgivings in connection with the word "trends" contained in the title of his contribution. If my memory serves me right, we had originally hoped that he would include not only a description and analysis of trends and tendencies within the religious sphere, but also a few words about the role of religion in contemporary Anglo-Jewry. I am glad to note that his remarks did include some references to this subject. For it is a basic point which we must bear in mind that since the beginning of the era of emancipation, i.e. about 150 years in the Western countries, Jewish communities everywhere are recognized as religious entities only, an approach that determined in the long run also the minority policies towards the Jews in Eastern Europe during the inter-war period. I stress this point also because though it might be self-evident to Jews in the Diaspora, it is not so with us in the State of Israel. I am under the impression that our students have to make quite an effort to grasp fully this fact. As is well known Israeli youth, as Israeli Jews in general, are only to a rather small extent what is called "religiously" orientated, and whatever may be the extent of knowledge we in Israel have about the Diaspora, it is known there that world Jewry too is religiously motivated only in part. Nevertheless, there can be little doubt that the number of avowed non-believers or "agnostics" within the Jewish Community in the Diaspora has diminished to a negligible minority in comparison to what it used to be in the last generation before the holocaust. Things being as they are, Diaspora Jewry at large looks upon itself officially as a community bound together by religious, even if undefined, affiliation. Mr. Cohen has stated that "the great bulk of the community has only the slightest concern with Judaism". I submit that this holds good not only for Anglo-Jewry as implied by the author, but for Jewries everywhere.

'As we have no intention to dwell here today on doctrines and beliefs, nor to analyse them, I am glad to use the phrase "concern with Judaism" as applied in this context. For if we are considering certain fundamental practices in use by the "great bulk" of our people, we cannot but concede that these practices are originally and essentially of a religious nature. This is so even though many (or even most) members of the community may not be aware of it, or, more than that, be opposed to the religious significance contained in them. I have in mind, of course, the fact that the great majority of Jews everywhere require religious ceremonies at the

Discussion

cradle (in the case of males) and at the grave, i.e. Brith Mila and interment. As far as I know there has nowhere been any overt dissociation from these practices. Every observer of the contemporary Jewish scene will confirm the fact, at first sight paradoxical, that in quite a number of countries organized Jewish life has come into being with the foundation of a Chevra Kadisha, and the establishment of consecrated Jewish burial grounds. I hope that no one has concluded from what I have said up to now that the adherence to these two basic practices—to which we could add the Bar Mitzvah ceremony, which Mr. Cohen has called "a central feature of Anglo-Jewish religious life" and which we might modify and say "of religious life everywhere"—are sufficient connection with Jewish religion. But, after all is said and done, their religious origin, albeit far remote, could not and cannot be denied.

'It should be clear that we should consider the situation in this regard not as a phenomenon isolated from its environment. Professor Ginsberg in his opening of the discussion on Mr. Brotman's paper, already has referred to British Christianity, by quoting the late Bishop of Durham.[1] I would like to draw your attention to the following extracts from a letter to *The Times* (January 22, 1962) which read:

"We already know that the very great majority of our people insist on being married in the Church, and are equally insistent on having their children baptized into the faith. That surely indicates that we still may be called a Christian people. We also know, and the Church will not deny it, that 80 per cent of our people seldom use the Church for anything but baptism, marriages and burials."

'These remarks throw light on a situation with English Christians strikingly similar to the one mentioned within the Jewish community.

'Now if we leave the massive category of the generally indifferent and come to consider the religiously conscious and active group, one thing clearly emerges. In British Jewry too there are now several trends clearly established, as there used to be in Germany until the destruction and as they exist in the U.S.A. and other countries. The contention that there is no more than one "brand" of religious Judaism, so fervently advocated by the leaders of modern orthodoxy, cannot honestly be maintained any longer, for it is contradicted by fact. Be it noted that this is not a question of numerical strength but of ideological and organizational crystallization. It even seems that the process of various trends crystallizing within Anglo-Jewry has not yet come to an end. Perhaps some of the difficulties felt in this field are due to some confusion in the terminology. Similar to what was rightly observed by Mr. Brotman in his paper that "the terms 'liberal' and reform' in Britain have a connotation different from that in the U.S.A. and in other parts of the world", and, for that matter, from what it had in Central Europe before the holocaust—the term "orthodoxy" in Anglo-Jewry also has a connotation different from that used in the greater diasporas and centres of Jewish life. If, as another authority put it, the "characteristic picture of the Anglo-Jewish bourgeoisie" (and that is the big majority of the British Jews) is "religiously conforming, even orthodox,

[1] See above, p. 20.

and yet anglicized", one has to remark that according to Continental standards this term means what was called there at most "conservatism".

'But now, as we have also heard today "there has been a remarkable change in the whole atmosphere of orthodoxy in Anglo-Jewry" in the last generation. In order fully to appreciate this change, one has to see it in its wider context. There can be little doubt that a change in the atmosphere of modern Western orthodoxy began to be felt in its stronghold, i.e. in Central Europe, in the twenties and thirties. On the one hand there were signs that the appeal of what has been called the Frankfurt type of Judaism had weakened. Jewish knowledge in the second and third generation was not enough to sustain the enthusiasm instilled by Rabbi Samson R. Hirsch in his followers. On the other hand, the closer contact with the daily life of the East European Jewish masses and their learned institutions brought about by the First World War and continued through organizational connections (notably amongst them the "Agudath Israel")', caused an inferiority complex which has never since been overcome, to say the least. Most characteristic seems to be the fact that the maxim "Torah im Derech Eretz" used by Rabbi Hirsch to connote the synthesis between strict adherence to Jewish orthodoxy and modern life and civilization, and brought forward against reformers of all shades, has nowadays become a defensive slogan used within orthodoxy itself, and sometimes rather weakly, against the rigorous trend of the pro-emancipation type. This has come a long way and it indicates too a growing differentiation within the religious sector, the acknowledgement of which should in my opinion be the basic starting point for unbiased discussion as well as for the future research worker.

'What we should ask ourselves and put before the scholars interested is, it seems to me, the question of scientific clarification of the religious situation. One may envisage the conducting of a survey—perhaps even on a local scale—about affiliation to different types of synagogues; the frequency of participation in their services on weekdays, Shabbatot, Holy days and High Holy days; the mode and measure of observance of those Mitzwot considered to be the criteria of religious behaviour—Shabbat and Kashruth. I may point out that in this field some very interesting—even if preliminary—inquiries have been carried out lately in the U.S.A. among the various religious trends constituted there; and lastly, such a survey may furnish us also with data on the influence of the religious attitude on natural demographic movements such as births and marriages.

'All these data when collected will serve not only the demographers among us, but they will for the first time supply a factual basis on which the religious situation can be appreciated as it really is.'

Mr. Julius Gould spoke next, and said:

'I would like to raise two rather concrete points, one perhaps more concrete than the other. In reading Mr. Cohen's general argument I was impressed by the case he presented that in the past twenty-five years there has been, in some quarters of the leadership of the Anglo-Jewish community, a return to religious ideology. This trend (if it is indeed a trend) stands out in such stark contrast to the general trend in Britain that it

Discussion

would surprise me very much if the Anglo-Jewish congregation as a whole participated in it. This is precisely the kind of thing which more detailed investigation would substantiate or disprove. Secondly, Mr. Cohen has illustrated very well the kind of difficult and delicate problems which specific investigations would encounter. For example he says (p. 53): "Many ministers themselves feel intensely frustrated and no clear or inspiring leadership is given to their congregants. And in truth, if a minister stays with a congregation for thirty years and more, it is the congregation which suffers more than the minister." Which minister, which congregation, and how much suffering? If I were asked to investigate this, what method would I use? Where would I get my data?'

The third speaker was Professor Moshe Davis.

'My comment will be directed to the area which I know a little better than Anglo-Jewish life, and that is the American scene. The purpose of the comment is to report on some of the questionnaire studies that were undertaken in the United States and which reveal basic attitudes towards the underlying problems of Jewish religious behaviour and religious habits. I shall bring some of these data to your attention, for they point to the possibilities of research studies which might be indicated in England.

'In a symposium conducted by *Commentary*, April, 1961, with Jewish intellectuals, it is asked, "Considering that you are at least partly the product of Jewish tradition, do you feel any sense of obligation and reverence to that religion?" The consensus seems to have been, No. On the other hand, in the inquiry "My Jewish Affirmation", also directed to a group of Jewish intellectuals, it seemed there was a central significance in the Jewish tradition; one respondent stated that he grew up on Proust and Camus but that he now credits Rabbi Akiba and Maimonides with considerably more influence upon him.

'Many of these surveys in America are organized not only nationally but also on a local basis. One of the most interesting of these studies was the Riverton study,[1] where questions were asked about Jewish belongingness. For example: What customs do your parents observe? What do you feel about their observance of these customs? If your parents do not observe customs, do any of your family? There were also questions which referred specifically to the habits and behaviour of young people—questions of social relations such as, How do you feel about working with non-Jewish boys and non-Jewish girls? And about associating with non-Jews?

'Out of these surveys have come the answers to some of the questions raised by Professor Ginsberg earlier and they have a direct bearing on our discussion. Those who will assume responsibility for the direction of research into Jewish religion in Britain should take note that the results of the American inquiries indicate clearly that the figures indicating greater attendance at the synagogue do not at all mean a revival of religious feeling.'

Dr. Highet referred to Mr. Cohen's statement: 'In this connection, therefore, it is pertinent to point out that, in the non-Jewish world, standards of religious observance and of religious interest are at a low

[1] *The Riverton Study*, M. Sklare and M. Vosk, New York: American Jewish Committee, 1957.

Trends in Anglo-Jewish Religious Life

ebb.' 'It depends, I suppose how one defines the term "Anglo" in "Anglo-Jewry",—if our context is England rather than Britain . . . England is a notoriously unreligious (I will not say "irreligious") country. The situation, as I have shown in several publications, is markedly different in Scotland, within whose bounds some at least of Britain's Jews reside.

'And I must also point out that there are several non-Jewish religious denominations who have recently been making world-wide progress—e.g. the Pentecostalists and the Jehovah's Witnesses. So that the picture is not quite as Mr. Cohen's generalization would suggest. Further, it is not true that "the Roman Catholics are probably the only group who can show real progress". The concept of "membership" does not apply in a Roman Catholic context. They speak of their "population", and in this are counted baptized infants. Growth in their numbers indicates their birth-rate as much as anything else, and their figures are not comparable with those for non-Catholic denominations. In the latter case, some sort of affirmation of faith is required before an individual will be counted as a "member", although the age at which this takes place varies from one Church to another.'

Dr. George Webber sensed the difficulty there is in drawing the correct inference from the "facts". 'For example: what is the correct inference to be drawn from the falling away from traditional observance? How far does it statistically extend? Mr. Cohen has said that immigration had stopped and that for its spiritual life Anglo-Jewry today depended upon the immigration of the past thirty years. When I was very young they also said that immigration had stopped. But immigration continued both after 1914 and after 1920. The present state of Anglo-Jewry is due, both on the right and on the left, to immigration since the 1930s. I do not know whether we would be right in assuming that the present trends will continue for the next decade. For myself I deplore the state that Anglo-Jewry has reached today. Homogeneity has gone; there is too clear a dichotomy between the right and the left. Will the children of today follow the practice of their fathers? Anglo-Jewry thirty years ago was acquiring the empirical English quality. It was finding a sort of *modus vivendi* which combined the English with the Jewish way of life. Today the trend is the reverse. I do not know whether it will continue and, if so, in what form. It has shown itself in particular in the recent conflict over the appointment of a principal at Jews' College but how this will develop nobody can say. I was disturbed by one of Mr. Cohen's observations: "Anglo-Jewish religious life might be improved or worsened by alterations in its leadership but the underlying situation will remain unchanged." The lesson to be derived apparently is: it does not matter what you say or do; it is all the same because nothing that you say or do will help; we are the agents of historical forces. What a moral!'

Dr. Cecil Roth said that the session seemed to be discussing the visible part of the iceberg. 'One of our tasks here is to see how large the invisible part of the iceberg is. We have been told that the community is basically religious because at the beginning and end of our lives we come within the influences of religion. If you look at the obituary columns of *The Times*

Discussion

you will see the names of Jews who did not come within this influence. It may surprise some of those who are here to learn that in the last few months there have died "secularly" both a former editor of the *Jewish Chronicle* and a former editor of *Young Israel*. They have simply been cancelled out. In the same way Mr. Cohen says that 70 per cent have no synagogal affiliations, whether orthodox or non-orthodox. I would like to suggest that there is one criterion of orthodoxy which might also serve as a method for a statistical survey of the orthodox—that is, the mikve. It should be easy to find out how many women attend the mikve. It should be possible to use this as the measure of the really orthodox element, rather than those who buy kosher meat. The number will probably be surprisingly if not regrettably small.'

Professor Bachi followed Dr. Roth. 'We have recently in Israel had occasion to do research on a number of women, asking them what is their general religious outlook and whether they are really adhering to the regular use of the mikve. The number of women actually using the mikve is much lower than those who declare themselves to be religious. In one particular field we have found that the mikve test is really an excellent test. The number of women who declared themselves religious but did not attend the mikve had about the same birth-rate as non-religious women, whereas those who used the mikve had a much higher birth-rate. So we see that the mikve test is quite an interesting one of real religious adherence and of influence of this adherence in social life.'

The next speaker was Rabbi Dr. Leslie I. Edgar. 'I do not propose to comment, to any extent, on Mr. Cohen's paper, but I would not like my silence to be misinterpreted as agreement with his views. I dissent from very many of his statements, though I fully appreciate that he has a particularly difficult task since this subject is not, like the subject of most of the other papers, susceptible to precise, statistical analysis. I must, however, specifically associate myself with Dr. Webber in questioning Mr. Cohen's conclusions in his last paragraph.

'My purpose, however, is to suggest three lines of investigation. First, I believe that by modern "sampling" methods, much valuable information could be obtained concerning the very considerable number of Jews who are either not affiliated to Synagogues or who, though affiliated to Synagogues, have only a slight concern with Judaism so that their affiliation has little or no religious significance. It should be possible to gauge more accurately what their position really is. I think that the depth of their religious perplexity and the exact nature of their religious problems in this difficult and perplexing age would be revealed and would correct a widespread tendency to underestimate the hidden religious worries of the average Jew and Jewess. Moreover, from such an investigation, I myself believe that the need for a much greater concentration on theology would be indicated as a way of assisting them through their religious perplexities. I would challenge the commonly held view that Judaism is not really theological: I think this is due to a confusion between the character of Christian theology, deeply influenced by Hellenism, and the different character of Jewish theology. I believe that, if we are going to assist this generation of Jews, we should investigate much more clearly the nature and depth of their religious perplexities and that this would lead to constructive action.

'Second, we should encourage an investigation into Synagogue organization and the extent to which it is, or is not, adapted to present conditions of Jewish life. I note that Mr. Cohen has directed some attention to this problem. And I believe that an inquiry into the position and problems of the Anglo-Jewish Ministry would be most valuable. I think that Mr. Cohen wholly underestimates much very hard and important work by the Ministry, especially in the pastoral sphere; but there are problems concerning the Ministry in relation to modern conditions which require most serious and careful investigation.

'Third, an investigation into the effect of social adaptation in Anglo-Jewry, and particularly concerning the religious problems which it has brought, would be very helpful. We ought to know more exactly the nature of the various problems which have resulted from the virtual elimination of social segregation from the life of the majority of British Jews.'

The Reverend I. Livingstone said that he disagreed with Mr. Cohen's view that a middle of the road idea in regard to traditional Judaism implied 'no set purpose'. 'I believe,' said Mr. Livingstone, 'that the alternative to "Reform" is not "ultra-orthodoxy", but a combination of religious observance with an intelligent approach to Jewish teachings. Traditional Judaism is something in which heart and head can work together in a rational harmony.'

Professor H. Goitein offered the following phenomenon for analysis by sociologists. 'Forty years ago Judaism was generally thought of as something for grandfather ("Passover with Grandfather" as the B.B.C. put it). Now, most young parents ask themselves what is there in it for their children and the grandchildren after them. Again, in his autobiography Humbert Wolfe, the poet, maintains that the Jews of his boyhood in Bradford were somewhat shamefaced about their observance. Going to synagogue, they went by the back streets. Today it is quite different; Jewish observance is practised openly. Compared with the sentimental frigid formalism of the big London synagogues of my boyhood, the devout congregations of the suburbs today are indeed noteworthy. In such matters it is quality, not quantity, that counts.'

Mr. S. S. Levin argued that, while Mr. Cohen had given a very interesting paper, it had consisted largely of personal views, very often not based on fact. 'Professor Ginsberg has questioned the number of Jews who have affiliations with the synagogue. One or two fairly authentic figures might be of interest in this connection. As an Honorary Officer of the United Synagogue, I can tell you we have 40,000 members; the Federation of Synagogues has, I calculate, some 10,000 members; the Sephardi, and other orthodox synagogues, as well as Reform and Liberal synagogues, have a total combined membership of 15,000, giving London a synagogue membership of some 65,000. If we regard these as heads of families, and multiply by three, or 3.5, we get a London Jewish population of some 200,000 affiliated to synagogues. That would be consistent with a total

Discussion

London Jewish population of 280,000 making allowance for those non-affiliated in any sense and those affiliated for burial purposes only, through Workers' Circles and Friendly Societies, etc.

'It is most probably true to say that in England we are not going to get any further large-scale immigration of Jews. Even in the remote possibility of Russian Jews being allowed to come here, they are hardly likely to provide spiritual forces for Anglo-Jewry as in past generations. It is clear, therefore, that Anglo-Jewry must become self-sufficient in the provision of spiritual forces.

'In this sense there is a crisis in spiritual leadership in Anglo-Jewry. And it has to be admitted that Jews' College has failed. The College was founded 107 years ago, and had, as its real purpose, not the provision of Rabbinic scholars, but of Jewish clergy who would help the Yiddish-speaking immigrant community to Anglicize. This process of assimilation and Anglicization has gone too far, and the need today is to Judaize. We have to think in terms of providing Dayyanim and Rabbinic scholars for our own Beth Din as we cannot look abroad for our "foreign scholars" who, in my opinion were disgracefully maligned not so long ago. We have to realize that a three-year course for a B.A. in Semitics, even extended by several years, will not produce the required Rabbinic scholarship. There must, therefore, be a more positive approach on the part of those who, in this country, are responsible for producing spiritual leaders, and it is essential that they should seek to link up with the old type of Yeshiva in this country who are turning out a considerable number of Rabbinic scholars.'

Miss S. Strizower drew attention to Mr. Cohen's argument that the importance of the orthodox trends 'cannot be over estimated. They guarantee the future of the community better than the most expensive synagogues'. Nevertheless, we know far less about orthodox trends in Anglo-Jewish life (in any accurate and detailed way) than we like to think.

'For example, Mr. A. G. Brotman suggests that the Union of Orthodox Hebrew Congregations represents in the main the orthodoxy of Central Europe rather than that of Eastern Europe. Surely, this is not—or no longer—the case. It seems to me that nowadays the Union of Orthodox Hebrew Congregations represents in the main the orthodoxy of Eastern Europe. Indeed, even in the Golders Green Beth Hamidrash, the citadel of Central European orthodoxy, persons of Eastern European origin now play a quite important part. And when one considers the almost unbridgeable gulf which existed between the Central European Jews and those of Eastern Europe, the significance of the change cannot be overestimated. Certainly it ought to be studied.

'Mr. Norman Cohen says, "large numbers of Anglo-Jewish youth spend at least a short period at the Yeshivot". But writing on *Jewish Education in Great Britain*, Dr. Fishman and Mr. Harold Levy say that the number of full-time students in all the main Yeshivot is 392, the number of part-time students is 162.[1] Do 554 Yeshiva students represent "large

[1] Below p. 78.

numbers of Anglo-Jewish youth?" (True, there are also small Yeshivot in Leeds, in Liverpool, and in Glasgow—but if twelve full-time students and seven part-time students represent a large Yeshiva, what constitutes a small one?)

'Mr. Cohen also says that in districts such as Hampstead Garden Suburb there are now considerable numbers of persons who have found it possible "to combine social emergence, and even affluence, with a high standard of observance". One wonders whether they are also finding it possible to pass on a high standard of observance to their children.

'We also read that "instead of competing for a place at a non-Jewish establishment with a Jewish quota", Jewish parents now "accept the reality of a Jewish approach to education".

'But how many non-Jewish establishments are there at which the Jewish quota is not fully taken up? How many headmasters of non-Jewish establishments are there who have not been thoroughly irritated by Jewish parents' attempts to get their children admitted even when told that the Jewish quota is more than fully taken up? True, there are a number of popular Jewish schools; but clearly, it is very necessary to distinguish between primary and secondary schools. I fear that only our primary schools may be termed "popular". Indeed, there are many who look upon attending a Jewish Grammar school as an admission of failure. And I doubt whether this is due only to the impression that Jewish primary schools are better than Jewish grammar schools; other factors are involved. (Moreover, if many members of the orthodox section of the community feel apprehensive about sending their children to a Jewish grammar school, how much stronger must this apprehension be among the non-orthodox section!)

'Mr. Cohen stresses the "extraordinary reliance" on the works of Samson Raphael Hirsch. But is there even a *minyan* of people of whom this can be said?

'I agree with him that the orthodox trend is of crucial importance for the future of the community. Hence insufficient information about it is not only a pity but also a great danger.'

Dr. Kochan spoke next, and asked whether Mr. Cohen would explain his statement that the orthodox synagogue is too much geared to the requirements of the wealthy.

Mr. Henry Shaw raised the matter of religious trends among the community's youth. 'As a result of strong educational influences—usually the effect of an outstanding local Rabbi—some young people from completely irreligious homes of second or third generation Anglo-Jews, have returned to strict observance of traditional Judaism—many of them becoming students at University.

'Unfortunately, there is a strong tendency among these particular young people to form a closely knit group and mix only among themselves, freezing out those of a different religious outlook.

'This tendency is very dangerous, and is particularly noticeable in the ancient universities. It has even been remarked upon in London University Jewish circles.

Discussion

'However, it should be realized that the number in this move back to orthodoxy is small, and certainly much smaller than the young people who move from nominal orthodoxy to Liberal and Reform groups.'

Mr. M. Richardson took up the assumption that a generation or two ago there was a virile orthodox Anglo-Jewish community. 'It is a myth and this myth must be exploded. The assumption is that the East End of London where there was a population of 100,000 Jews was very orthodox. This is complete nonsense. The vast majority of the people had no connection with the synagogue. They were Jewish because they lived in a Jewish milieu. A greater proportion belongs to a synagogue today than in a previous generation. My own experience is that many people only became members of the community when they moved to a suburb. Then they became formal members of the Jewish community and joined a synagogue. It is also not true that in the immediate past the synagogue itself was the centre. In the East End, although there was quite a rich synagogal life in terms of worship, there was no room—no space. Hebrew classes and Talmud Torahs were not part of the synagogue establishment, nor was social work. Don't exaggerate the past. My impression is that there has been a trend towards joining the community. And the final assumption that I want to challenge is that we are more integrated in the general community. We have a large number of M.P.s, but this is no proof that we are more integrated. It is only nominally true. Ideologically we are moving towards a greater ghetto than ever before.'

Rabbi Dr. Van der Zyl regretted that 'so little has been said in the report on Jewish youth. The vigorous life of Jewish youth in the synagogue would perhaps show that the scenery of religious life in Great Britain was not so bare'.

Dr. Levenberg said that there were two weaknesses in Mr. Cohen's paper. 'Firstly, no sources whatever are given. It is an individual assessment of the situation but there are no proofs. In my view, the scholarly approach requires proof. No one will accept judgement without asking on what the judgement is based. The second weakness is, that no attempt is made to give us very briefly an indication of the general religious climate in the British community. After all, in this respect the Jews are definitely a part of the country and the Jewish youth is a part of the general youth. One must begin by trying to ascertain what the general position is and then proceed from the general to the particular.

'I would like, especially, to question Mr. Cohen on three points. He says, "In a community that shows every sign of distintegration and drift, the one institution which still has the power to attract loyalty and impose some degree of unity is the Chief Rabbinate." This may be correct as far as the orthodox community is concerned. Does this apply to what he calls the 70 per cent of the indifferent people?

'The second point: Mr. Cohen gives us the figure of 15 per cent of those who inter-marry. On what is this figure based? What is the scientific basis of this very important figure from the point of view of development in Anglo-Jewry?

'Thirdly, Mr. Cohen says, "Zionism has not much of an influence on the religious life of Anglo-Jewry." Can we accept this statement? What about the Mizrachi? Would they accept this statement? The Zionist Federation would not accept it. I believe that Zionism brings certain categories of Jews closer to religion. On the other hand, there are certain categories of Zionists whose Jewish emotions are satisfied by Zionism and Israel and, therefore, they do not show any inclination to attend a synagogue.'

Mr. Armin Krausz argued that there was no doubt that the religious structure of Anglo-Jewry is undergoing a considerable change. 'Although it is difficult to assess trends in all matters, which emanate from the mind or the heart of people, nevertheless, in religious matters there are many outward signs, from which we may discover some indication which will help us in our speculations.

'On the one side we notice with considerable apprehension the numerical increase which is taking place within the Reform and Liberal folds. On the other end, we are pleased to see vigorous orthodoxy expand daily and assume a growing voice in the councils of the Community. Those extreme tendencies however do not give us a reliable indication of the real trend in Anglo-Jewish religious life. It is the attitude of the massive core of Anglo-Jewry, whom Mr. Cohen describes as the "middle-of-the-road Jew" and the attitude of the large number of unidentified Jews that give us a better clue.

'Within this massive core we see a strange development—a struggle between "inconsistency" and "uncertainty". The controversy raging round the principalship of Jews' College is a classic example of this struggle. No person can claim to be above criticism. The Chief Rabbi is no exception to this rule. Certain sections in the community, however, under the cloak of criticism are trying to wrest authority to make decisions even in matters on which they are incompetent to adjudicate. Could it happen in a University that a layman will select the scientist, for example, who should head the department of pathology?'

Dr. Homa observed that Mr. A. G. Brotman and Mr. Norman Cohen had drawn attention to the split in the orthodox community, with the formation of independent groups, outside the jurisdiction of the Chief Rabbi. 'This is largely due to the unusual character of the British Chief Rabbinate, unparalleled elsewhere, in which members of the Beth Din are regarded merely as ecclesiastical assessors, and the Chief Rabbi may override their views. In a properly constituted orthodox *Kehilla*, the Chief Rabbi (Av Beth-Din) must abide by a majority decision of the Beth Din over which he presides.'

Mr. Norman Cohen replied to the points that had come up in the discussion. He dealt first with the questions raised by Dr. Levenberg. He believed that the influence of the Chief Rabbi was still important with regard to the 70 per cent unaffiliated members of the community. The figure of 15 per cent inter-marriage had been quoted recently in the *Jewish Chronicle* in the course of their report of remarks made by Dayan Steinberg. On the subject of Zionism, it was true that individual Zionists played an important part in synagogal affairs, but this was due to their

Discussion

own personal qualities and did not mean that Zionism, as such, was influencing the course of Anglo-Jewish religious life.

Dr. Kochan had queried his statement that traditional Judaism was 'geared to the requirements of the wealthy', but this statement did not refer specifically to synagogues. 'I had in mind such matters as the high cost of supervised functions and holidays.'

Replying to Miss Stritzower's remarks on Yeshivot Mr. Cohen observed that according to returns made by the yeshivot, some thousand young men were now receiving either part-time or full-time instruction at these institutions. The number was, apparently, growing, and increasingly the yeshivot were drawing their material from students resident in this country and were importing far fewer from abroad.

'Miss Strizower's pessimism leads her too far on the question of education. The fact that many parents try to enter their children at a quota-establishment does not mean that many others do not make every effort to enrol their children at a Jewish school. This is a simple fact which would be confirmed by all headmasters and headmistresses.'

He finally took up the question of the need for statistical information. There was an obvious need to obtain current statistics regarding religious affiliations, standards, and so forth. 'It was, however, important that any survey should be properly run. There had been an awful warning some years ago when a small survey had been carried out. This survey included a question on affiliation, roughly on the following lines:

'Do you belong to (*a*) the Anglo-Jewish Association? (*b*) the Jewish Fellowship? (*c*) a Zionist Society?

'With questions loaded in this way, no reliable information could be expected. We also needed to establish a climate of opinion in which a frank discussion of the Anglo-Jewish religious scene could be held, in which participants were able to put all their cards on the table. No real advance in scholarship could take place if there were not the freest interchange of views.'

Jewish Education in Great Britain

ISIDOR FISHMAN and HAROLD LEVY

THE United Kingdom of Great Britain and Northern Ireland has the largest Jewish population in Europe.[1] Although there is no official census it is estimated that at the present time there are some 450,000 Jews living in Britain, 62 per cent of whom live in Greater London. The number of Jewish children of school age 5–15 is estimated at about 52,000.

The majority of Jewish pupils have always attended ordinary secular schools and received religious education outside school hours in special classes maintained by various educational organizations in London and the Provinces. Before the Second World War the three largest in Greater London were the Jewish Religious Education Board (whose origins go back to 1860) arranging and supervising Hebrew centres for pupils attending L.C.C. schools; the Talmud Torah Trust (founded 1905) for pupils whose parents strove to keep alive the tradition of intensive Jewish education; and the Union of Hebrew & Religion Classes (founded 1907) responsible for centres held at synagogues throughout the Metropolis. In addition, there was the Association of Non-Provided Schools in London, a co-ordinating body dealing with problems of voluntary Jewish Day Schools under the local education authority. The Central Committee for Jewish Education was established in 1921 to promote adequate and co-ordinated Jewish religious education in Great Britain. It had a special responsibility for promoting Jewish education in the Provinces.

The outbreak of war in 1939 created a new problem and all the major educational organizations in London agreed upon a provisional

[1] Since the time at which this was written French Jewry has become enlarged to such a degree that it is now considered to be the largest Jewish Community in Europe (Editors).

plan for merging their resources in finance and personnel as soon as the emergency arose. Thus the Joint Emergency Committee was formed which included provincial representation and care for the religious educational welfare of the thousands of Jewish children evacuated throughout the country. In 1941 a conference of lay and education leaders was held at Oxford to review the situation and to plan for the future. The most important outcome was the conviction that Jewish education must be the responsibility of the community as a whole, and that a communal and not a sectional approach was the most effective to meet post-war conditions.

At the end of hostilities a communal conference met in November, 1945, to deal with the reconstruction of Jewish education in Great Britain. As a result two central bodies were established in May, 1946, viz. the London Board of Jewish Religious Education for the Greater London Area and the Central Council for Jewish Religious Education for the Provinces.

We give here a skeleton account of the structure of Jewish education in this country, it reflects, of course, the variegated structure of English secular education.

(1) The London Board of Jewish Religious Education[1]

The London Board is administratively and financially responsible for seventy-eight part-time schools attached to synagogues in Greater London, for twelve Talmud Torahs mainly in North and East London, and for 'Withdrawal' Classes held in twenty-four secular schools during the periods set aside for religious instruction.

The total number of pupils rises and falls with the increase and decrease of the general primary school population. The peak was reached in 1957, since when the numbers have gradually declined as the following figures for representative years show:

	Nov. 1950	Nov. 1957	Nov. 1958	Nov. 1961
Synagogue Classes	5,735	10,167	10,130	9,120
Talmud Torah Classes	1,517	1,613	1,488	1,127
Withdrawal Classes	3,145	2,805	2,639	2,328
	10,397	14,585	14,257	12,575

It may well be that when the primary school population increases, as it is expected to do after 1965, the number of Jewish pupils receiving religious instruction may increase likewise.

[1] The London Board issues an Annual Report, obtainable on request, giving full details of its activities and a statistical analysis of the rolls, attendances and age-groups at each of its Centres.

Jewish Education in Great Britain

The London Board is responsible *inter alia* for the drawing up of curricula, the provision of text-books, inspections, the holding of annual examinations and the payment of teachers' salaries, in accordance with a scale depending on qualifications. In addition, it is responsible for the J.F.S. Secondary School (see below); its educational work is controlled by a Director of Education and an Education Officer, who will be joined later this year by an Assistant Education Officer.

Its income is derived chiefly from a religious education rate levied on the members of the United Synagogue and the Federation of Synagogues.

Other aspects of the work of the London Board in the fields of teacher-training and day schools will be treated later in this survey.

(2) Jewish Day Schools in London

In London there are the following Jewish Day Schools:
- (a) Two state-aided primary schools, the Stepney and the Solomon Wolfson schools, each with 250–300 pupils, continuing a history begun in the middle of last century.
- (b) The J.F.S. Secondary School, which is a denominational school owned by the London Board of Jewish Religious Education. There are 500 pupils at present with a projected roll of 1,400 when the premises are extended within the next few years. The school replaces the old Jews' Free School founded in 1817 and the majority of its Governors are appointed by the London Board.
- (c) Two grammar and four primary and kindergarten schools which are associated with the Jewish Secondary Schools Movement that developed between the Wars and which have a combined roll of 1,400.
- (d) One grammar and two primary and kindergarten Yesodey Hatorah Schools with a combined roll of about 900.
- (e) Four primary and kindergarten schools associated with the Zionist Federation which have a combined roll of about 750.
- (f) One grammar and four primary schools independent of a central organization.

(3) Other Organizations active in London

In addition to the part-time classes administered by the London Board there are part-time classes organized by:
- (a) The Board of Orthodox Jewish Education;
- (b) The Sephardi Community;

(c) The Lubavitch Foundation;
(d) The Association of Synagogues of Great Britain (Reform);
(e) The Union of Liberal and Progressive Synagogues;
(f) One or two independent synagogues.

(4) The Central Council for Jewish Religious Education and the Provinces[1]

The Central Council for Jewish Religious Education inspects classes in England outside Greater London and in Wales, Scotland and Northern Ireland; advises on curricula, text-books and methods of teaching; and organizes Jewish Youth Study Groups both in London and the Provinces. The Central Council is supported by a contribution from the London Board, by affiliation fees paid by provincial communities, and by contributions from individual associate members, trust funds, and central organizations, particularly the Jewish Memorial Council.

The Central Council has one education officer, an Inspector. The communities he visits vary very much in size and in internal organization.

The variation in size is best set forth in the following table:

GROUP	NUMBER OF PROVINCIAL COMMUNITIES	APPROX. JEWISH POPULATION	NUMBER OF PUPILS PER COMMUNITY IN HEBREW CLASSES AND DAY SCHOOLS	TOTAL NUMBER OF PUPILS IN THE GROUP	PERCENTAGE OF PROVINCIAL JEWISH SCHOOL POPULATION
A	1	28,000	Over 1,000	2,700	31·4
B	4	6,000 to 20,000	400 to 999	2,788	32·4
C	5	2,000 to 3,500	150 to 399	981	11·4
D	14	500 to 2,000	50 to 149	1,299	15·0
E	17	200 to 500	20 to 49	540	6·3
F	31	under 200	under 20	304	3·5
Total	72			8,612	

[1] The Central Council issues an Annual Report, obtainable on request, giving full details of its activities.

Group A is represented solely by Manchester. Group B comprises Leeds, Glasgow, Birmingham, and Liverpool; Group C communities like those of Cardiff and Newcastle; Group D such towns as Belfast, Bradford, Fdinburgh and Nottingham; Group E smaller communities like those of Bristol, Coventry, Harrogate and Portsmouth; and Group F the smallest communities like those of Aberdeen, Norwich and York.

The variation in internal organization is just as striking.

Manchester is almost a counterpart on a smaller scale of London. There is a Central Board for Hebrew Education which has a Director of Education and undertakes tasks similar to those of the London Board in London. There are the state-aided King David (Jews') Schools with 1,000 pupils in Infants, Primary, and Secondary departments continuing, like the J.F.S. school in London, a century-old tradition; there are newer schools like those of the Secondary Schools Movement, and there are independent schools and independent part-time classes to meet special needs.

In Leeds Jewish education is provided almost exclusively by the Talmud Torah Jewish Education Board which maintains a Talmud Torah meeting five times a week, a number of branches, a network of Withdrawal Classes and, in co-operation with the Zionist Federation, a growing day school. Leeds is the best example in the provinces of one board controlling Jewish education. The position of Education Officer has been vacant for some years.

In Glasgow the Board of Jewish Education directly administers a Talmud Torah with its branches, maintains a Hebrew College for post-Barmitzvah education and loosely co-ordinates the work of a number of synagogue classes.

Liverpool presents a different picture. The synagogue classes are all independent of one another and of the long-established Jewish Primary School and the new King David Bilateral Secondary-Modern/Primary School. In Birmingham the Hebrew and Religious Education Department of the Hebrew Congregation has an Education Officer who organizes Jewish education in part-time classes and supervises the Jewish side of a Hebrew Primary School. There is an independent Talmud Torah. There is also a full-time Director of Education in Sheffield. In most of the other communities Jewish education is organized by the Rabbi or minister with the assistance of an Education Committee. Some of the smaller communities have to depend on a visiting teacher from a neighbouring town or on a resident layman. There are new day schools in Southend and in Sunderland.

We turn next to the statistical background. To arrive at an estimate of the Jewish child population we begin with figures taken from the

Isidor Fishman and Harold Levy

'Registrar-General's Statistical Review for England and Wales', 30th June, 1958.

(1) Child Population of England and Wales

	All figures in thousands	Percentage of Total Population
Total population	45,224	—
5 and under 15	6,950	15
5 and under 16	7,577	16.7
5 and under 17	8,148	18

(2) Estimate of Jewish Child Population
  (*a*) Assuming
    (1) that the Jewish population of Great Britain and Northern Ireland is 450,000 (*Jewish Year Book*, 1962); and
    (2) that the age distribution of the Jewish population is the same as that of England and Wales
  the figures for the Jewish child population are as follows:

Total population	450,000
5 and under 15	67,500
5 and under 16	75,150
5 and under 17	81,000

  (*b*) Since there are great variations between the age distribution in urban areas and the age distribution in rural areas, and since the Jewish population is largely an urban population, it seems better to base the estimate for the Jewish child population on the Registrar-General's figures for Greater London, available only for the 5 and under 15 age-group.

	Figures in thousands
Total population Greater London	8,222
Population 5 and under 15	964
Percentage of total	11.7

On this basis the number of Jewish children between the ages of five and under fifteen is 52,650. Of this number it is estimated that there are around 32,500 Jewish school children in London and 20,000 in the Provinces.

(3) Number of children receiving Jewish instruction in organized groups (excluding pupils taught privately)
LONDON
  Part-time
    London Board of Jewish Religious Education (after deducting 1,000 for overlap

Jewish Education In Great Britain

between Withdrawal classes and other classes)	11,575 (Nov. 1961)
Union of Orthodox Hebrew Congregations and Sephardim	860
Reform and Liberal Congregations	1,000
Day Schools (including some pupils over 16)	4,800
Yeshivot (97 part-time, 132 full-time)	229
	18,464

PROVINCES

Part-time

Provincial communities	7,000
Sephardim	140
Other Organizations	500
Day Schools and Boarding Schools (including some pupils over 16)	3,500
Yeshivot (65 part-time, 260 full-time)	325
	11,465
Grand Total	29,929

(4) Percentage of children receiving Jewish Instruction

The foregoing figures suggest that, allowing for some overlap between attendances at day schools and attendance at part-time classes, around 30,000 children out of the estimated 52,650, that is to say, 57 per cent, are enrolled for part-time or full-time instruction at the present moment. This does not mean that the remaining 22,000 never received any religious instruction. The startling disparity between the total Jewish child school population and the total roll of the Hebrew class is to be explained by the very large proportion of late beginners and early leavers. Only a small proportion of the five to eight age-group are represented in the Hebrew Class; the same is true of the incomparably more important age-group thirteen to fifteen, of which certainly less than 10 per cent continue their attendance. Jewish education thus suffers from an early leaving age combined with an erratically floating starting age. In other words whilst at any given time no more than about 57 per cent of Jewish children of school age are on the roll of the Hebrew Class, it may be reasonably assumed that about 75–80 per cent of all children receive Jewish instruction during some period of their school career.

This point was well brought out in a statistical survey made in

March, 1958, by the Central Council. Headmasters were asked to complete for each class in their school a form giving the number of boys and girls on their roll and their distribution by age. Sixty-six schools in forty-nine towns submitted returns. Setting aside the towns, six in number, from which complete returns were not received, and in which there were day schools and therefore overlapping enrolments, the figures for the remaining forty-three towns were collated and the following picture emerged:

	Age last birthday											Total
	under 5	5	6	7	8	9	10	11	12	13	14	15+	
Boys	8	51	101	125	145	171	123	186	158	72	26	21	1,187
Girls	10	42	87	116	116	125	127	127	98	51	16	12	927
Total	18	93	188	241	261	296	250	313	256	123	42	33	2,114

These figures give precision to the impressions of all educational workers, making it quite clear that in part-time schools:

(a) many enrolments are made at 8 or 9 years of age or even later;
(b) girls enrol in fewer numbers than boys;
(c) most boys have ceased attendance by Barmitzvah age and many girls earlier;
(d) the average boy is on the roll of the Hebrew Class for about four or five years, the average girl for a little less.

In interpreting the table it is important to remember that at the date of the survey there were more children of 12 years in the country than of any other age and that the age distribution of Jewish children may or may not have followed precisely the age distribution of the general child population.

(5) Duration of the period of tuition

Part-time Classes
In London the average synagogue class meets for a total of six hours a week, on Sunday morning (10 a.m. to 1 p.m.) and on two evenings (5–6.30 p.m.). But mid-week attendance averages only 33 per cent, and teaching Sundays may not exceed forty-five per year, so that most children receive only 135 hours of tuition per year. If the average child attends for only four years then all his Jewish instruction has to be given in about 540 hours. In many Talmud Torahs the position is better. The hours of tuition are longer and mid-week attendance exceeds that on Sundays. A similar situation is to be found in the Provinces. Where there is a Talmud Torah-type school midweek attendance is good. In Synagogue classes the London pattern is repeated.

Day Schools
Jewish day schools vary considerably in the amount of time afforded to Jewish studies. Some give as little as three hours per week, others almost three hours per day.

Of obvious importance is the question of the educational standards that are attained.

(a) Part-time Classes
Since there is such a wide variation in the period of years during which a pupil studies at a Hebrew class or Talmud Torah, it would be difficult to attempt a succinct statement of average attainment. One child in his fourteenth year who attends regularly for a number of years may be thoroughly at home in *Chumash* and *Rashi* and may have embarked on the study of the Talmud. Another whose attendance is limited to Sunday mornings for a short period, may still be at a very elementary stage.

The minimum aim of the London Board's Centres is the School Certificate Examination of the Central Examining Board under the auspices of Jews' College, which is taken when a pupil reaches the age of 14. The syllabus for the examination is set forth in Appendix III. Since only about 8 per cent of pupils attending classes remain beyond the age of 13, the number of candidates is limited.

Most pupils, however, proceed to the London Board's Junior examination (for pupils under 12 years of age) and to the senior examination (for pupils under 14 years of age). The number of entrants is growing annually and in 1962 346 pupils entered for the Junior and 190 for the Senior grade. The syllabuses are set forth in Appendix II.

Few students go beyond the School Certificate stage to study for the Intermediate examination of the Central Examining Board which requires a more intensive knowledge of Bible and Rabbinics, and includes selections from medieval and modern Hebrew literature.

In the Withdrawal Classes attached to Secondary Schools, pupils are prepared for the G.C.E. Examinations at 'O' level in Classical and/or Modern Hebrew and Religious Knowledge.

In an effort to encourage pupils to continue their Jewish studies beyond the age of 13, the London Board has adopted a scheme of regionalization whereby in a given locality the Centres are re-organized into Junior and Secondary Schools housed in separate buildings. With the establishment of Secondary Hebrew Centres courses are provided for pupils between the ages of 12 and 16 designed to retain their interest in Jewish matters. They are divided into various streams and the academic stream is prepared for the

School Certificate and G.C.E. Examinations. A special session is set aside for all pupils for the study of the Hebrew language. The history of the modern period also finds its place in the curriculum. A number of regional classes have already been established and have proved their value thus giving encouragement to similar schemes which are under consideration.

Ventures of this nature have been established, with success, in the Provinces notably in Glasgow and in Manchester.

Another step has been the formation of girls' classes especially in the Provinces. These are popularly known as Batmitzvah or Eshet Hayil Classes and sometimes simply as Senior Girls' Classes.

(b) Day Schools

The most outstanding contribution to the recent progress of Jewish education in Anglo-Jewry has been the development of Jewish Day Schools. On April 28th, 1961, the *Jewish Chronicle* published a statistical review by Dr. J. Braude which shows that the number of pupils attending Jewish Day Schools has almost doubled during the previous seven years. There are at present thirty-eight Jewish Day schools in this country with a total roll of 8,000 children (in London there are twenty-two schools with approximately 4,800 children). About one Jewish school-child in seven now attends a Jewish Day School as compared with one in eight in 1959. The standards in Primary Day Schools, as in the case of Synagogue Classes and Talmud Torahs, varies considerably. The long established state-aided primary schools generally attempt to reach a standard similar to that of the Junior examination of the London Board. The Primary Schools associated with the Secondary Schools Movement follow a more intensive course of studies and give great emphasis to *Chumash*, *Rashi* and in some instances Mishnah. The schools associated with the Zionist Federation place greater stress on spoken Hebrew. A few schools such as those organized by the Yesodey Hatorah and the Lubavitch Foundation use Yiddish as the medium of instruction.

Secondary schools are fewer in number, there being only five in London, three in Manchester (two of them very small) and one in Liverpool. The first attempt to establish a Jewish school on the model of the English public school is Carmel College in Berkshire which has proved very successful and is recognized by the Ministry of Education. It is a private school and does not come under the jurisdiction of any communal organization. Most of these schools aim at the General Certificate of Education in Classical and Modern Hebrew but a number give a considerable amount of time to Limmudei Kodesh.

Finally we would like to indicate the provision that is made for further (and higher education) and for teacher training. A number of organizations cater for the further Jewish education of young people in adolescence and early adult life. The education offered is sometimes formal, sometimes informal. It is particularly useful because the Jewish education of many children ceases so early. In some cases even those who have been entirely bereft of Jewish education in childhood are attracted and influenced.

Among the organizations that provide such educational opportunities are the following:

(1) Youth Groups
(a) Jewish Youth Study Groups under the auspices of the Central Council for Jewish Religious Education comprise a number of groups that meet weekly for study. Some groups study elementary Hebrew reading, some groups Mishnah, some history and some the fundamentals of Judaism. At Summer and Winter Schools the forenoons are devoted to lecture courses mainly on basic sources.

(b) The Zionist Youth Groups, such as B'nei Akiva and Habonim each with its own emphasis try to foster a knowledge of Hebrew and of Jewish History especially in relation to Zionism.

(c) Organizations such as Ezra and Yavneh aim at strengthening the religious ties of young people.

(2) For students the Inter-University Jewish Federation in association with the Hillel Foundation arranges valuable central courses and week-end schools.

(3) The Jewish Agency Department for Education and Culture arranges Summer and Winter Seminars and shorter seminars at other periods of the year at which many hundreds of young people have developed their knowledge of Hebrew and been introduced to many branches of Hebrew literature and Jewish thought. A network of classes in Modern Hebrew is also maintained.

(4) The Hoveve Torah movement in London organizes Shi'urim in Tanach, Mishnah and Talmud.

All these organizations together, while they have a strong influence on their members, attract only a small fraction of Jewish youth.

In the field of higher education the premier institution is Jews' College which trains ministers, Rabbis, Hazzanim and teachers.

Students preparing for the ministry take the London University B.A. Honours degree in Semitics and the Minister's Diploma of the College. At the date of the last published report (for session 1959–60) there were thirty-one students following this course of study. The number has since decreased. At the same time in the Hazzanut class there were twelve students. Post-graduate students prepare for the Rabbinical Diploma of the College or the London University degree of Doctor of Philosophy. The Sephardi community maintains the *Judith Lady Montefiore College* as a Rabbinical College and Teachers' Training Seminar. There are about a dozen students mainly from Mediterranean countries.

The Reform movement maintains its own *Leo Baeck College* for the training of its ministers. The main *Yeshivot* have altogether 392 full-time and 162 part-time students as follows:

	Full-time	Part-time
Gateshead		
Yeshiva	135	—
Institute for Higher Rabbinical Studies	25	5
London		
Etz Chaim	23	66
Law of Truth	69	12
Horomo	28	12
North-West	12	7
Manchester	40	60
Sunderland	60	—
	392	162

It should be noted also that at many universities there are degree courses in Classical Hebrew and in Modern Hebrew.

It is estimated that just over 800 persons are engaged in Jewish full-time or part-time teaching. Some are graduates of the institutions mentioned above or of similar institutions and are academically equipped to teach in any of the part-time classes. Although few have had pedagogical training this does not mean that they are unsuccessful as teachers.

A small number of teachers are graduates of secular training colleges. They have much to offer particularly in junior classes but their Jewish knowledge is often insufficient to warrant their allocation to senior groups.

The number of teachers who combine adequate Jewish knowledge with sound pedagogical training is small. They are outnumbered by those whose Jewish knowledge is elementary and whose pedagogical training is nil.

[1] There are also small Yeshivot in Glasgow, in Liverpool and in Leeds.

The facilities for the training of Jewish teachers are as follows:

(*a*) The Gateshead Seminary for the Training of Teachers with about ninety women students combines a thorough training in Judaism with courses in pedagogy and is doing most valuable work.

(*b*) On a smaller scale the Beth Ya'akov Seminary in London works on similar lines.

(*c*) The Jews' College Institute for the Training of Teachers is younger and the first cycle of students is only now completing its studies. Students take a B.A. (General) degree at London University, and simultaneously pursue Jewish studies by working for the Intermediate and later the Hebrew Teachers Diploma Examination of the Central Examining Board. It is intended that students take a post-graduate course at the London University Institute of Education. There are thirty-five students.

(*d*) The Evening Institute for the Training of Teachers under the auspices of the London Board is newer and aims primarily at improving the academic qualifications and the teaching ability of its part-time students. There are thirty students.

We must frankly admit that unless young people can be offered a full-time teaching career, with an adequate salary and a dignified status, there is little likelihood of obtaining the large number of qualified teachers the community requires for its day schools and part-time Hebrew Centres. The prospects are certainly brighter in view of the rapid growth and expansion of Jewish day schools in London and the provinces, but we do not believe that any local community or private body can deal with this complex problem on its own. More than consultation is required. A permanent council has to be established representative of the whole country, with its own professional officers who can devote their full time to this pressing need. Many alternatives have to be investigated. Should not a renewed effort be made to establish a denominational Jewish Teachers' College? If under present circumstances this cannot be achieved, should not selected certificated teachers specializing in secular subjects be encouraged to study for two or three years at one of the established teachers training institutes to qualify for the Hebrew Teachers' Diploma of the Central Examining Board of Jews' College? Has not the time arrived for unqualified part-time teachers to be obliged to undergo practical training before they are allowed to stand in front of the class?

APPENDIX I

Text-Books

The most widely used *Alef-Bet* primer is still the traditional *Reshit-Da'at* but a number of Centres are now using more attractive books such as *Reshit Hochma* published in America. N. Morris's *Hayeled* and V. Schonfeld's *Sefat Mosheh* have still their devotees. Israeli primers are on the whole not considered suitable. They are often based on a rural background which would be strange to our urban children and they are designed of course for children who come to school already lisping Hebrew.

Chumashim and Siddurim are produced in England though some editions are brought from abroad.

Rabbinic texts (e.g. Mishnah, Shulchan Aruch) are usually brought from Israel. Dr. Fishman's *Gateway to the Mishnah* is used very generally as an introduction.

The Hebrew Grammars used are by and large produced in this country. M. Adler's *First Steps in Hebrew Grammar* is popular for young beginners. Senior pupils use such books as J. Weingreen's *Practical Grammar for Classical Hebrew* and S. Fundaminsky's *New Hebrew Grammar*.

For Modern Hebrew a variety of American and Israeli books is used as well as a Central Council publication, Harold Levy's *Hebrew for All*.

For the principles and practice of Judaism teachers now have at their disposal a number of books, among them Dr. Fishman's *Introduction to Judaism*; *A Guide to Jewish Knowledge* by Pearl and Brookes, and Dr. Epstein's books on the Jewish Religion.

The range of books available for the teaching of History is small especially for younger children. For senior pupils there are J. Halpern's *History of our People in Bible Times*, the companion volume for *Rabbinic Times*, and Lady Magnus's *Outlines of Jewish History*. These are supplemented by a number of American books. Important teaching aids are a wall-map of Israel in Hebrew and English published by the Central Council, and a magnetic blackboard devised by R. Brookes. Audio-visual aids are not widely used.

APPENDIX II

LONDON BOARD OF JEWISH RELIGIOUS EDUCATION

Syllabus for the Twelfth Annual Prize Examination, March 1962

JUNIOR: *Pupils under 12 years of age on February 28th, 1962.*

1. HEBREW
    Translation:
    (*a*) Genesis xl, xli, xlii.

Exodus xix and xx.
Numbers xiii and xiv.
(b) Weekday Amidah; Sabbath Morning Amidah; Ahavah Rabbah; Three paragraphs of the Shema; first four paragraphs of Grace after Meals;
Kiddush and Havdalah for Sabbaths and Festivals; Blessings on various occasions (Authorized Daily-Prayer Book, pp. 287-92); Alenu and Adon Olam.
(c) The Passover Haggadah; Ma Nishtanah, Avadim Hayinu, Pesah, Matzah, Maror.
(d) Translation of simple sentences from Hebrew into English and vice-versa.

2. GRAMMAR
  (a) A simple knowledge of the noun including gender, number, prefixes and suffixes.
  (b) The adjective, position and agreement.
  (c) The definitive article.
  (d) The verb: Kal (regular).

3. HISTORY
  (a) Patriarchs; Joseph; Moses; Joshua; Ruth; Samuel; Saul; David; Solomon. The Division of the Kingdom; Elijah; Elisha; Hezekiah; Josiah; The Destruction of the Temple. Jeremiah.
  (b) Hillel and Shammai; Johanan ben Zaccai; Bar Cochba; Rabbi Akiba; Judah the Prince.

4. GEOGRAPHY
  The elementary geography of the Holy Land and of the State of Israel.

5. RELIGIOUS KNOWLEDGE
  Jewish Observances—in particular, the Laws of Kashruth; The Sabbath and Holy Days; the Calendar; Tephillin, Mezuzah and Tzitzith.
  The main features of the Synagogue Services.

LONDON BOARD OF JEWISH RELIGIOUS EDUCATION
Syllabus for the Thirteenth Annual Prize Examination, March, 1962
SENIOR: *Pupils under 14 years of age on February 28th, 1962.*

1. HEBREW
  Translation:
  A (a) Genesis i, ii, iii, xii, xiii and xxiv.
     Exodus i, ii, iii.
     Leviticus xxiii.
     Deuteronomy xxix, xxx, xxi and xxxiv.
     II Kings iv, 1-37
     Isaiah vi.

Appendices

Jeremiah i to ii, 3.
The Book of Jonah, Chaps. iii and iv.

(b) Prayer-Book (Authorized Daily) pp. 2 to 9, line 3. Morning Service, pp. 37-54, omitting the Kaddish. Evening Amidah for New Year and Day of Atonement up to Oseh Hashalom.
All four Amidot for Sabbath.
Hallel.

(c) The Passover Haggadah; Ha Lachma, Ma Nishtanah, Avadim Hayinu, Dayenu, Pesah, Matzah, Maror, Bechol Dor Vador, Lefichach.

(d) Mishnah; 'Gateway to the Mishnah', paras. 19 to 23, 52 to 58.
OR
Talmud: Baba Kamma p. 55 (b) from the beginning of the Mishnah to two lines from bottom of page.

(e) Rashi: Exodus xviii to xix, 6.

(f) Kitzur Shulchan Aruch (Ganzfried);
Chap. 1, paras 1 to 4;
Chap. 143, paras. 1 to 12 and 21.
Selections from the Laws relating to the Sabbath.

B (a) Translation of unseen passages from Hebrew into English.
(b) Translation of sentences from English into Hebrew.

C GRAMMAR

The Noun, gender, number, simple declension; the adjective; the definite Article; prepositions (including prefixes); the regular verb—all seven conjugations.

2. HISTORY

(a) Solomon; the Temple; the Division of the Kingdom; the House of Omri; Elijah; Elisha; the House of Jehu; Amos, the End of the Northern Kingdom; Hezekiah; Isaiah; Jeremiah; Exile of Jehoiachin; the Destruction of the Temple; the Babylonian Captivity; Ezekiel.

(b) The Return; the Rebuilding of the Temple; the Book of Esther; Ezra and Nehemiah; Judah the Maccabee; Herod the Great; Hillel and Shammai; the Roman War; Johanan ben Zaccai; Bar Cochba; Rabbi Akiba; Judah the Prince.

(c) Saadiah; Maimonides; Yehudah Halevi; Rashi; Abrabanel; Menasseh ben Israel; Vilna Gaon; Moses Montefiore; Theodor Herzl; Hayyim Nahman Bialik.

3. GEOGRAPHY

The Geography of the Holy Land and of the State of Israel to include the following:

(a) Position, size, population, boundaries, neighbouring nations.
(b) Physical regions; coastal plain, highlands, Jordan gorge, the Negev.
(c) The more important towns, rivers, plains, lakes and mountains.
(d) Climate, agriculture, natural resources and main exports and imports.

4. RELIGIOUS KNOWLEDGE
Jewish Life, Faith and Practice. To include:
The Bible, its constituent parts.
The Calendar; Sabbath and Holy Days; Special Sabbaths; the Minor Fasts and their significance.
Our distinctive observances. Tzitzith, Mezuzzah, Tephillin, Dietary Laws.
The Ten Commandments.
The arrangement of the Siddur.
The Synagogue and its ritual; the main features of the different Services.
Duties in daily life especially as to honesty, charity, truth, humility, the dignity of labour, kindness to animals.
The Unity and Fatherhood of God; God's Justice; love and fear of God; the Messiah.

APPENDIX III

SYLLABUS FOR THE SCHOOL CERTIFICATE EXAMINATION OF THE CENTRAL EXAMINING BOARD
1962

1. TRANSLATION (No candidate will pass in this section who does not satisfy the Examiners in sub-section (c)).
    (a) Bible:
       (i) Genesis i, ii, iii, xii–xiv, xviii, xxii, xxiv, xxxvii, xl–xlv; Exodus i–v, xix, xx; Leviticus xix, 1–18, xxiii; Numbers xiii, xiv; Deuteronomy vi, xv, xvi, xxix, xxx, xxxi and xxxiv.
       (ii) The following Haphtarot: Joshua i; I Samuel xi, 14 to xii, 21; II Kings iv, 1–37; Amos ii, 6 to iii, 8; Isaiah i, vi, xl; Jeremiah i to ii, 3; Ezekiel xxxvii; Jonah.
    (b) Prayer-Book (Authorized Daily): pp. 2–9, line 3; Morning Service, pp. 37–54 (omitting the Kaddish); Avinu Malkenu, pp. 55–57; Evening Service, pp. 95–101; Ashre, pp. 29–30; Friday Evening Psalms, pp. 108a–111; all four amidot for Sabbath; Evening and Musaph Amidot for the three Festivals; Evening Amidah for New Year and Day of Atonement up to Oseh Hashalom; Hallel; Alenu; Yigdal and Adon Olam; Grace after Meals, pp. 279–85; Kiddush and Havdalah for Sabbath and Festivals; Hamappil, p. 293. Blessings on Tzitzit, Tephillin, Lulav and Sukkah; Blessings on Various Occasions, pp. 287–92; Pirke Avoth, Chap. 1.
    (c) Passages from the Bible or Prayer-Book not specified above.
    (d) The Passover Haggadah; Ha Lachma, Ma Nishtanah, Avadim

Appendices

Hayinu, Dayenu, Pesach, Matzah, Maror, Bechol Dor Vador, Lefichach.
(e) Mishnah: 'Gateway to the Mishnah', paras 19 to 23; 41 to 46; 52 to 58; 90 to 93; 117 to 119.
(f) Rashi: Genesis xxii; xxxvii; Exodus xviii, i to xix, 6.
(g) Kitzur Shulchan Aruch (Ganzfried), Chap. 1, paras. 1 to 4; Chap. 2, paras. 1 to 4; Chap. 143, paras. 1 to 12 and 21; selections from the Laws relating to the Sabbath. (Texts obtainable from the London Board of Jewish Religious Education).

2. HEBREW GRAMMAR AND COMPOSITION
   (a) Regular Verbs (including those with gutturals)—all seven conjugations. Kal only of ע״י and ל״ה verbs.
   (b) Nouns, the definite article, adjectives and prepositions.
   (c) Translation from English into Hebrew and Simple Composition in Hebrew.

3. HISTORY AND GEOGRAPHY
   (a) Scripture History and post-Biblical History to the Compilation of the Mishnah, together with a knowledge of the geography of Palestine in relation thereto.
   The following is a list of the general events and personages of which a knowledge will be expected:
      (i) The Patriarchs; Joseph; the Bondage in Egypt; Moses; the Exodus; the giving of the Torah; the nature of the contents of the Five Books; the Wanderings in the Wilderness; the conquest of the Eastern side of the Jordan; the Death of Moses.
      (ii) Joshua; the conquest and division of the land; the Judges (general characteristics of the period); Deborah; Gideon; Jephthah; Samson (the Philistines); Eli (Shiloh); Samuel; Saul; Ruth; David; the Wars of David; the capture of Jerusalem.
      (iii) Solomon; the Temple; the Division of the Kingdom; the House of Omri; Elijah; Elisha; the House of Jehu; Amos; the end of the Northern Kingdom; Hezekiah; Isaiah; Josiah; Jeremiah; Exile of Jehoiachin; the Destruction of the Temple; the Babylonian Captivity; Ezekiel.
      (iv) The Return; the rebuilding of the Temple; the Book of Esther; Ezra and Nehemiah; Judah the Maccabee; Herod; Hillel and Shammai; the Roman War; Johanan ben Zaccai; Bar Cochba; Rabbi Akiba; Judah the Prince.
   (b) Outline of later history to the present time, with reference to the following personages: Saadiah, Rashi, Judah Halevi, Maimonides, Abrabanel, Menasseh ben Israel, Karo, Vilna Gaon, Moses Montefiore, Herzl, Bialik.

4. RELIGIOUS KNOWLEDGE
   The Torah as our inheritance. The written and the oral Law and of what they consist.

The Bible; its constituent parts and the nature of the different books. The teaching of the Prophets.

Our Beliefs; unity and fatherhood of God; the choice of Israel; God's justice; the golden age of the Messiah; the resurrection of the dead.

Duties in daily life, especially as to truth, honesty, purity, considerateness, charity, repentance, devotion in prayer, diligence in work and study, loyalty to the State.

Our distinctive observances. Outward signs; Tzitzit, Mezuzah, Tephillin, Mila, Dietary Laws.

The Calendar; Sabbath and Holy Days, Special Sabbaths, the minor fasts and their significance.

The Synagogue and its ritual. Congregational and private prayers. The arrangement of the Prayer Book. The main features of the different Services.

Discussion

WELCOMING the contribution on Jewish education, Dr. Esh felt that the authors had dealt almost exclusively with one aspect of the educational field. 'The picture that emerges from their very competent analysis is that a lot is done in this country for instruction in Jewish knowledge; as regards Jewish "education" in the particular sense referred to, namely, transmission of Jewish values and creating a Jewish atmosphere, it remains an open question, at least for me, if much is done in this respect. It seems that British Jews have arrived at quite a considerable degree of administrative efficiency in the field of Jewish instruction. That this well organized educational effort does not include all Jewish children of school age is duly stressed in the paper itself. The statisticians among us might be rather sceptical about the information regarding the percentage given by the authors of children receiving some Jewish instruction at all (they assume it to be 75–80 per cent). The question, as I see it, is that, of these, almost 30 per cent seem not to reach, let alone retain a working knowledge of even reading Hebrew. If this assumption is right, then we arrive at the rather sad conclusion that about half of the growing Jewish generation will be unable to take any active part in Jewish religious life, and it is difficult to see how this half of the future community can be retained as an integral part of our community. For them religious identification will be void of any content, nor will there be a substitute for it, conceivable at least in theory, namely by way of "group identification" based on *secular* Jewish *nationalism*.

'It does not seem to be out of place to add a word about secular Jewish instruction. In this field, as in others, the holocaust has made grave inroads as far as the Diaspora is concerned. The once flourishing secular educational institutions in Eastern Europe are no more. What is left of them, is to be found mainly in the Western hemisphere. I only mention it because in Anglo-Jewry apparently even the idea of this type of Jewish education never came to mind and was not brought into discussion. It might be useful for people to bear in mind that Jewish *religious* education is not a matter of course and not the only possible course of Jewish education.

'Anyway, practically all Jews in this country are agreed (as I have learned today) that Jewish instruction should be a religious one, centred around the various branches of our traditional literature. I think we should be grateful (as in fact I am) for the various syllabuses added by the authors

Discussion

to their paper, for they enable us to learn the aims and targets of the main stream of Jewish education. Perhaps it might be useful to take these syllabuses as starting-point for our discussion, as I assume them to be a kind of resumé of the school programme. Far be it from me to pretend that the situation as it appears from the programme is peculiar to England. From what I know from my stay in Switzerland and my work there some years ago, and also from what I read about the situation in other countries, in and outside Europe, it seems to be quite clear that the educational situation in most of these countries is rather similar to that found here.

'What strikes one most is the impression that the tremendous events which happened to the Jewish people in our generation, and which have made so great an impact on Jewish life, have hardly made any impact on Jewish education in this country.

'One cannot but ask if the study of the Hebrew language and the traditional literature written in it, is still carried on as if Hebrew were only a sacred language used in the synagogue and Beth Hamidrash. Do pupils learn the language exactly as their fathers and grandfathers used to learn it, translating the text word by word or sentence by sentence? Can it be that the achievements made during the past decades in the method of teaching foreign languages, remain almost unnoted in our own field of Hebrew instruction in the Diaspora? In fact, I can understand that the inclusion of modern Hebrew literature in the general programme of Jewish instruction may be a matter of discussion, but I can hardly imagine a reason for treating Hebrew nowadays as a non-spoken language. I am aware, of course, of the barrier of the Ashkenazi pronunciation, but this should not prove to be insurmountable. Sooner or later the Sephardi pronunciation used in spoken Hebrew will also have to be recognized by all those Diaspora communities which are connected in other aspects with the State of Israel—even if only to remove one of the divisions between Israel and the Golah.

'No less interesting in my opinion is the impression one gets of an almost complete absence of knowledge about Jewish history in modern times. Even in the advanced Certificate of Examination (to say nothing of the Senior and Junior Prize Examinations) there seems to be very little, as far as I have been able to see, about the very things that have stood in the centre of Jewish life and discussion in modern times. Could it really be that some knowledge about Montefiore, Herzl and Bialik will compensate for not learning the essential facts about *Binyan Ha'aretz* and the establishment of the Jewish State, or about the fundamental shift of the Jewish people all over the world?

'This is, of course, not the place, nor is it for me, to discuss possible remedies for this situation. I intended only to indicate certain points that seem to be characteristic of the contemporary scene in Jewish education.'

Dr. Esh ended by underlining the quite spectacular development of Jewish day schools in this country in recent years. 'From the statistics presented,[1] we learn that about 25 per cent of the children receiving Jewish instruction in London are pupils in Jewish day schools, whereas the per-

[1] See above (p. 73).

Jewish Education in Great Britain

centage in the provinces is even higher than one third. It would be quite important to supplement this information by an inquiry about the motives lying behind this development, which seems to continue vigorously. Does this trend not contradict the widely-held opinion that indifference to all things Jewish is the main characteristic of contemporary Anglo-Jewry?'

Dr. Esh was followed by Dr. Steinberg, who argued that, valuable as the paper had been, 'the basic purpose of Jewish education was omitted. The question which arises is: What kind of Jewish personality can be formed in this country in 400 hours of Jewish education? When I consider the things which occupy the mind of the general public in this country; when, for instance, I study the debate on Youth which took place in the House of Lords on the 21st February in which I find this sentence: "The young people of today are very different from any generation in human memory", I ask myself whether such thoughts affect the syllabuses of Jewish school teaching? Perhaps they do, but I find no reference to this aspect in the paper under consideration. If we follow the way of tradition, I ask myself whether our ancestral tradition, which I cherish so deeply, is sufficient to cope with the many primarily moral problems facing the young men of today, and the young men after Barmitzvah in particular. And I must say that it is great worry to me not only in relation to Jewish education in this country, but also more generally. When we start investigating the position of Jewish education, we must concentrate first of all on this problem and turn our minds and hearts to solving it.'

Dr. Prais observed that like Dr. Fishman and Mr. Levy he too had attempted estimates of the *proportion* of children receiving religious education. 'Not surprisingly, we have arrived at somewhat different answers, and I should like to comment briefly on the reason for the discrepancy. On the numerator in the fraction, namely the number of children receiving education, there is agreement (in fact I am indebted for these figures to Dr. Fishman and Mr. Levy); but on the denominator, namely the total number of Jewish children in the country (both those receiving and those not receiving instruction), we have made different assumptions. And the reason we have had to base ourselves on assumptions is that no one knows how many Jewish children there are in the country; I have in mind a possible way of obtaining this figure more directly (by the Yom Kippur absence method), but until this is adopted we have to rely on rather indirect calculations.

'In both our calculations we took the number of Jewish children as being a certain proportion of the Jewish population; I took that proportion as equal to that of the general population in England and Wales, and Dr. Fishman and Mr. Levy took it as equal to that for London where, for various reasons, children are less frequent. Hence there is a discrepancy; but, in any case, I think I may say we agree that somewhere between a quarter and a third of all children never have any religious instruction at any time in their life. And that surely provides sufficient cause for reflection.

'I should like to put a further question to the authors on an important related matter. Would it be at all possible to say, on the basis of present information, how many Jewish teachers should be trained each year to provide adequate instruction for the children? And how does the number of teachers required compare with present training facilities?'

The next speaker was Dr. Raphael Loewe. 'Dr. Fishman and Mr. Levy are to be congratulated upon producing so clearly intelligible a summary; but it is not unfair to claim that it ought properly to have been entitled *Jewish Educational Organization in Great Britain.* Something is said of educational standards and syllabuses are appended. The impression is conveyed that the admittedly small proportion of children that ever get as far as taking an examination, emerge from it, if they qualify, with a fairly competent knowledge of the area covered by the syllabus. It is perhaps idle to think that that is more than an aspiration, if one has had much to do with the finished product. It is further stated[1] that the best pupils—the so-called academic stream—are prepared for the Hebrew General Certificate of Education examinations offered by various non-Jewish examining boards.' Having read the answers offered by candidates in such examinations, Dr. Loewe expressed himself as unhappy at their small number and indifferent quality. 'The reason, I suspect, is in part only due to the inadequate supply of competent teachers deplored in the report. Sufficient parental demand would elicit that supply, were it known that parents and/or Jewish educational authorities were prepared to pay the rate for the job. The absence of any such demand is, in my view, in some degree attributable to the emphases implicit in the syllabuses recited in the report, and to the attitude of mind that prevails in too many Jewish classrooms that there is something un-Jewish about construing Hebrew biblical text as carefully as one would a Latin or a French one. Indeed, the very size of the set book syllabus[2] (the so-called School Certificate Examination), which I reckon to contain some forty-seven chapters of the Bible, to say nothing of other prescribed Hebrew texts, is such as seems to me virtually to condone, if not indeed invite, an intellectually slipshod approach from a candidate at the very stage in his educational career that he is being mentally stretched at school by his ordinary G.C.E. courses.'

Dr. Braude stressed that the authors had shown that the number of children who continue to attend Jewish religious classes after the age of 13 is extremely small, even if we add those who find themselves in Jewish grammar and secondary schools at that age.

'This underlines the importance of the other medium of education, the Jewish youth organization. Since none of the contributions to the conference has dealt with this subject I would like to add a few observations.

'The number of young Jews in this country aged between 13 and 22 is approximately 50,000, but not more than 20,000 of them can be found in any Jewish youth organization. Most of those organizations serve a social purpose only; they provide very little real education and their main achievement—which must not be underestimated—is to keep their members within the fold until they are married to a Jewish partner.

'The 20,000 who are organized include about 1,750 Jewish students in thirty societies which are affiliated to the Inter-Universities Jewish

[1] Above p. 75.
[2] Above p. 83–85.

Jewish Education in Great Britain

Federation. This is less than half the number of Jewish students in this country.

'It appears that only youth organizations with specific aims and ideals—Zionist and especially religious—can achieve any lasting influence on their members. The ultimate effect of these groups on the Community will, therefore, be much greater than their present numbers would lead one to expect.

'What happens to about 30,000 young people between the ages of 13 and 22 who are not attached to any Jewish school, youth organization or club? Since the world in which most of them live is predominantly non-Jewish, a great number will ultimately be lost to the Jewish community. It is very important to investigate their actual position which, I believe, depends to a great extent on the atmosphere in their homes. Experience shows that the more religious their home, the less are they likely to be lost. The attachment of a home to Zionist ideals only, has today frequently not sufficient and lasting influence on children, unless they emigrate to Israel.'

Mr. Levi Gertner urged the importance of a wider approach. 'I think that an account of the contemporary Anglo-Jewish educational scene should also contain an appraisal of the spiritual, cultural and social developments of Jewish Youth—their desire to organize themselves into various groups, the aim of these groups, the problems that interest them, the Jewish problems which are of vital concern to young people. This is particularly important because in a community like ours, the father generation is not always in a position to impart its concepts and values to the children. Jewish youth, in consequence, is frequently choosing its own way and direction.'

Mr. S. S. Levin said: 'The numbers given for the pupils in Jewish day schools were a total of 4,800 in London. Of these, 1,500 go to secondary schools and 3,500 to primary schools. If one breaks down this further it is found that of the 1,500 in secondary schools, 900 are in State-aided establishments and 600 in independent schools. I maintain that ultimately the permanence of a school depends on its becoming part of the educational fabric of the State and that requires a very high standard. It is not difficult to maintain a number of small primary schools by the conversion of houses, though they would never achieve State aid. But when it comes to secondary school provision there is a good deal of glib talk, for private means cannot provide and maintain great secondary schools. To build a secondary grammar school requires 500 pupils, each with an I.Q. of 120 plus. The cost would be £300,000 and the annual wage bill would be £40,000. In the J.F.S. Secondary School we shall shortly start building the second stage, adding to the present 500 pupils, 900–1,000, making a total number of 1,500. The whole cost of that school, when complete, will be £950,000, of which a very large portion will be borne by the State. For the Jewish community the problem will then be to find the children for the school, and people should not talk glibly of building further secondary schools. There has to be overall planning for school provision for London Jewry.

'A further important factor in Jewish day schools is the division of

Discussion

education into "Limmudei Kodesh" and "Limmudei Chol", and unless a school is successful in both these departments, it would be a failure so far as the Jewish community is concerned. The London Board for Jewish Religious Education, allowing for the fullest development of Jewish day schools, recognizes that education for the greater number of Jewish children lies in the Talmud Torah and synagogue class on Sundays, and two or three evenings a week. We are keenly alive to the need for new stimulus. In this regard the question of Ivrit is no longer regarded as a problem for discussion. Our decisions have been made. Ivrit must come and we must add additional hours to our part-time system of education in places where it is suitable. We are already adding an additional evening for teaching Ivrit in some places.

'I would like to refer briefly to the statistics concerning Leeds. The Central Council report by Mr. Levy gives Leeds 850 pupils in its Hebrew and Religion classes. The Leeds Jewish population is some 20,000 to 25,000. If you take from these statistics that one-in-nine of the Jewish population must be a school child, then the Leeds Jewish child population must be in the region of 2,000 to 2,500. Where are these children? It may be that a number of them attend withdrawal classes as provided by the law of the land. In primary schools such withdrawal classes are of little value. It seems to me that Leeds is the ideal community for statistical investigation and survey. Time was when Leeds was the most compact community within Anglo-Jewry. They lived closely together on both sides of North Street and Chapeltown Road. What has been the rate of dispersal and marriage with non-Jews? Here is a field for a pilot scheme for the investigation to which this conference might give encouragement.'

Professor C. Domb, Miss B. Barwell, Miss S. Strizower and Mr. Armin Krausz also participated in the discussion.

Mr. Harold Levy and Dr. Fishman then both replied briefly.

The Anglo-Jewish Community in the Context of World Jewry

CECIL ROTH

IT was nearly seventy years ago that Joseph Jacobs, one of the most eminent historians and one of the finest brains ever produced by British Jewry, delivered before the Jewish Historical Society of England a masterly lecture on 'The Typical Character of Anglo-Jewish History'. In a way this was intended as an apologia for the subject to which he had made such fundamental contributions. Anglo-Jewry was not and had never been very significant numerically. Yet Anglo-Jewish history was a microcosm of Jewish history generally, and hence its study (facilitated by the remarkable state of preservation of the medieval English records) not only reflected, but also helped in the understanding of, the wider scene, quite apart from its natural antiquarian appeal to those who belonged to this restricted group.

British Jewry does in fact mirror—and as we shall see has continued to mirror—the most significant phases and facets of world Jewish history in general. It is probable, if unproved, that Jews were living in the principal urban centres of these islands in the Roman period. None of the evidence assembled to demonstrate this is conclusive, but the possibilities are overwhelming: and it is well to remember that even for France or Spain (for example) where it is universally accepted that the Jewish settlement at this period was considerable, the concrete evidences are trivial, and as it were accidental.

Anglo-Saxon England lay probably within the sphere of activity of the Jewish international merchants so significant to European economy in the Dark Ages, though here again positive evidences are lacking. But with the Norman Conquest we are on sure ground, and medieval English Jewry between the eleventh and the thirteenth centuries was the type of the medieval Jewry in a feudal setting—

dependent mainly on money-lending though with sufficient exceptions to prove the rule, and devoting its enforced leisure to Talmudic studies of the same type as those so widely spread in northern France. However in England too there were Mediterranean contacts and Sephardi intellectual influences, as evidenced in the activities in London of Abraham ibn Ezra. Thereafter came the expulsion of 1290—the prototype of the great medieval Expulsions, as was realized by the contemporary Jewish chroniclers: sufficiently comprehensive to make it possible to study the medieval record in self-contained isolation, yet at the same time with just sufficient exceptions and subsequent infiltration to emphasize the point, that no such exclusion of the Jews could or can be quite impermeable.

In the sixteenth century (as has been realized only recently) England came into the orbit of the New Christian emigré world centred in Antwerp, with ramifications as far as Turkey and the Holy Land, personified in such outstanding figures as Joseph Nasi, Duke of Naxos, and Solomon Abenaes, Duke of Mytilene—both of whom incidentally visited England: Lucien Wolf showed how this group played a role of some importance in creating the Anglo-Turkish alliance against Spain, which became so significant at the close of the reign of Elizabeth I. This interlude was succeeded by the more familiar Marrano period properly so-called (if one may so differentiate the two) which constituted the background to the Resettlement under the aegis of that protean dreamer, Menasseh ben Israel. For a generation, this element, whether coming direct from the Peninsula or via Guienne, Hamburg, or especially Holland, dominated or rather all but monopolized English Jewish life, London becoming in these years one of the principal centres of what I have termed the Marrano Diaspora, and sharing as well as contributing to its life and activity.

Before the end of the seventeenth century, the Ashkenazi immigration began, stemming largely from Germany, and England was brought into close relations with the coterie of Court Jews and gem merchants whose world is depicted so graphically in the memoirs of Glückel von Hameln. But at the same time there was an influx, far more important numerically, of Jews of the lower social stratum, who, as on the Continent, earned their living in the classical Jewish proletarian callings followed at this period throughout the western world, as pedlars and old-clothes men. This element, gradually rising in the social scale notwithstanding all obstacles, before long far outnumbered the Sephardim, and by the middle of the eighteenth century had not only achieved numerical primacy in the Metropolis but also created the rapidly-increasing diaspora of provincial Jewry. On the other hand, it was this element too that gave rise to the not inconsiderable problem of delinquency among English Jews in the reign of George III, when, as on the Continent, perhaps one-third of those of the Metropolis were actually paupers. What is noteworthy, and has a considerable general significance, is the rapidity with which this problem disappeared with acclimatization and increasing opportunity, thus showing clearly that it was the result of circumstances. Noteworthy too is the speedy economic advance of this element, who became the fathers of the 'older' English Jewry who still dominated the scene when Joseph Jacobs delivered the memorable address to which I have referred.

By this time however (though it was too early as yet for him fully to realize the fact), the Anglo-Jewish community had already entered a new phase in its history, no less typical of Jewish history as a whole than those earlier phases to which he had called attention, and in the long run more significant.

Already during the previous fifteen years, from the time of the beginning of the *pogroms* in Russia and the enacting of the May Laws, Eastern European Jewry had, as it were, burst its banks, and the trickles of emigration from the Tsarist Empire which had been manifest during the previous century (more important to be sure both in England and in America than was formerly believed by our chroniclers), had become a mighty flood, which was destined to change the face of the Jewish world. There is no need for me to go into details. It is enough to say that large segments of Russian and Polish Jewry were in these years catapulted as it were into Great Britain, with their language, standards, ideals and institutions: and Anglo-Jewish history for the next generation was largely the history of the interaction of this most vital group and its environment. There are aspects of this which even today are insufficiently explored—such as the history of the beginnings of the Socialist movement in London's East End (a very significant episode in Jewish history, and indeed in that of English Socialism), with which was closely connected the history of Jewish trade-unionism and the record of the Yiddish press and ephemeral publications. This immigration has continued with varying intensities throughout the past eighty years, though now obviously it has finished, the reservoir being alas drained tragically as a result of the horrible Nazi devastation. (Incidentally, the last wavelet, in very recent years, appears to have coloured some superficial aspects of Anglo-Jewish life more obviously than the tidal waves of the previous generations.) Moreover, the annihilation of Eastern European Jewry and other events of the past generation have completely altered our perspectives. The result has been, that Anglo-Jewry, numerically insignificant in Jacobs' day (the population of, say 60,000 when he began his literary activity did not comprise much more than one-half of one per cent. of that of the Jewish world as a whole—in the same range as that of say Italy (30,000), about one-tenth the size of that of Germany (500,000), a hundredth that of the Russian Empire (5,000,000)), is at present of considerable importance statistically and very much more so proportionately. Leaving out the Jews of Russia (as unhappily we must) the half-million Jews of Great Britain comprise the second largest community of the world outside Israel, being exceeded only by that of the United States. Moreover, its importance is emphasized by reason of the role of leadership that it continues to fill in the life of some at least of the communities of the Commonwealth. We are almost in the position of King Saul: 'Though thou be little in thine own sight, art thou not head of the tribes of Israel?' It may be noted that the corollary in this case was the imposition on the ruler of a highly unwelcome responsibility, which he tried in vain to shelve. . . .

One facet of the Anglo-Jewish experience in the modern period has been of particularly great significance in Jewish history as a whole. In this country, alone or almost alone in the Old World, the Jews have at no time since the resettlement been subject, *qua* Jews, to a special legal status. The results of this were far-reaching and wholly beneficent: yet it was the result, not of any original virtue or far-sighted statesmanship, but of sheer historical accident. I have on more than one occasion indicated the reason. Owing to the ostensible failure of Menasseh ben Israel's mission to Oliver Cromwell, the Jews were not formally recalled or readmitted to England: but at the same time the Judges who attended the Whitehall Conference decided that no law prevented their residence in the country. The decision of the Council of State of June, 1657, subsequently torn out of the Minute Book, merely recognized their presence *post facto*, permitting them to maintain the organs of public worship. They were hence not subject as they would have been otherwise, and had the spectacular movement for Recall been successful, to any special conditions leading inevitably to a special status; and whatever proposals may have been made subsequently (whether by Jews or Gentiles) no legislation was at any time passed which imposed on them specific disabilities or a discriminatory régime.

Except for a period of a few months in 1690/1, no special taxation was imposed on the Jews *qua* Jews (only the wealthy Jewish merchants being envisaged, even so): and even in this case I do not know that there is any evidence that it was actually exacted. This absence of special taxation, inevitably leading to a discriminatory status, was the case I believe in no other country of Europe in which Jews were resident, not excepting even Holland.

The disabilities from which the Jews suffered, or rather which they experienced, were in every or almost every case not positive and specific, but negative and accidental—they were unable to sit in Parliament for example not because they were Jews, but because, as Jews, they were unable to subscribe to a certain form of oath. Israeli scholars, systematically collecting historical records relating to the Jews from the specific sections of the archives relating to them in almost every European country, here find themselves faced with an entirely different situation, because so far as the modern period is concerned there can be no concentration of material of this type. The English Jew, one may say, was a normal citizen, subject down to a certain date to various restrictions of diminishing severity, on the whole shared with others who were not members of the dominant Church: he was not, as on the Continent, a person in an abnormal situation whose inferiority was qualified by various privileges, rights and protections.

Herein lies perhaps the principal significance of the Anglo-Jewish experience in modern Jewish history. Moreover, this served as a model for the former British dependencies, colonies, and countries of the Commonwealth, where conditions in this respect were similar; as well as, with far-reaching results (and this is all-important), for the United States of America. For the significance of our experience in the modern world is enhanced because of its close interrelation with, and up to a certain point, influence on, that of the transatlantic Jewish community. Our histories indeed run parallel—from the trickle of ex-Marrano immigration in the seventeenth century diluted with Ashkenazi immigration in the eighteenth: then the Continental immigration of the nineteenth, far greater indeed proportionately on the other side of the Atlantic, and setting up therefore its own institutions, to a wider extent than was the case here: and finally the great Eastern European tidal wave from 1882 onwards, largely of a similar type and relying on the same economic factors for its maintenance and livelihood. The reception of the successive waves of immigrants in the two countries was moreover not dissimilar. As I have pointed out on so many previous occasions, owing to the circumstances of the resettlement and the relatively tolerant outlook of the British people at large, English Jews enjoyed what may be termed social emancipation from the moment of their arrival here—quite apart from the absence of specific local discrimination—with nothing in the nature of the Ghetto and Ghetto discrimination. Without doubt, this example influenced the treatment of the Jews in the American colonies as well, where the circumstances of a frontier society, composed entirely of the newly-arrived and without historic roots, helped the process still further. The formal emancipation of the Jews in the United States at the end of the eighteenth century owed not a little to English experience and antecedents; which indeed proved more solid in the long run than the doctrinaire enfranchisement of Continental Jewry.

As compared with some other countries, the complete implementation of Jewish political emancipation in England was somewhat retarded, precisely because the disabilities were relatively inconsiderable. Yet in some ways it has perhaps gone farther in this country than in any other. It is not that Jews have risen to higher dignities, but that those Jews who have risen to high dignity have not done so at the expense of their Jewish loyalties. The Jewish statesman who is at the same time a broadly conforming Jew, of the type that Viscount Samuel was, is by no means a universal European phenomenon. And Disraeli, with his ostentatious Jewish sympathies, may be said to have been in the literal sense the exception that proved the rule.

English Jewry constitutes indeed a test-tube for determining the answer to one question of paramount importance: how far a Jewish community can resist assimilation in the modern world under conditions of emancipation. On the one hand, during the generations immediately following 1858, the English Jews were accepted into their environment more fully perhaps than in any country of Europe, other than Italy. On the other, more than in any country of Europe, they generally maintained in full measure their Jewish allegiances and their attachment to the synagogue if not (and this was perhaps their major shortcoming), their awareness of the Jewish cultural tradition. This was obviously facilitated by the religious conservatism of the British people, and by the fact that English Liberalism, and even radicalism, were generally speaking bound up with Church and Chapel, and not, as in so many Continental countries, in sharp opposition to organized religion. Indeed, the most notable drift from Judaism in this country, among the well-to-do German immigrants in the middle of the last century, was neither to the dominant Church nor to agnosticism, but to liberal Unitarianism. Nevertheless, on the whole Anglo-Jewry was able in the past to develop a satisfactory synthesis of considerable general significance between its two attachments. I am by no means sure on the other hand that this phase is not now passing—of the Jews in the public eye today, in particular perhaps in intellectual and literary life, an increasing number seem to be of the type that formerly prevailed in Germany, of Jews in the ethnic rather than the religious sense. This is a phenomenon which may as it seems to me affect our future drastically.

Our Anglo-Jewish experience demonstrates on the other hand the recessiveness in a tolerant environment of what were once regarded as Jewish characteristics. A generation suffices for the children of the immigrant to be converted into persons whose lives and outlook have, religion apart (and even this reservation cannot always be made), little in common with that of their parents. It may be remembered that the father of Major Lionel Wigram, the initiator of the new system for the training of a citizen army in World War II, was the son of that Maurice Wigram, egregiously foreign down to the end, who gave evidence before the Royal Commission on Aliens Immigration in 1903 as a typical immigrant manufacturing tailor.

Yet it is as well to remember that in this country too there have been manifestations of anti-semitism in more or less recent years of the type that one would prefer to forget, but should not. There was over a long period, even in the pre-Nazi era, an 'intellectual' anti-semitism associated with names such as Goldwin Smith, Arnold White, G. K. Chesterton or Hilaire Belloc. Nor was it always academic. Without taking into account the Limerick boycott of 1904, there were the South Wales riots against the Polish Jewish miners in 1903 and again during the strikes of 1911, when troops were called out by Winston Churchill; there was the Leeds outbreak of 1918, and there was the dangerous friction at the time of the rise of the British Union of Fascists in the 1930s. One should mention in connection with this the tense situation in 1947–8, at the time of the disturbances when the British mandate was drawing to its close in Palestine, though this is in a somewhat different category. All this is enough to remind us that violent expression of anti-Jewish feeling is not out of the question even in this country—and therefore, assuredly (the point that I wish to emphasize), in any country whatsoever.

On the other hand, it is worth while to notice at this point that English experience demonstrates how far it is possible for national attitudes to change. England was down to the eighteenth century the principal medium for carrying on the infamous slave-trade: yet only a generation later England led with supreme altruism the movement for the abolition of slavery. England is today regarded as the centre (though perhaps with certain reservations) of the movement of humanitarianism towards animals—in part, we may remember, through the untiring efforts of the Jew, Lewis Gompertz. In the eighteenth century however it was the specific home of bull- and bear-baiting, and the cruelty of the English nation in this respect was noted by foreign visitors as something wholly exceptional: the change had come about in little more than half a century. Similarly in Jewish history: it is worth while recalling that the centre of opposition to the Resettlement of the Jews in England in the mid-seventeenth century, and of opposition to the Jewish Naturalization Bill a hundred years later, was the City of London: while in the mid-nineteenth century the City of London was the pivot of the movement for Jewish Parliamentary emancipation. In part this was of course due to the changes in economic outlook during the previous generation: yet nevertheless, the persons who persistently returned Baron Lionel de Rothschild on the hustings in the Guildhall time after time from 1847 onwards were the great-grandchildren of those who had led the opposition to the innocuous naturalization measure a century before. At the time of the anti-alien agitation sixty years ago, a distinct anti-Jewish feeling was discernible amongst the London working classes, who imagined that their interests were threatened by the influx from abroad: but this too was dissipated with remarkable rapidity. All this has its significance in the wider historical setting. National attitudes do change: a point which in view of the tragic experiences of our people in the past generation we may have to bear in mind, once the scars are truly healed.

While the typical elements in the Anglo-Jewish experience are readily discernible, it is not so easy to recognize aspects in which our experience has provided a model. There is perhaps an exception in the emergence in England earlier than in any other country in modern times and under modern circumstances of an inter-communal Jewish organization. Such organizations came into being much earlier —even in the Middle Ages indeed—as governmental fiscal agencies which took over some internal jurisdiction (e.g. the Council of the Four Lands in Poland) or as *ad hoc* bodies meeting in times of emergency and for a specific purpose, such as was designated in England in the Middle Ages by the title of the 'Universitas Judeorum Anglie'. But English Jewry evolved in the typical inconsequential English fashion, in the second half of the eighteenth century, its rudimentary Board of Deputies, which before the beginning of the Victorian era had become a fairly effective mouthpiece for expressing the opinions and desires of English Jews as a body regarding matters of common interest: an organization both earlier and more effective than the disciplined and more or less disciplinary Consistories which emerged from the Napoleonic era onwards on the Continent, and as soon became manifest with wider potentialities than these. Because of the geographical extent of the British interests overseas, almost from the beginning, when it was still virtually only a sub-committee of the Sephardi Mahamad, the Board interested itself in the lot of fellow-Jews living under the British flag elsewhere. Hence it was an easy step for it to concern itself with Jews living overseas generally who were suffering because of their faith. Thus Sir Moses Montefiore's Damascus Mission of 1840 marked the beginning of systematic intervention by Western Jews in a political sense to protect their suffering brethren anywhere in the world: already foreshadowed here at the time of the expulsion of the Jews from Prague in 1745, and more recently when the House of Rothschild headed the attempts to safeguard Jewish interests in parts of Germany after the Napoleonic Wars. The 1840 precedent on the other hand was the forerunner of systematic intervention of this type sponsored by an established and responsible representative body. British Jewry had of course specific advantages at the time owing to the dominant position of Great Britain in the Western world, its leadership in the humanitarian field, its general protection of the Jews for political if not wholly altruistic reasons, and the remarkable personality and prestige of Sir Moses Montefiore—as well as the affluence which enabled that personality and prestige to be placed perpetually at the service of his co-religionists, and the physical stamina which put him for an entire generation in the category, always irresistible to British sentiment, of the Grand Old Man. After the ill-starred unification of Germany, the improvement of communications with America by the laying of the Atlantic cable, and the establishment of the *Alliance Israélite* in France as a specific result of the Mortara Case of 1858, the unique position of England in this respect came to be qualified—though in the early years of the present century the first Lord Rothschild could figure in the eyes even of Herzl as the contemporary Prince of the Captivity. It is probably true to say that British Jewry was responsible for the initiation of what one might call the humanitarian Jewish Foreign Service which today is of such considerable moment in the world, even though the leadership has passed from Europe.

Another aspect of Jewish history in which the contribution of Great Britain and of British Jewry was significant was in the implementation if not evolution of Zionism in its modern sense. Whether it was actuated by high idealism, or sordid political considerations, the close association of the British Consulate in Jerusalem with the general protection of the Jews in Palestine in the nineteenth century was of the utmost importance in the development of the *Yishuv*, and owing to the personal enthusiasms of the Consul James Finn of the beginnings of the agricultural movement among them: while Sir Moses Montefiore, representing England as well as its Jewish community, is one of the key figures in the renewal of Jewish Palestine. Later, the adherence to the Zionist movement of some outstanding English Jews such as his nephew Sir Francis Montefiore, the bearer of the most honoured name in Anglo-Jewry, Israel Zangwill, perhaps the foremost European Jewish writer, and Colonel Goldsmid, the prototype of the modern Maccabee, conferred on Zionism even here something of its cachet as a 'respectable' and practical movement: and the opening of negotiations with Herzl by the British government, in connection first with El Arish and then with the Uganda scheme, gave it the international prestige which was to find its culmination in the Balfour Declaration—addressed not to the Zionist Organization as such but to the personality who was considered to be the outstanding British Jew. Had it not been for the existence of an Anglo-Jewish community, some eminent members of which displayed an intense interest in the Zionist idea, the renewal of the Jewish National Home in Palestine could probably not have been effected in our day—with far reaching and tragic consequences in the history of our people.

We must now leave the past and turn our attention to our own times. I would like to determine what the Jewish chronicler of the future will consider to be the salient historical events and tendencies of the present day, and see how far these too are likely to affect the destinies of this Anglo-Jewish community of ours.

There can be no doubt that the two foremost events in recent Jewish history—indeed, in Jewish history as such during the past two thousand years—have been the annihilation of Eastern European and much of Continental Jewry; and closely interconnected with this, and towering above it, its providential sequel, the emergence of the State of Israel. In conjunction with the former we must take into consideration also the secularization of the surviving Jews of the former Russian Empire and the beginning of a similar process, the implementation of which is unlikely to take long, in the other communistic states of Central and Eastern Europe. Simultaneously, we have witnessed a complete change in the circumstances of the Jews in the Moslem and Asiatic world: the result in part only of the Arab-Israel hostilities. What with the liquidation of Jewish life in the very ancient communities of the Yemen, Egypt, Syria and Iraq, the attraction of the anticipated delights of the State of Israel on the poverty-stricken but Zion-centred Jews of Turkey and Iran, and the changed political circumstances in North Africa, the number of Jews in the Moslem world has declined perhaps by one-half in the past fifteen years, and the process is likely to be virtually completed before long. The events to which I have referred have been accompanied by the inevitable decline of Yiddish as the international language of a large part of the Jewish world, and the emergence in its place of spoken Hebrew on the one side and of English on the other: American Jewry is by far the largest of all Jewish groups, and English-speaking Jewry now about as numerous as was Yiddish-speaking Jewry a century ago—a fact which enhances what we may term the focal significance of the Jewish community of England. It may be added, though the relevance to us here is less direct, that to compensate for the undermining or disappearance in our days of

The Anglo-Jewish Community in the Context of World Jewry

Ladino, a Spanish-speaking Jewry of nearly a million strong is now re-emerging in Central and South America.

Meanwhile, in those western countries in which the Jews have been able to develop or reconstitute their lives without serious interruption, certain universal tendencies are manifesting themselves. Whereas during the past century the Jews tended to become concentrated in the great cities, in our generation we see them everywhere concentrating in the greatest cities, the metropolises of a million inhabitants or more: not a fortunate development perhaps in the event of atomic warfare, when precisely such centres would be the primary military objective. There is throughout the Western world a perpetual advance in economic well-being: the Jewish proletariat of a generation ago has well-nigh disappeared in many countries, though it is less certain that the North African immigrants of our day will be able to emulate in this respect their more alert Ashkenazi predecessors. It is perhaps true that the Jews now constitute in some countries taken as a whole the most affluent recognizable group among the population—by no means a healthy sign in every respect, and a phenomenon very different from that which formerly prevailed, of the presence of a small wealthy element contrasted with a very large semi-pauper proletariat. This has been accompanied by the emergence of the new phenomenon of the 'Gilded Ghetto' in which the Jews constitute a recognizable social group with the same preoccupations, interests and diversions as their neighbours; distinguished from them indeed by origin, name and tepid adherence to the Jewish religion, yet increasingly isolated from the rest of the Jewish world in a sense that was not true formerly because of the absence of a common language and culture. The circumstances of intellectual life cannot of course be left out of account in any survey of the Jewish scene. Up to the beginning of the present century, and in large measure down to the beginning of the Nazi persecutions, the Jewish cultural centres were in Central and Eastern Europe: the *Jüdische Wissenschaft* in Germany, the traditional Talmudic disciplines in Poland and Russia. Now both centres have been blotted out, and if either of these cultures so essential to our existence is to be maintained outside Israel, it can only be in the English speaking world, that is, in England and America,

I have tried to distinguish some basic tendencies in Jewish experience in our day. The relevance to English conditions has not always been obvious, and I must revert to some of the points which I have raised.

Throughout its history, Anglo-Jewry has had as it were a satellite existence, at least so far as its spiritual and intellectual life was concerned, reflecting to a great extent the attitudes, activities and moods of one of the great Continental groupings. In the Middle Ages, it was virtually a colony of Franco-Rhenish Jewry: at the time of the Resettlement an offshoot of Sephardic Amsterdam, in the eighteenth century and to some extent in the nineteenth closely associated with Germany, while after the Russian immigration it looked for its spiritual sustenance and reinforcement largely as I have said to Eastern Europe. Whether it can be self-dependent in the future is now one of our great problems. But obviously it must henceforth have in any case a different centre of attraction. There are two possibilities only, if we leave out of account the anomalous great residue under Soviet rule: Israel on the one hand, the United States on the other. Both influences are exerting themselves in an increasing measure: the future course of the history of our community will be decided by the answer to the question, which of them will triumph.

But will either, in this sense?

As I emphasized before, the two salient events in Jewish life in our day have been the emergence of the State of Israel, and the annihilation of the great part of Continental Jewry, with the result that, in Eastern Europe, only the Jewish masses living under Soviet rule now survive. I am not quite sure that the corollary to this has been fully realized: nor on the other do I know what the ultimate results will be. Until not so long ago, Eastern Europe was for English Jews an inexhaustible reservoir of traditional Jewish life, and Palestine, though its Jewish population was small, was the Jewish religious focus; for the bond was essentially spiritual. Now, this is no longer so. Whether or no traditional Judaism flourishes or is to flourish in Israel; whether or no it is to be the focus of a Jewish religious revival, is beside the point. The fact is that it is a secular state, largely inhabited and controlled by persons whose Jewish loyalties are not expressed primarily through the synagogue and its spiritual heritage. In Eastern Europe, the 'religious' Jews of Poland (whose religiosity was already indeed much diluted in a vast number of cases) have been annihilated; what is left is only the secularized Russian Jewry, who cannot escape from their Jewishness since they are officially reckoned to belong to the Jewish nationality, but whose Judaism has lost its significance. The same circumstances are likely to prevail before long in the other countries behind the Iron Curtain, some of them with still significant Jewish populations. The background of Anglo-Jewry is a world in which the touchstone of Jewishness was, if not observance, at all events a positive attitude towards the Jewish religion. We are now in a world in which for nearly one-half of the Jewish population the criterion of Jewishness is ethnic or political. This cannot fail to have in the long run a considerable influence on our own outlook. Were emigration from Russia to be resumed for any reason, the impact on our innocent communities would be something wholly unprecedented. Hitherto, this non-Judaistic Jewishness touched only individuals, but in the future it cannot fail to affect to some degree the whole of the communal outlook.

This is being accentuated by another universal change in the life of the Jews in the Western world. The continued exigencies of the past generation—first the tragic conditions in Europe, then the perpetual emergency in Israel—have made imperative the raising of funds in hitherto unprecedented amounts. Hence the large-scale donor has become more and more important: while the giving of money has become the fundamental expression of Jewish activities and loyalties. The 'magbit' (to use a convenient term) has taken its place as perhaps the dominant force in Jewish life, to the exclusion of scholarship, piety, or personal sacrifice.

Thus the influences making for utter secularization are becoming increasingly strong. There can be no doubt that they are discernible in a growing measure in Anglo-Jewry as well, hitherto the most synagogacentric community of the Western world.

Anglo-Jewry typifies the extent to which the Jews as a whole threw in their lot inextricably within the past few generations with the Occident. But Spengler prophesied long ago 'the Decline of the Western World'. Since he wrote, the process has taken on a new urgency, and we are today, quite literally, at the turning of the ways. The change in Jewish circumstances in some parts of the Mediterranean and farther south, as well as east, is due in great measure to the fact that, during the past centuries, the Jews identified themselves to a very great extent, so far as this was possible for them, with the colonizing European powers. That this was necessarily wrong I am unconvinced, but whether it was or no, the process has now become reversed. Colonialism and all that is bound up with it has become unfashionable and therefore execrable, and the colonizers and those elements in the population who associated themselves with them have receded. This, as well as the Israeli-Arab conflict, and the rise of nationalism, is responsible for the critical state of affairs for the Jews of North Africa at present, which is likely to become exacerbated in the immediate future. But the repercussions do not remain restricted there. They have already affected the Jewish communities of India and the Far East, and they are surging down the African continent. The only open question now—with considerable significance from the Jewish point of view—is whether in our day the tidal wave will stop at the Zambesi or the Cape of Good Hope.

Almost from the moment of the Resettlement, England has figured in Jewish life as a distributive as well as a reception area.

Throughout the three hundred year period in question Jews—sometimes barely acclimatized in the country—have gone out from England as part of the British and European colonization abroad: already in the seventeenth century to India, throughout the eighteenth to the American colonies, in the nineteenth to the United States, to Australia, to South Africa, to Rhodesia, to every other part of the world where English was spoken or where the British rule was established. The same has been the case with the Jews of other European countries. Now we are confronted with the reaction: though to be sure the quantitative vacuum caused by the withdrawal is being in part filled by the qualitative action of the Israeli diplomats and technical experts.

One incidental result of this process of colonial recession is that the position of the Sephardi body in particular, in the world and in our community, is rapidly changing. There is no need to remind you how at the close of the Middle Ages there was a remarkable shift of emphasis in Jewish history. Hitherto, Sephardi Jewry in its widest sense (including the Mediterranean and Levantine Jews) had played a dominant role, and, so far as we may conjecture, was numerically preponderant. In the course of the sixteenth and seventeenth centuries, notwithstanding the prominence and distinction of the newly-found communities of the Marrano Diaspora, this element to a great extent lost its vitality, while the Ashkenazi forged ahead. In the first quarter of the twentieth century, one may say that the Sephardim numbered only some 10 per cent of the Jewish people—say, 1,500,000 out of a total of 16,500,000. As a result of the Nazi persecutions, the balance changed to some extent, the German devastations raging especially in the Ashkenazi areas (though indeed the sufferings of the Sephardi communities of the Balkans were appalling—a fact which is generally forgotten). In 1948, the Ashkenazi element had been reduced to only some 10,000,000, whereas the Sephardim had not lost more than some 100,000. Moreover, at this time, partly owing to the annihilation of Eastern European Jewry and isolation of those under Communist rule, partly to the increasing difficulties of the Jews in the Moslem world, the Sephardim became to an increasing extent the facet of the Jewish Problem which engaged outside attention, and the Sephardi and oriental immigration into Israel changed the face of that community which had become the nerve centre of the Jewish world.

I recall that when I returned from my first visit to the Continent and the Middle East at the close of the war, I foretold that the centre of the 'problem' Jewry which would henceforth occupy the attention of the Western world was rapidly shifting from the Ashkenazi to the Sephardi element. No one of course paid any attention: but it has

The Anglo-Jewish Community in the Context of World Jewry

happened. The change in circumstances on the other side of the English Channel is already drastic. The face of French Jewry is likely to alter fundamentally in the course of the next few years (so at least many of its leaders believe) as a result of the Algerian settlement, which seems about to result in the addition to the metropolitan communities of that country of a vast mass of new immigrants, who would increase its numbers in a short time by one-half and in due course perhaps transform it into a predominantly Sephardi agglomeration. Incidentally, we see here how the *Loi Crémieux* naturalizing Algerian Jewry, so long considered to be a triumph of beneficent statecraft, for the renewal of which we all strove so zealously after 1944, may turn out to have been a double-edged weapon, in the long run perhaps deleterious to the ultimate interests of those it was intended to benefit.

This emphasizes a further point which is worthy of some attention here. In this country we have never been faced with the agonizing Jewish quandary which has been and is being felt in so many parts of the world—whether or no to maintain the traditional loyalties, in the name of respectability, to an alien government at a time of rising nationalism, or to a reactionary government at a time of rising liberalism. Whereas for others this is a matter of personal choice, with Jews there are far wider repercussions. If they throw in their lot with the malcontents, they become as a group an object of governmental distrust; if they remain loyal to the government, the malcontents are encouraged to regard them as an extraneous and expendable element in case of victory. We see at both extremities of Africa today the pitfalls that await the Jews in this respect. In England, owing to its more fortunate history, the more placid character of its inhabitants, and its unconquerable conviction that Revolution must be achieved at the ballot-box and not in the streets, this unhappy quandary has never arisen, to our great good fortune.

There can be little doubt that the change of circumstances in France to which I have referred, arising out of the North Africa crisis, would have its repercussions here as well. But even without this influence from across the Channel, the new facets of the Jewish world picture are already beginning to make themselves manifest. The obvious changes in the Sephardi and Oriental elements in London Jewry in the course of the past decade may prove to be only the small beginning, like the first trickle of Russo-Polish immigration in the 1880s. Last year, the majority of the newly arrived immigrants who engaged the attention of the Jews' Temporary Shelter in London—established to help Ashkenazi Jews of Eastern European origin—were 'Sephardim' from the Middle East, India and Aden. This may well be the pattern of things to come. In view of what is so often said, however, we will be well advised to remember that our experience here, more perhaps than that of any other community of the world, demonstrates what intellectual reserves there are in North African and Oriental Jewry, and their potential contribution to the national life as well as to our own community. Such names as those of Philip Guedalla, Leslie Hore Belisha, S. L. Bensusan, and the versatile Farjeon family, not to mention the Sassoons and the Davids from another segment, are a sufficient testimony to this fact. Our past experience thus has very actual implications, not only for ourselves.

It is a commonplace of Jewish sociology that (as I have already observed) a distinguishing facet of Jewish life in every part of the world in the past century has been the constant flow of Jews from small towns to large, and from the large to the largest. In Italy, the village communities which still flourished at the beginning of the nineteenth century gave place to town communities at its end, and today two or three of the large cities (Rome, Milan, Turin) seem to be engulfing the rest. In India, the Bene Israel surnames largely reflect the names of villages from which they have long been absent. Strasbourg has engulfed to a great extent the Jewries of the country centres of Alsace, while the capital of the country has more Alsatian Jews than there are left in that province. So too in England, the 'country town' and small port communities of the Hanoverian period (Canterbury, Exeter, Gloucester, Kings Lynn, Penzance, Falmouth, Yarmouth, Bedford and so on) had disappeared out of existence or almost so by the end of the reign of Queen Victoria. The early years of this century were the heyday of the 'small town' Jewish community. But now, as in other lands, the 'small town' Jew has drifted more and more to the large towns, so that there seems to be here too the probability that in a generation's time only a handful of large Jewish communities in great cities will maintain an effective existence—a fact of very considerable historical as well as sociological importance.

England indeed led, rather than followed the current tendency of urbanization and metropolitan concentration in Jewish life: one reason for this being perhaps the exceptional dominance of London in English life generally (with about one-fifth of the total population of the country); another being the fact that the capital is at the same time a principal port of entry for immigrants from the Continent as well as a main centre of communications. Hence, whereas before the holocaust, while normal conditions prevailed, Berlin had something more than one-seventh of Germany's Jews, London has never had much fewer than two-thirds of the entire Jewish population of the country; 80 per cent of England's Jews, but only 24 per cent of the general population, live in the six largest cities: while 62 per cent of the Jews, as against only 16 per cent of the whole total, live in the capital. Largely for this reason, Anglo-Jewish life has been centralized in the metropolis more than is the case probably in any other country—perhaps a dangerous symptom. This tendency moreover is likely to increase with the constant flow thither of population and of ability.

There is another side to the question, which is perhaps overlooked. Parallel with the drift of the Jews to the towns there has been another process of irradiation from the towns—partly of traders looking for new opportunities, partly of the well-to-do settling in rural retirement. But there is the following to be noted: whereas the Jew who lived in the small towns a generation ago maintained the basic Jewish religious institutions, those who settle in them now in moderate numbers fail to form local organizations, being at the best attached to the Jewish communities in the capital or some neighbouring large centre. The nature of Jewish life in the smaller centres has moreover changed during the past generation: and here too we face a universal phenomenon, true of most countries, which is an obvious cause for anxiety. It should never be forgotten that the average Jewish community of the past was numerically very small, but its smallness did not qualify the intensity of its Jewish life. The communities of medieval England other than London probably did not number more than a hundred souls or so: Troyes, when Rashi taught there, cannot have comprised more than a score or so of Jewish householders. The Italian Ghettos which maintained such vitality in the seventeenth and eighteenth centuries had for the most part only two or three hundred, very few of them exceeding one thousand; and so throughout the Jewish world. But these groups, notwithstanding their small size, were able to maintain a fully rounded communal life. The same was the case in this country up to a generation ago. At the beginning of the twentieth century, as a glance at the old editions of the *Jewish Year Book* is sufficient to demonstrate, a community of say 300 souls in this country (and the same is true of France or Belgium or Holland) would be able to maintain not only its synagogue, which would be open for service daily, but all the ancillary institutions, and a full complement of officiants. Today on the other hand they will be content with only occasional (at the best, weekly) services and a single communal factotum. The minimal dimensions of the viable Jewish community, as one might put it, have become much larger. This is, I believe, one of the important differences between the provincial Jewish community in all countries today and that of fifty years ago, and a universal socio-historical tendency.

Cecil Roth

As you will have seen and heard, I am not wholly an optimist as regards the long-distance prospects and potentialities of English Jewry. Yet the fact remains that of the Jewish groupings of the Old World it is the one whose future is, if not the most bright, at all events the least depressing. What with uprooting and menaces of uprooting in some areas, lack of roots and the inevitable assimilation in others, the role of our community seems likely to increase constantly proportionately, even though it may diminish absolutely, in the years before us.

Among the Jewries of the Old World, moreover, that of England is unique in one respect. We hardly realize it, but it is the only considerable Jewish body in Europe—and indeed almost in the Old World—which has not experienced a violent convulsion in the course of the past generation (save in the Channel Isles, a fact which we should certainly not overlook): the only exceptions are the communities, far less significant in every way, of Switzerland, Portugal and Sweden, to which we may perhaps add Finland. In every other community of Europe without exception there has been an interlude of German occupation and Nazi anti-semitism, translated into appalling practice. We, almost alone, have been spared.

The events of the past thirty years have thus fundamentally changed the position of the Anglo-Jewry in other respects besides the numerical. A generation ago, we were considered, correctly, among the youngest of the Jewish communities of the world, our roots barely going back beyond the eighteenth century: as compared with the vigorous communities of Germany, Poland, Greece, and so on—not to mention the Moslem lands—we were newcomers. But now, these ancient groupings are for the most part annihilated or reduced to impotence. Of the more or less healthy Jewries of the Old World—indeed, of the world generally—we are now among the most venerable, if not indeed—it sounds a curious statement, but it is not far from the truth—the most venerable of all.

Our historical experience—whether we are aware of it or no, and whether we deserve it or no—has therefore come to be far more significant than was ever previously the case. That is one reason why the present Conference is so timely and so important.

We cannot divorce our present from our past. We cannot divorce ourselves from the history of the British nation to which we belong. We cannot divorce ourselves from the history and the destiny of the Jewish people.

Statistical Research: Needs and Prospects

S. J. PRAIS

1. Developments in the past half-century

Whilst much is known on a firm statistical basis about the Jews of certain countries, such as Switzerland or Canada (to take an example from the Commonwealth), there is hardly a single figure that can be quoted with any firmness for the Jewish community of Great Britain today. Again, in some countries statistical research centres have been established by their Jewish communities many decades ago; yet in England, despite the relative sophistication of the community, there is little that can be pointed to today in the way of comprehensive statistical research.

It was not always so. At the end of the last century some noteworthy contributions were made by the eminent Joseph Jacobs in his *Studies in Jewish Statistics* (1891); and, while Jacobs was editor of the *Jewish Year Book*, original contributions appeared year by year in its statistical section. When Jacobs left London for New York to help edit the *Jewish Encyclopedia*, the good work in the *Year Book* was continued under the editorship of I. Harris. As a result of their efforts, the issues of that annual preceding the 1914 war remain of considerable interest to the statistician of today, both on grounds of method, and as providing valuable source material for historical series. In the same period there was formed in London a Society for Jewish Statistics at which members read prepared papers; S. Rosenbaum (later Rowson), whose paper in the *Journal of the Royal Statistical Society* (1905) is well-known, was secretary of the Society.[1] What has happened to the records of that Society, I do not know; but perhaps its mention here may lead someone to come forward with information.

---

[1] For references to this Society, see *Jewish Year Book*, 1904–5, p. 237; and 1905–6, p. 229.

S. J. Prais

After the First World War, interest in statistics lapsed (the *Year Book*'s statistical section did not even appear every year); but, by the 1930s, we find a Jewish Health Organization newly established with a Statistical Committee engaged in research. The papers by Trachtenberg (1933) and Kantorowitsch (1936) were prepared for that Committee; again, there are possibly other papers of that committee hidden in some cellar for which a future student would be grateful. These published contributions, however, all remark on the general sparseness of information, and indicate that the hopeful start made by Jacobs was not pursued by the community. More recently Dr. Neustatter (1955) has made a brave survey (to which the present paper is much indebted) of the available material on the contemporary community, but I feel sure she would be the first to emphasize the complete lack of straw to help make satisfactory bricks today.[1] Indeed, the comprehensive information on births, deaths and marriages that were centrally collected by the community at the turn of the century are today no longer available.

As is clear from the well-known works of Ruppin on the sociology of the Jews, statistical material is of profound interest both for the serious student of the Jewish social trends, and for the general sociologist and demographer studying minority groups in Western societies. One would also have thought that statistics on population movements, educational level, etc., would be highly valuable to communal leaders and organizations making long term plans (for the siting of schools, their size, etc.). The ordinary observer, unaided by long-term statistics, is generally more impressed by a multitude of short-term factors than by the longer term trends which ultimately govern the fate of the community; a statistical reporting service would be justified on these grounds alone. If, so far, little has been done in this field by Anglo-Jewry, the reason perhaps is that the benefits from a statistical service are not always to be reaped immediately; it requires a certain long-sightedness to appreciate that a modest but regular effort is sufficient to yield, in the course of time, a body of extremely valuable information. The governments of all advanced countries (including, I may say, the government of Israel) are constantly engaged in improving their statistics on social, economic and demographic matters and, in the post-war period especially, many advances have been made in techniques and coverage; it is to be hoped that the Anglo-Jewish community will also in due course show the necessary vision so that certain basic statistics, at least, may be put on firm ground.

The statistics generally quoted on Anglo-Jewry are little more than

[1] Further references to statistical publications on Anglo-Jewry will be found in Prais (1959), and Schmelz (1961).

Statistical Research: Needs and Prospects

rather informal estimates. For the smaller communities, where all members are personally known to one another, these estimates may not be wide of the mark; but it must be remembered that the coverage of these communities is not complete, and isolated Jews living in the smaller townships are of course never reported. For the larger communities the available figures quoted are often nothing more than a shibboleth—such as the figure of 25,000 for the Jewish population of Leeds which has appeared for the last forty years in the *Year Book*[1]—and both the proportionate and absolute error for the larger communities is apparently serious; the opinion of individuals, however well placed they may be, is not of much value here as a source of statistics. For the largest community in the country, London, we have fortunately a more scientific estimate of the Jewish population due to the works of Rosenbaum, Trachtenberg, and Kantorowitsch already referred to, and described in more detail below; the most recent estimate using such methods is now thirty years out of date and needs to be repeated.

My task is not, however, confined to lamenting present deficiencies but is, rather, to indicate what could be done further by way of academic research and with the help of a positive approach from the central institutions of the community. We shall consider the main heads under which statistics are required, the methods by which they may be obtained in practice, difficulties of interpretation, and certain of the topics which may be of research interest—as far as may be judged on the basis of research elsewhere. Finally, certain first steps are suggested which, it is hoped, may commend themselves as being of immediate interest.

Of the various heads under which statistics may be collected, I propose to deal here more fully with: population estimates, and statistics of births, marriages, and deaths. To keep the paper within reasonable length, I shall consider only briefly statistics on education, religious observance, and occupational structure, though each of these topics deserves very much fuller treatment.

2. The definition problem

It is as well to begin by referring to a problem of definition which is often raised as an obstacle to research in this field. Whether one is considering statistics of Jewish births, or population, or what have you, there always arises the question—as regards a certain proportion of the cases—who is, and who is not to be counted as a Jew?

This is, no doubt, a profound question but I would like to suggest that it can, and should, be satisfactorily ignored for the present

[1] I take the example from Neustatter (1955), p. 65.

purposes. Definitional issues of this kind are familiar grist to the applied statistician; consider, by way of example from another field, the measurement of unemployment. Persons who are habitually employed for only part of the week, though a varying part, always lead to difficulties in counting the number who are unemployed at any particular moment; there are, again, certain housewives who are willing to work in boom conditions when wages are high, but prefer to stay at home when the industrial climate is cooler and wages are lower: are they, in the latter conditions, to be considered as unemployed? The treatment, possibly cavalier, that statisticians often employ in problems of this kind is to adopt some simple, if arbitrary, criterion (in the case of unemployment, for example, one might count only those applying personally at a Labour Exchange in a given week) and to collect statistics on that basis. Every attempt is then made to measure the phenomenon as correctly as possible on that criterion; the resulting statistics measure what they say, though, if the marginal cases become of importance, the help of an 'expert' may occasionally be necessary in their interpretation.

Similarly, statistics on the Jewish community would be of value on whatever basis they were computed, if that basis were reasonably maintained in making comparisons from one year to another. Questions of consistency of definitions, employed in different statistical series (for example, in comparing death and population statistics, there arises the question whether all who make use of Jewish burial grounds are also members of synagogues during their lifetime), may I think be deferred until our basic information is very much more satisfactory than it is at present.

3. Population Estimates

A direct population estimate for the Jewish community is difficult to obtain unless as part of the national general census. In this country religious information was collected as part of the decennial census on only two occasions, in 1841 and 1851; the Registrar General has otherwise not taken any notice of religion in official population statistics. The opinion is often heard that it would be undesirable to change this approach for that of the European continent, where religious communities are officially recognized, and statistics on them are collected as an integral part of routine official statistics. Those expressing such opinions are however generally unaware that in many other English-speaking countries a religious question appears in the Census (and, need I add, without undesirable consequences). The most notable of these is Canada, for which very full statistical analyses have subsequently been prepared by Rosenberg (see, for example, his 1959 article on the demography of Canadian Jews).

Statistical Research: Needs and Prospects

Statistics are similarly collected for Australia, New Zealand, Ireland and certain other countries in the British Commonwealth. In the United States a religious question does not appear in the Census of population; but one was included in one of the regular sample surveys carried out by the Bureau of the Census in 1957, with highly interesting results.[1] Such a sample survey, carried out under proper statistical auspices, is for many purposes quite as satisfactory as a full census.

While there are no signs that the scope of the census in this country will be increased to cover religion, the possibility of doing so on a sample basis, as on the American pattern, may well be kept in mind. If proper approaches were made by the major religious communities of the country, such an addition could conceivably be made to one of the pre-tests for next census in 1971.[2]

In the absence of direct estimates we have to rely, as is familiar, on various *indirect* methods of estimating the size of the Jewish community. These are based on counts of (*a*) school attendances, or (*b*) deaths, or (*c*) marriages; such figures can often be obtained more easily because, for example, of some existing registration procedure. This number is then inflated by the reciprocal of the corresponding proportion in the general population.[3]

(*a*) The method based on *school attendances* has a particular application in what is known as the 'Yom Kippur method', since it is based on a count of the absentees from general schools on that day. This count is taken to represent the number of Jewish children of school age, after allowance has been made for normal absenteeism at that time of year. The method has been widely used in the United States; Horowitz, in his recent study (1961), still considers it the most practical method for New York. It seems to me that it could, with advantage, be applied again in London today and, in view of their interest in the basic figures, the London Jewish Educational Board would perhaps be the appropriate body to do so.

Once the number of Jewish school-children is known, an estimate of the total Jewish population can be made by assuming that the children represent the same proportion of the total as in the general

[1] See *Current Population Reports*, 2nd February, 1958, U.S. Department of Commerce, Washington D.C.

[2] Registrations at Kosher butchers after the war might be thought to provide a direct figure on the population; but the number was only 190,000 (see Neustatter, 1955, pp. 113–15), and much below the 450,000 who are thought to comprise the Jewish population.

[3] To illustrate the principle involved, let us suppose the death-rate in England is one in fifty, and we find 100 Jewish burials a year in a particular town; then the estimated Jewish population for that town would be 5,000.

population. The use of this approach by H. Llewellyn Smith at the end of the nineteenth century is of interest.[1]

(b) A population estimate based on *death statistics* is somewhat easier to apply, at least in this country, in view of the relative accessibility of the basic data (as noted further below). As far as the reliability of the method is concerned, it is often objected that the Jewish death-rate is not necessarily the same as that of the general population, partly because of the different age and sex structure resulting from migrations, and partly because of differing economic or other conditions of life. The former need not prove an obstacle if the statistics are classified by sex and age-group, and death-rates specific to each group are applied; whether any adjustment is advisable on grounds of social class is, in my opinion, doubtful, but some idea of the effects could be obtained from the Registrar General's decennial analysis of mortality by social class. In any case, the magnitude of the possible error has, in my opinion, been exaggerated: the problem mainly exists for the younger age-groups, say 0–15, where Jewish mortality appears to be lower; but some adjustment of the estimates for these age-groups may be made on the basis of other information.

The Jewish population of London has been estimated on the basis of burial statistics (classified by sex and age) by Trachtenberg (1933) and Kantorowitsch (1936). The latter's estimate, which relates to the years 1929–33, forms the basis of the latest available estimate by Dr. Neustatter (1955), after adjusting as well as possible for natural increase and migration in the intervening period. It would, however, be desirable today to prepare a new estimate based on more recent burial statistics; this should, indeed, be done not only for London but for the whole country.

(c) For the sake of completeness I mention that calculations of the size of the London population have also been made on the basis of *marriages* by Rosenbaum (1905, p. 542), though the method has rather more serious limitations.[2]

Even if the underlying assumptions are precisely correct, the above methods may be subject to error, more especially in estimates for the smaller communities, where the number of cases of (for example) death may be small and subject to random fluctuations from year to year. In such circumstances it will be desirable to consider the average number of deaths over a period of years. For

[1] See his chapter on 'The influx of population' in C. Booth (1902, Vol. III), esp. pp. 104–6, with the reference to Dr. Adler's calculations based on marriages and deaths, and to the Statistical Committee of the Board of Deputies.

[2] His paper has to be read rather critically; there is an element of circularity in reasoning when he derives a marriage rate later in his paper (p. 553).

Statistical Research: Needs and Prospects

the benefit of statisticians, I note that the statistical margin of error due to sampling has been given by Trachtenberg (1933, p. 93); the percentage standard error for a population of N based on d observations of deaths is given approximately by

$$\frac{\sigma}{N} = \frac{1}{\sqrt{d}} = \frac{1}{\sqrt{(\rho N)}}$$

where ρ is the death rate for the community. Taking a death-rate of twelve per thousand, it will be seen that the sampling standard error will be less than 5 per cent provided the expected size of the community exceeds 35,000. The same margin of error will apply to a community half that size if statistics for four years are taken. Greater accuracy may be expected if the data are stratified by sex and age.

These indirect methods are thus not of much value for very small communities, considered individually, except as providing a rough order of magnitude. For groups of communities taken together, the accuracy, of course, increases according to their combined total.

The preceding paragraphs have considered methods of estimating the total population by towns; these methods, however, will not be suited for an allied research topic, namely an examination of the geographical dispersal of the community within and about the major towns. This phenomenon is of the greatest interest; the pattern of life of the American suburban community, where communication depends on the car, is quite different both socially and ritually from that of the densely populated town community. The measurement of the trend towards greater dispersion is thus a subject worthy of study; interesting results would, I suspect, emerge, from a study of the addresses of members of, say, half a dozen synagogues over the last fifteen years, in order to find their average distance from the synagogue or communal centre, and other characteristics of the distribution of those distances. The methods put forward by Professor Bachi for measuring the geographical mean and dispersal of a population may be mentioned in this connection.

4. Births, marriages and deaths

Continental statistics for the years preceding the war have generally shown the Jewish *birth-rate* to be lower than the general birth-rate; this possibly reflects the urban characteristics of the Jews (the urban birth-rate is generally lower than the rural) and, again possibly, that the general decline in birth-rates during that period took place somewhat earlier among the Jewish community. In England births are not registered by religion, so no comparable information exists from official sources.

Unofficial sources are equally disappointing so far as the past is concerned, though it appears from the *Year Book* that the Board of Deputies collected figures on births at the turn of the century. If the attempt were now made, the number of boys born could be obtained by requesting annual returns from the Mohalim, possibly with the help of the Initiation Society; the latter society, founded over two hundred years ago, is in contact with all Mohalim in the country. Some Mohalim already keep records for their personal use and would find it easy to provide the precise number for previous years; those who do not keep records could presumably provide a rough estimate for the preceding year, and for future years could be asked to maintain records, perhaps in a suitable book provided by the Society.

I understand that a scheme is now under consideration whereby Mohalim would be obliged to register all male births with the Beth Din; if this were to come into effect, the necessary statistics could, of course, easily be made available.

If the total number of boys born were known, the number of girls could be deduced by assuming the general sex-ratio; if it were further desired, a check could easily be made on the latter by examining the maternity records of a few London hospitals with a large number of Jewish maternities. The aid of the hospital visitation committees, attached to the synagogues, could also be invoked to provide separate returns for maternity cases: whilst their coverage would not be complete (owing to home births, etc.), they would provide a satisfactory sample to check the sex-ratio.[1]

The principal difficulty with statistics based on the returns of Mohalim would be one of definition; there are undoubtedly many cases attended by doctors not registered with the Initiation Society (and hence not authorized to officiate by the Beth Din). Such births would on this approach not be classified as Jewish though, for other purposes, the families concerned may regard themselves as Jewish. As already indicated, I do not think this difficulty should prevent the compilation of such statistics; I am convinced that the trend they reveal will be of great interest.

If Birmingham is at all representative of experience in the U.K., I suspect that the level of births revealed by inquiries from Mohalim

[1] Continental statistics have in the past occasionally shown some extraordinary values for the sex-ratio at birth: an extreme case (see *Jewish Encyclopedia*, art. 'Births') is that for St. Petersburg in 1866–72 where the ratio of boys to girls was 1·47. No doubt this was due to a deficiency in the registration of girls (which are still regarded today in certain circles as a 'consolation prize'); analogous omissions in registration take place in the Census of Population, even in the U.K. today, where the returns for babies are always found to be smaller than is otherwise known on the basis of direct birth registrations.

may be found to be lower than usually thought. In Birmingham it appears, from an informal inquiry I have made, that the birth-rate is now about five to seven per thousand; this may be compared with the eighteen per thousand recorded generally for the U.K. in recent years, and the much higher figures (in the region of thirty) that applied both to the Jewish and general communities a generation or two ago.

I turn now to the statistics of *marriages* where, because of official and rabbinical requirements, the possibility of obtaining satisfactory coverage is more promising. We have here two parallel primary sources. First, there are the records resulting from the authorization of marriages by the Chief Rabbi's office for all communities under his authority; this source provides details on probably over 90 per cent of all marriages. The records are readily accessible and go back to 1840; besides the number of marriages, they would also provide some information on the age at marriage, birth-place, etc. (though, I understand, these details are not always completed on the forms).

A second approach would be to make use of the marriage register books maintained under Act of Parliament by the officially appointed marriage secretaries of the various synagogues. In this case the details as to age, etc., are always included since they are required by law. An abstract of these records is prepared by the marriage secretary at regular intervals for the Registrar General's purposes; and, as far as the future is concerned, it would be a simple matter to arrange for a copy of the abstract to go to the Board of Deputies so that statistics could be compiled centrally for the community.

From an administrative point of view, it would, of course, be desirable to obtain the co-operation of the orthodox, Reform and Liberal communities (each of which is, on this topic, governed by a separate Parliamentary Act), but if the results were required purely for statistical purposes, one need not expect this to cause difficulty. It has to be kept in mind that a certain number of marriages, for one reason or another, are solemnized separately at a civil register office and subsequently at a religious ceremony;[1] these would not appear in the synagogues' official register books and would therefore have to be requested separately in any scheme of centralized returns. While for particular communities their number may be important, over the country as a whole the proportion is probably negligible.

As far as information on the *number* of marriages is concerned, it

[1] In the earlier days, certain of the ultra-orthodox synagogues did not have marriage secretaries, nor did the Liberal Synagogues (apart from St. John's Wood); accordingly they would adopt the above procedure. It has also been suggested to me that this procedure may be adopted by couples wishing to benefit from income-tax relief by marrying civilly before 5th April; and by those wishing to arrange for passports: it is not thought, however, that such cases would form a significant number.

is pleasing to report that the Registrar General has recently resumed the publication of an analysis by religious ceremonial, after having ceased to do so in 1934.[1] This provides us with the one firm and very important figure that is now available for the Anglo-Jewish community; I should perhaps add that other information that could be abstracted from marriage certificates (average age at marriage, occupation of the groom, literacy, etc.) is not summarized by the Registrar by religion, and a central compilation by the community thus still remains desirable.

TABLE 1. Jewish marriages solemnized in England and Wales, as recorded by the Registrar General, 1844–1957.

Year	Number	Year	Number
1844	175	1924	1,972
1864	349	1934	2,233
1884	867	1952	1,876
1904	1,815	1957	1,713

Table 1 shows the number of Jewish marriages recorded in selected years; for the most recent year available, 1957, it will be seen that their number is over a fifth lower than in 1934 and, in fact, below even the figure shown for as long ago as 1904. In the five most recent years available, 1952–7, the number of marriages fell by nearly 10 per cent. As the Jewish population is thought to have risen, according to our 'informal' estimates, by some 60 per cent in 1904–34 and a further 30 per cent subsequently, these figures for marriages will, I suspect, cause concern.

Accepting, for the moment, the estimate of the Jewish population of 450,000, the marriage rate according to the 1957 figure would be rather under four per thousand. This may be compared with the general rate of close on eight per thousand in the U.K. It is true that from European statistics we would expect the Jewish marriage rate to be lower than the general rate, but the difference is of a smaller order of magnitude; from a table compiled by Ruppin (1940, p. 85) for Europe in the 1930s the Jewish rate is seen to be about seven per thousand, about one per thousand lower than for the general population. A comparison with recent Canadian Jewish statistics, as analysed by Rosenberg (1959, p. 225), is perhaps of greater relevance: he finds seven per thousand for 1955 (which apparently is a low rate by Canadian standards), while a rate of ten per thousand was recorded for 1951. The figure of nine per thousand for Jews in Israel is also of interest in this connection.

A marriage rate of four per thousand may well seem implausibly

[1] See the Registrar General's *Statistical Review for 1952, Civil volume*, pp. 178–84; *Text volume*, p. 53.

Statistical Research: Needs and Prospects

low: should one then conclude that the accepted population figure of 450,000 is too high? One could work backwards (as discussed in section 3 above) by starting from the recorded figure of marriages and, assuming that the general rate of marriages applied to the Jewish community, one would arrive at a population about half as great as assumed above. I would not have thought that the error is in fact so large; a more likely explanation, in my opinion, for the low number of Jewish marriages is that a large number of Jewish persons must today be marrying only civilly, whether on account of intermarriage or otherwise.[1]

Further comment on these highly interesting figures would perhaps be out of place in the present paper, which is intended to do little more than sketch the background. I therefore merely add that a geographical breakdown is given by the Registrar General and, in addition, a figure for marriages involving divorced persons (in 1952, of the total of 1,876 Jewish marriages there were 122, or 6·5 per cent, which involved divorced persons—a proportion that is about half that in the general population).

The traditionally early age of marriage among the Jews was often thought to be the cause of their fruitfulness. Today matters are somewhat different; when carrying out my study of Birmingham Jewry (Prais, 1949) I analysed the local marriage records, over a period of some forty years before the war, and found the average age of Jewish grooms similar to that of the general population. Jewish brides were however a year or two younger. It would be interesting to have similar information for the whole community.

Owing to the often limited choice of marriage partners in small communities, there tends to be an unduly high rate of consanguineous marriages among Jews. The early investigation by Jacobs (1897, p. 3) may be recalled, based on a count of marriages where bride and groom had the same surname, as shown in published marriage announcements. He applied a rather ingenious analysis to these figures and concluded that marriages between first cousins among the Jewish community were then five times as frequent (relatively) as in metropolitan London.

A word must be said also about the subject of intermarriage, on which it is very difficult to obtain, with any accuracy, even any general impressions. The interviews with fifty hospitalized soldiers by Slater

---

[1] If the community were declining for natural reasons (that is, due to a true low birth-rate), one would also expect to find a low marriage rate in due course; but can one really believe that the community is halving itself each generation in this way? In any case, this only changes the question to one of the cause of decline (whether it is natural or due to assimilation), but leaves the fact of the decline undisputed.

(1947) led him to the conclusion that one person in eight married out of the faith; this proportion, to be sure, is much lower than the 20, 40 or 60 per cent recorded for Budapest, Berlin and Trieste, respectively, in the inter-war period (Ruppin, 1940, p. 108). But in view of what has been said above about the low recorded marriage rate, I suspect that the intermarriage rate may be higher than Slater's small sample suggests. A larger investigation of that type would be of interest.

Statistics of *deaths* could be obtained from burial societies and synagogues without too much difficulty since they all maintain records. It would be desirable to have a return showing each year the numbers classified by age and sex. As already indicated, such figures have previously been centrally collected by the Board of Deputies, and it would be highly desirable to re-institute this practice. Such figures would provide the most comprehensive possible coverage of the community, and would provide a convenient basis for estimating the population. There are, I understand, a certain number of cremations (perhaps of the order of 5 per cent of total deaths), and a separate return should be attempted for these.

Studies of the causes of death and the incidence of diseases among Jews are undoubtedly of interest (see the article by Kallner, 1961), and the possibility of such studies at some of the London hospitals might well be considered by a medical statistician.

5. Education

Educational questions are considered more fully in this book by Dr. Fishman and Mr. Levy[1] accordingly I shall mention here only one or two thoughts of a statistical nature. I take it that the figures in which we should be interested are (*a*) the proportion (not merely the absolute number) of Jewish children receiving Jewish education, and (*b*) the number of hours a week the average child devotes to such studies.

On the basis of the information at present available, it is difficult to estimate the latter figure, but an estimate of sorts can be made for the former. The number receiving education, whether full-time or part-time (including 'withdrawal' classes) is given by FL as 30,000 (of which 18,500 are in London and 11,500 in the Provinces); these figures roughly allow for overlapping between the various types of classes (a child at a 'withdrawal' class may also attend part-time classes, as may a child at a full-time school). The amount of overlapping could be verified by a survey, but is perhaps not too large— the estimate of FL puts it at about 3 per cent.

The main difficulty in the calculation is to know the total number

[1] Referred to below as FL.

Statistical Research: Needs and Prospects

of Jewish children of school age. As indicated in a previous section, this figure could in future be obtained, with some hope of precision, by applying the 'Yom Kippur' method; but in the present state of knowledge, we have to rely on the indirect method of assuming they form a certain proportion of the total community. But what proportion should we assume? FL take a proportion of 12 per cent, which corresponds to that for the general population in Greater London. In England and Wales as a whole the proportion is rather higher, at 16 per cent; London is, I imagine, exceptionally low owing to the migration into London, from the surrounding country and from abroad, of people in the non-school age-groups. If we look at the Jewish population of Canada, for which we have official census information, the proportion aged 5–14 is found to be 14 per cent; in the United States the corresponding proportion given by the 1957 survey for the Jewish community is 16 per cent (I have had to interpolate from the published figures which relate to the age group 0–13). For working purposes I would thus prefer to use a proportion of 15 per cent for the Jewish population in this country.

Accordingly the number of Jewish children in this country would be some 67,000; and the proportion enrolled for religious education is thus about 45 per cent. Weekly attendances at synagogue classes, it is important to note, are less than half the enrolment.

The number receiving Jewish instruction at any period in their life, however short that period may be, is clearly greater than the average enrolment per annum. Some limit on that number may be obtained by using the figures on the age distribution of pupils, as compiled by Mr. Levy; these show that the largest class (in the sense of pupils, of a particular age) exceeds the average class by about a half.[1] If pupils who ever receive religious instruction may be assumed always to attend this largest class, the 45 per cent—derived in the previous paragraph—has to be raised in that proportion; we thus find that the total proportion ever receiving instruction is about two-thirds.

The above proportions would of course be raised if it were thought that the population were declining, and that there were therefore fewer children available for enrolment.

The numbers receiving full-time education at Jewish day-schools in England has recently risen and is now about 8,000, of which 5,000 are in London and 3,000 in the Provinces (based on Dr. Braude's survey in the *Jewish Chronicle*). But for the historically minded, I note that in 1900 the number was also 8,000 (see the *Year Book* for

[1] There are certain peculiarities of the age distribution as shown in that inquiry; but these are not very large and may be ignored here.

1901–2, and Gartner, 1960, p. 224), at which time the population was less than half its present size.[1]

6. Other Statistics

It is not widely known that the Registrar General publishes the number of *buildings registered for worship* by religious denomination. Some of these figures are abstracted in Table 2 below; the number registered is seen to have doubled between 1911 and 1952, which roughly parallels the change in population. But in the subsequent years, 1952–7, the number has fallen by over 10 per cent.

TABLE 2. Number of synagogues registered with the Registrar General, 1911–57.

1911	208
1924	270
1934	310
1952	428
1957	377

In relation to the population, it would appear that there is now one synagogue for some 1,200 individuals, or, say an average of 300 families per synagogue. This is of the correct order of magnitude, as far as one can tell from general impressions; but taking into consideration the smaller size of the typical provincial community, I think it is rather on the high side. There is undoubtedly a proportion of the community not affiliated to any synagogue, and the true average membership is thus probably well under 300.

It should be remembered that synagogues may have changed in size over the years; for this and other reasons it would be desirable to have independent and direct figures on membership and seating capacity. By way of further qualifications to the above figures, it may be noted that some of the smaller Minyanim may not be registered with the Registrar General; and that a few of the older synagogues, those in existence before 1850, are not included in these registration requirements.

I would like to add a word or two on some other social statistics. A study of the *occupational* distribution of the community, and its changes, would be of considerable interest; here the Registrar General's marriage records would prove a convenient source (cf. Prais, 1949, for a study of the Birmingham records for the past century). The use of trade directories in such studies never yields results that relate to more than a fraction of the community. The

[1] An extraordinary trend is shown in the enrolment at Talmud Torahs in London which, in two years (1958–60), fell from 1,488 to 1,170, that is by 21 per cent.

Statistical Research: Needs and Prospects

problems of *poverty* are fortunately no longer of pressing importance; but interesting figures for earlier years may be gleaned from reports of Boards of Guardians, giving the number of families receiving Matzot for Passover, and the like.

A final question that may merit discussion at this Conference is the desirability of a comprehensive *social survey* of the community by means of questionnaires addressed to all known members. Dr. Neustatter (1955) reported on the results of two questionnaires circulated in 1950–2: the first was addressed to communal organizations and requested estimates of population, average size of family, births, deaths, Jewish schools, etc.; the second was distributed to individuals and requested for each member of the household, their occupation, educational level, marital status, etc. The number of replies received was not large (from only 1,700 households in the second inquiry), and it is thus not known to what extent the results can be regarded as representative. My own opinion is that surveys of this kind require a degree of organization, both at a central and local level, which the community does not possess at the moment; and such surveys are thus rather over-ambitious, even if the necessary funds were available.

7. Summary

The above brief survey has emphasized the present paucity of statistics on the community, and the need for many purposes of comprehensive and soundly based figures. The few trustworthy statistics that are available all point in one direction, namely, to a decline in numerical strength: the number of synagogues is declining, the number of marriages is low (half the national rate) and declining, the proportion of children receiving religious instruction is low (about a half) and has been declining since before the war.

It is suggested that some central institution should revive the collection of figures on births, deaths and marriages, as previously compiled by the Board of Deputies, so that long-term trends may be judged more accurately. An attempt to obtain the number of male births may be made with the help of the Initiation Society; marriages could be analysed in some detail on the basis of the Chief Rabbi's authorization forms or, perhaps better, from the abstract prepared for the Registrar General; and statistics of deaths could be obtained from burial societies. The last is especially important as providing a source for an indirect estimate of the size of the population.

S. J. Prais

POSTSCRIPT (*April 1964*). The Registrar-General's Review for 1962 has now appeared and shows a further decline in marriages of some 10 per cent over the quinquennium for 1,713 in 1957 to 1,549 in 1962. The alarming trend shown in table 1 is thus apparently continuing at an unabated rate. The number of places registered as synagogues is shown at 400 for 1962 which is about half-way between the figures for 1952 and 1957 in table 2 above.

REFERENCES

R. Bachi (1958), 'The analysis of geographical series', *Bull. I.S.I.*

L. P. Gartner (1960), 'Notes on the Statistics of Jewish immigration to England', *Jewish Social Studies*, **22**, 97.

—(1960), *The Jewish Immigrant in England* (London: Allen and Unwin).

C. M. Horowitz (1961), 'The estimated Jewish population of New York, 1958: A study in techniques', *Jewish Journal of Sociology*, **3**, 243.

J. Jacobs (1891), *Studies in Jewish Statistics* (London: Nutt).

G. Kallner (1961), 'Differences in morbidity among Jewish groups in Israel', *Jewish Journal of Sociology* **3**, 264.

M. Kantorowitsch (1936), 'Estimates of the Jewish Population of London, 1929–33', *J. Roy. Statist. Soc.*, **99**, 372.

H. Levy (1958–9), *Inspector's Report* (Central Council for Jewish Religious Education, London).

H. Neustatter (1955), 'Demographic and other Statistical Aspects of Anglo-Jewry', in M. Freedman (ed.), *A Minority in Britain* (London: Vallentine, Mitchell).

S. J. Prais (1949), 'The Development of Birmingham Jewry', *Jewish Monthly* **2**, 665.

—(1959), 'Statistical publications on the Jewish Population of Great Britain: A bibliography', *Jewish Journal of Sociology*, **1**, 136.

S. Rosenbaum (1905), 'A contribution to the study of vital and other statistics of the Jews in the United Kingdom', *J. Roy. Statist. Soc.*, **68**, 526.

L. Rosenberg (1959), 'The demography of the Jewish Community in Canada', *Jewish Journal of Sociology*, **1**, 217.

A. Ruppin (1940), *Jewish Fate and Future* (London: Macmillan).

O. Schmelz (1961), *Jewish demography and statistics: Bibliography for 1920–60* (Jerusalem).

E. Slater (1947) 'A note on Jewish-Christian intermarriage', *Eugenics Review*, **39**, 17.

H. L. Smith (1902) 'The influx of population', in C. Booth, *Life and Labour of the People in London*, Vol. III (London: Macmillan).

H. L. Trachtenberg (1933), 'Estimate of the Jewish population of London, 1929', *J. Roy. Statist. Soc.*, **98**, 87.

Discussion

THE discussion on Dr. Prais' paper was opened by Professor R. Bachi. 'The emphasis put by Dr. Prais on the proper organization and utilization of the statistical sources on Jewish demography shows that he, too, considers that the main problems in Jewish demographic research today are lack of information, and lack of co-ordination of demographic statistics. I concur completely in this view and I must add that the steady deterioration reported by Dr. Prais in respect to reliable sources of Jewish statistics for Great Britain is also true, alas, for the rest of world Jewry. This state of affairs is particularly sad, because it occurs in an era of widespread and ever increasing interest in population problems all over the world, of continuous improvement in techniques for collecting and processing data, and of much progress in demographic research. Within this frame of continuous improvement in the field of population study, the place of research on demography of the Jews at the world level is conspicuous by its steady deterioration, in comparison with the situation which prevailed before World War I, and, at present, indeed by its almost complete absence. For instance, today it is almost impossible to give a clear and unqualified reply even to the most elementary questions about the number of Jews in the world, their demographic structure, their rate of natural increase, the degree of fusion with the Gentile population through intermarriage, the volume of internal and international migration, etc. For many other Jewish communities, besides the Jews of Great Britain, the statement by Dr. Prais that many statistics are little more than informal estimates or even guesses is unfortunately true: for this reason we cannot even state today whether the size of the Jewish population in the world is increasing or decreasing.

'The lack of the possibility of replying to such basic demographic questions in respect to the Jewish population does not stem from any lack of practical or scientific interest in these questions. On the contrary, there are probably few peoples in the world to whom demographic problems are of such vital interest as the Jews.

'The survival of the Jewish people is dependent upon the continuation from generation to generation of large or small bodies of population, acknowledging themselves and being acknowledged by others as Jewish. Such processes as insufficient reproduction rates, mixed marriages, ageing of the population, irregular age and sex structure, etc., might lead to dwindling or complete disappearance of these bodies. Hence the vital

Discussion

importance of the study of these demographic processes. Moreover, demographic documentation is acknowledged today to be of basic importance for the planning and administration of Jewish affairs and social services, both at the local community level and at the national level. As aptly pointed out by Dr. Prais, good organization of Jewish schools, synagogues, hospitals, etc., in a given town requires data on the distribution of the Jewish population by sex, by age, by district, etc., in order to make sure the services are given in the neighbourhood of the person to be served. From a national point of view, planning of educational services as discussed yesterday here, and even the organization of fund-raising campaigns, require a good knowledge respectively of age structure and of the size of the population by economic and social groups in each place, etc.

'Besides this, the analysis of demographic processes occurring among the Jews is extremely interesting from a scientific point of view. For instance many Jewish communities scattered all over the world show astounding similarities in regard to, say, smallness of mortality rates at young ages, low incidence of certain causes of death, high age and low frequency of marriages, low fertility, population ageing, etc. The questions arise, therefore, whether these similarities are due to Jewish peculiarities, or to specific influences of the Jewish religion or culture, or whether they are due simply to the fact that during the nineteenth and twentieth centuries the demographic evolution of the Jews has been similar to that of other Western populations, but has preceded it.

'If this last explanation is accepted, it is still necessary to explain why the Jews have led in time most demographic processes, whilst other population groups in the same places have lagged. In order to reply to such questions it is often necessary to ask ourselves whether demographic processes occurring among the Jews actually differ significantly from those which would occur among any population having the same degree of urbanization and having the same socio-economic distribution as that of the Jews. In this connection, a further question arises, namely, whether the urban and socio-economic concentrations of the Jews are strictly connected with their minority status. If this is so, it may be of great interest to follow up changes in the demographic structure and trends which occur among the immigrants to the State of Israel, where the Jews have attained majority status. From those few hints regarding the general scientific interest of Jewish demographic research, a further point immediately arises, namely the need to have data on the Jewish population analysed in a very refined way; only very detailed data may enable us to disentangle the influence on demographic processes of general or external factors (such as age structure, socio-economic distribution, and geographic distribution), from that of peculiar Jewish factors, if any.

'Despite all these reasons, which render the collection and analysis of demographic data of the Jews so important for both practical and scientific reasons—why are data lacking to such a large extent, and why the situation is deteriorating rather than improving?

'There are many reasons for this, mainly connected with the spread of Jews all over the world. We will quote only a few of them.

Statistical Research: Needs and Prospects

(1) Until the beginning of this century, the majority of Jews lived in a few European states where data on religious minorities were collected currently as a matter of routine; emigration to West European countries, to Great Britain and especially to the U.S.A., where such traditions did not exist, and the change in attitude of East European countries in this field, have destroyed the main base on which Jewish statistics were compiled in the past. Today official censuses furnish some statistical data in regard only to some 47 per cent of world Jewry.

(2) The official data on the Jews being published in some countries and the materials furnished by Jewish sources are spread over a very heterogeneous set of publications and in many languages; therefore, in the absence of a central institution collecting these data (as was done at the time of the *Bureau für Statistik der Juden*) the task of the Jewish demographer is indeed a formidable one. He must consider the entire world as the frame of reference for his research work and, at the same time, he is powerless to influence the methods by which the data on the Jews are being collected.

'However, Dr. Prais is right in stating that our task here is not confined to lamenting present deficiencies, but is to find ways to improve the situation.

'The analysis made above may be summarized by saying that there are two main difficulties in the way of Jewish demography:

(1) Information in regard to many Jewish communities is insufficient or even non-existent.
(2) Existing information is so scattered that it is difficult to collect and digest it systematically.

'The conclusion is therefore that if we wish to improve the situation, there is a need for two main lines of action:

(1) Fostering initiative for collecting data on the Jews in the various countries of the world.
(2) Establishing a world pool or focal point of information.

'Initiative for collecting statistical data on the Jews in the various countries of the world can and must come primarily either from the Governments or from the Jewish institutions of each country. In this field, prospects and methods are different in the different countries of the world.

'I will briefly review the situation and prospects
(1) in Israel,
(2) in other countries where there are official statistics on the Jews
(3) in countries where such statistics do not exist.

1. '*Israel*. The settlement of about two million Jews in the Land of Israel and the establishment of the State of Israel have opened up recently new vistas for Jewish demography.

'Among the Jews of Israel there are people hailing from almost all the countries of the world. Both for practical and scientific reasons, great interest is attached to information about the demographic, social, economic, cultural and pathological characteristics of these people at the time

Discussion

of their arrival in the country, and on the change which takes place in these characteristics—both among the immigrants themselves and their descendants. The problems of the adaptation of the immigrants to the economic, social and health conditions of the country and of the merging of the heterogeneous masses of the immigrants into a more homogeneous population, are considered very important in the life of the State. An acute demand for data on the demography of the Jews has therefore been created. In Israel, we have been fortunate in that the Government has given the means and technical possibilities for satisfying this demand; two detailed population censuses have been taken (in 1948 and 1961), a well integrated system of vital statistics has been established, and a fully fledged permanent register of the population is kept on punched cards.

2. 'In countries outside Israel in which population censuses ask questions on religion or other questions which enable to identify Jews, there are potentially good possibilities for Jewish statistics. Generally, these countries publish today only the total number of Jews and little additional information. However, if Jewish institutions in these countries would take some initiative, they could obtain at a low cost additional detailed data on Jews, by utilizing the punch cards or the tapes for electronic computers, regarding Jewish persons.

3. 'In countries like the U.S.A., Great Britain, France, most other European countries, etc., which include the majority of world Jewry, and where no questions on religion are asked in the official censuses, the initiative for obtaining statistics rests solely with Jewish bodies.

'Among these countries, there are a few, such as Italy, in which a permanent register of the Jews is kept by Jewish communities, from which data on population, births, deaths, and marriages, can be derived.

'However, for the largest communities, such as those of the U.S.A., Great Britain, France, etc., such a register does not exist, and it would be extremely difficult to try to establish it.

'However, even without a register, and even without a fully-fledged census of the Jews, there is considerable scope for obtaining more or less reliable demographic data on the Jews, by utilizing proper and by far cheaper techniques, which should be adapted to local conditions and needs.

'In the U.S.A., a host of such techniques have been suggested and employed—both for indirect estimates on size and structure of the Jewish population, and for direct Jewish community surveys. At present, at the request of the Institute of Contemporary Jewry of the Hebrew University of Jerusalem, the Council of Jewish Federations and Welfare Funds in U.S.A. is working on the preparation of a manual of methods to serve as a guide to communities in making demographic surveys. Proper use of modern sampling techniques is found to be of considerable help in lowering cost and enhancing the quality of results.

'In Great Britain, the possibilities of obtaining data on the Jews seem to be potentially better than in the U.S.A., since it appears possible with a moderate effort to compile yearly a systematic digest, at least, of deaths and marriages, and perhaps also of male births. From such a digest, extremely important information could be derived. This has been shown very well by Dr. Prais, whose main proposals in this field I wholeheartedly endorse.

'However, I must warn that these data on Jewish population movements may be considerably incomplete. For instance, a cursory glance at the marriage rates for British Jews, as estimated by Dr. Prais, would show that it is similar to that of Jewish marriages registered by Jewish communities in Italy (1926–55), where these marriages are known to include only some 53 per cent of marriages of persons of Jewish origin (1930–40).

'Therefore, the compilation of vital statistics, as advocated by Dr. Prais should, in my opinion, be integrated by a proper and thorough population survey on a medium-sized community, which should serve as a means for evaluating coverage, quality and meaning of Jewish vital statistics and for establishing organic links between vital statistics and estimates on size and structure of the Jewish population.'

Professor Bachi went on to stress that whilst techniques for demographic research on the Jews must necessarily be selected according to local conditions, efforts should be made to ensure that surveys and research conducted at a local level be organized in such a way as to enable comparisons to be made both at the national and world levels.

This brings us back to the problem of ensuring adequate contact among the people interested in the field of Jewish statistics all over the world, and also to the problem of pooling information on Jewish demography collected throughout the world.

'In this field some modest steps have already been taken, by establishing a Society for the Demography and Statistics of the Jews—which has recently started its work in Israel; and by developing a Section for Jewish Demography in the Institute of Contemporary Jewry at the Hebrew University of Jerusalem. This Section has been active in preparing a first draft of an International Bibliography of the demography of the Jews in the past forty years, which has appeared recently in a volume which includes some 5,000 entries.

'This bibliographical list serves now as a basis, in order to establish in Jerusalem a focal point for the collection of existing documentation on the demography of the Jews: copies of publications and microfilms are being collected, and in the long run it is hoped to start with the preparation of synoptical tables on the main demographic aspects of those parts of the Jewish people for which statistics can be obtained.

'In conclusion, despite the fact that the present situation of Jewish demographic research is admittedly bad, prospects for the future are not necessarily pessimistic. Considerable improvements seem possible if Jewish institutions will show more initiative than in the past, and if proper co-operation and mutual exchange are established among the institutions and people interested in this field all over the world.

'The fact that the subject of demography has been given so much attention here, seems to be both a symbol of readiness for such co-operation and a promise for the future.'

Professor Bachi was followed by Mr. J. Hajnal. He agreed with Dr. Prais

Discussion

that such data as are available must be assembled and would be very useful. 'However, I do not think that we should neglect problems of definition. Attempts should be made to find out what kinds of Jews are included in the different statistics that may be collected. Professor Bachi has already pointed out strong reasons why the birth and marriage rates quoted by Dr. Prais cannot be complete. I should like to underline that. It is almost inconceivable any country in the world has ever had, or will have, a marriage rate as low as four per thousand, or a birth rate as low as five per thousand. Such figures simply mean that the numbers on which they are based do not all refer to the same thing. For example, as Dr. Prais points out, the explanation of so low a birth-rate (calculated from the number of circumcisions) may be that many (it would have to be over half) of those included as Jews in the population figures did not have their sons circumcised, or that the circumcisions are performed by Mohalim or doctors not authorized by the Beth Din. If this is the explanation, such a "birth-rate" figure may serve to indicate the prevalence of the practice of circumcision by authorized Mohelim; it permits no inference whatever concerning the birth-rate.

'However, it is not merely for the interpretation of statistics that efforts are needed to investigate who is counted as a Jew in England today. Jewish life in England is rapidly changing and we cannot understand what is happening without understanding how the marginal Jews and the committed Jews interact. No one knows how many of those who have their sons circumcised may leave the life of the community, or how many who do not have their sons circumcised may want to take part in the life of the community. It would be desirable to know in what combinations the various aspects of Jewishness are found together in the same person and also how frequently people move from one category to another. How many people move from orthodox homes right out of the Jewish community; how many people move back again in various ways? We ought to study movement within a person's lifetime and also what happens over the generations. There are two basic ways of studying such questions. One is to take a body of people and go forward in time. Dr. Roth has suggested there might be data on people taken at the beginning of the century and one could attempt to see what had happened to their descendants since. Another way is to select a group of people and now ask them about their personal histories, their parents and so on; and thus go backwards. The problem here is how to select a suitable group for study, especially how to include those who are not actively attached to the Jewish community. I think there is no simple overall answer to this problem, but there are things that can be done. One could get in touch with groups which comprise a fairly large number of those not actively attached, for example groups of students. Another way to find people who have moved out of the community is through their relatives who probably in many cases still are actively Jewish. For example one could take a sample of Jewish marriages, or of readers of the *Jewish Chronicle*, or of contributors to communal appeals, etc. One could approach them and ask about their personal history, their grandparents, parents, uncles, aunts, sisters, and brothers, and thereby

Statistical Research: Needs and Prospects

get some information on how many people coming from different origins are now attached in various ways to the Jewish community. A population of relatives is inevitably a biased one for study, but methods are known of allowing for much of the bias. There may be in this approach also an opportunity of studying what happens within the same family, for the better understanding of such matters as 'Jewish values". One might perhaps be able to throw light on the strikingly different ways in which people may react to a common background—to take an extreme instance, how it happens that one brother becomes an orthodox Rabbi and another a Communist.

'Ideally studies of this problem of what happens from generation to generation should be planned in such a way that the foundation is laid for a series of studies over the years and one can follow the change in the nature of the community, as obviously it will change in the next decade. With an open community it is now easy to move out; but this possibility may come to be counter-balanced by the opening up of movement into the community. This is happening on the fringes of the American Jewish community. Attempts are being made to convert people to Judaism. In certain circles in the United States it seems that individuals move in and out of the Jewish community fairly easily. Movement in both directions may become more frequent in this country. Another possibility is that large parts of the community fall away entirely, but that a nucleus remains living a relatively isolated ghetto-like existence. There are all sorts of conceivable lines of development. Ideally we should be prepared with programmes of study to enable the changes to be traced as they happen.

'Now to turn briefly to another subject. There is one possibility of getting data easily which should not be left unexplored. In the last census, taken in 1961, the majority of the questions were put only to one household in every ten; but among the questions which were asked of everyone there were questions on birth-place and nationality. The Registrar General is willing to supply special tabulations of census data on payment of the additional cost. The possibility should be explored of getting from the Registrar General an analysis by birth-place of the population in certain districts of London and provincial cities where the Jewish population is concentrated. If, for example, we take the people over 50 or 60 who were born in Russia or Poland, etc., and live in Golders Green, we should have identified a group of whom the great majority are Jews. Various characteristics of such a group could be studied if the Registrar General could provide a cross-tabulation of birth-place with other information collected at the census. For example, it would be possible to study fertility since a question on the number of children borne by her was put to every woman who was or had been married. This opportunity of getting statistics should not be neglected because many of the people concerned will die before the next census.'

Mr. Harold Levy was the next speaker. He began by expressing his gratitude to Dr. Prais for the help he had given him on various previous occasions on matters relating to Jewish statistics. He went on to make two points—one regarding Glasgow and one regarding Nottingham.

Discussion

'My own town is Glasgow and I refer to Dr. Prais's remarks on the Yom Kippur method. Now in a town like Glasgow it is comparatively easy to get to know the number of Jewish children attending the secular schools and one can assume that one then knows the number of Jewish children in the community. It is not as in London where there are many independent schools and where many people send their children to private schools. In the 1930's, when it was customary to say that there were 15,000 Jews in Glasgow, an investigation of this kind was made, and the number of Jewish children was established and multiplied by $7-7\frac{1}{2}$, which gave a figure of 13,500 for the Jewish population in Glasgow, and I think this is now the accepted figure. It is therefore useless to take the figure in the *Jewish Year Book* and work backwards to find the number of children. If Dr. Prais and his friends could descend on Glasgow and establish independently a figure for the Jewish population, then by comparing this with the number of Jewish children we could find the ratio between the children and the general population.

'In Nottingham I questioned the figure for the Jewish population which is given in the *Jewish Year Book* as 2,300. I then found that a friend of mine had been asked for a figure on the telephone and had had to give an answer quickly! I asked the proprietor of a Jewish catering establishment how many Jews there were in Nottingham and he said he had to compile annually a list for selling *matzot*. He said, "My livelihood depends on making the list as complete as possible." According to his list there are 1,750 Jews in Nottingham and this figure may be more reliable than the official figure given in the *Year Book*.'

Dr. S. Roth spoke of the use that might be made of data on synagogue membership in assessing Jewish population figures.

Dr. Braude spoke next. 'I would like to correct an error in Dr. Prais' paper.

'The number of children enrolled in Jewish day schools in the whole country is about 8,000; 5,000 in London and 3,000 in the provinces. These numbers do not include boarding schools. The figures concerning schools are one of the few items about which we have exact details available. All the other figures which are given to us in the *Jewish Year Book* and other sources are carried on from year to year and it is generally known that these figures are not reliable. It is especially necessary to try to establish new figures for the Jewish population in this country.

'The Anglo-Jewish community is not reluctant to have such figures established, but the main difficulty is that it is easy here for Jewish people to disappear because the Gentile population is not as antagonistic to meeting socially or to mixed marriages as is the case in the U.S.A.

'In Switzerland, for instance, after the last war there occurred a change in the attitude of the Gentile population. They are no longer so much opposed to mixed marriages and unfortunately this has led to a great increase in these marriages which will eventually lead to the disintegration of a large part of the Swiss Jewish community.'

Dr. Highet said that he would strongly support 'these speakers who have suggested that, contrary to Dr. Prais' proposal, an attempt be made to

Statistical Research: Needs and Prospects

define "Who is a Jew?" I should have thought that, if not the whole point of, then a very important purpose in, attempting this research is to obtain data that will tell us something more about the corporate entity we are concerned with than simply that they are "not Gentiles".

'Otherwise we shall end up with something as vague as the results of the religious censuses carried out by some European countries, to which Dr. Prais refers. I cannot over-emphasize how singularly worthless these data are. They derive from answers to such vague suggestions as "What is your religious affiliation?" or "To what religion do you belong?" This leads to figures purporting to show that 80 per cent, 85 per cent or 90 per cent of a country's population claim to belong to a church—very often in just these countries whose ministers of religion are anxiously looking about wondering where all "their people" are.'

In reply to the discussion, Dr. Prais said that he welcomed the comments made on his paper. 'With regard to the comprehensiveness and coverage of the statistics—a matter touched on by many speakers—one could argue that if in 1957, for example, we found 1,700 Jewish marriages recorded in synagogues, there might well be a further 1,700 marriages of persons of Jewish origin at registry offices of whom we know nothing. But if we disregard questions of biology, and look at the matter purely from the point of view of the organized community, I think it should be said that the latter are not Jewish marriages (the descendants of such marriages would have certain difficulties in regarding themselves as being members of the Jewish community). The way I interpret the figure, mentioned in my paper, of four marriages per thousand, is that these are four marriages per thousand within the Jewish community. I am not sure whether we shall, in this country, ever be able to ascertain the larger figure of biological marriages relating to all persons of Jewish origin—that seems to me a very difficult task in present circumstances.'

Topics and Methods of Future Research: Sociological

MAURICE FREEDMAN and JULIUS GOULD

I

SOCIOLOGICAL research can mean different things, and it would be as well for us to begin with the proposition that the study of Anglo-Jewish social life can usefully be approached in several ways. (That this chapter is jointly written by a sociologist and an anthropologist is by itself a guarantee that no one special method of research will be recommended to the prejudice of others.) If we had been dealing with a community which had been well described in many of its aspects we might then have urged some concentration on a particular topic by a special method. As it is, we know precious little about the society of Jews in Britain, and we must think about devising research which will bring in the greatest body of data in the most economical manner.

We may conveniently begin a rapid survey of what has so far been accomplished by making a rough division between historical and contemporary studies. Contrary to popular misconception, the past is in principle as amenable to sociological inquiry as the present.[1] (The relative lack of sources about the past and the special problems of technique for handling what data exist are questions which in no

[1] See the work of Dr. V. D. Lipman (especially his *Social History of the Jews in England 1850–1950*, London, 1954; see also his history of the Board of Guardians, *A Century of Social Service 1859–1959*, London, 1959; 'Synagogal Organization in Anglo-Jewry', the *Jewish Journal of Sociology*, Vol. I, No. 1, 1959; and 'Trends in Anglo-Jewish Occupations', *The Jewish Journal of Sociology*, Vol. II, No. 2, 1960) and of Dr. Lloyd P. Gartner (*The Jewish Immigrant in England, 1870–1914*, London 1960); also several of the essays in *Three Centuries of Anglo-Jewish History* (ed. V. D. Lipman, Cambridge, 1961). This literature covers a field which could with great profit be still more intensively studied.

way affect the principle.) The past by itself is sociologically interesting; but it is also to be analysed in relation to the present; the study of contemporary Anglo-Jewry must not be left to float in the colourless fluid of an undefined past. At the very least, we need to understand trends in the development of modes of grouping and institutional life; they are untraceable unless the sociology of the past and the present are correlated.

In fact, of course, its past is one of the few aspects of Anglo-Jewry to have attracted the attention of its scholars. In the work of Dr. Cecil Roth (and under his aegis) we have an impressive body of historical material, the sociological aspects of which are to be used and extended. What is strikingly lacking are sociological studies of the present. To the best of our knowledge only two field studies have been carried out, and one of these was by a foreigner. Dr. Howard M. Brotz, an American sociologist, now teaching at Smith College, Northampton, Mass., did a field study in north London which was embodied in a Ph.D. thesis in the University of London, 1951, *An Analysis of Social Stratification within Jewish Society in London*.[1] Mr. Ernest Krausz, now a research worker at the London School of Economics, carried out a field study of the Leeds community.[2]

Nearly ten years ago one of us was responsible for putting together a provisional survey of what was known about Anglo-Jewish society. *A Minority in Britain, Social Studies of the Anglo-Jewish Community* (ed. Maurice Freedman, London, 1955) consisted of four papers. The first was an historical sketch by Dr. James Parkes and the second a demographic and statistical survey by Dr. Hannah Neustatter. The third paper, dealing with Jewish society in London, was by Dr. Brotz; it built upon the field research already referred to. The final piece was written by the editor of the collection; it was based on no systematic field research whatever, but attempted to outline the problems of analysing the position of the Jews in British society. Apart from the papers by Brotz and Krausz (and an additional paper by the latter on Anglo-Jewish Occupation and Advancement[3]) virtually nothing has appeared since *A Minority in Britain* to take its tentative analysis a step further.

Why? The question is itself a sociological one. If it can be answered it will help us to be realistic in our planning for the future. The

[1] See also his article, 'The Position of the Jews in English Society', *The Jewish Journal of Sociology*, Vol. I, No. 1, 1959.
[2] See his University of London (M.Sc.Econ.) thesis, 1960, *Aspects of Social Control in a Minority Community; The Leeds Jewish Community*, and his article 'An Anglo-Jewish Community: Leeds' *The Jewish Journal of Sociology*, Vol. III, No. 1, 1961: also his book *Leeds Jewry*, Cambridge: Heffer, for the Jewish Historical Society of England, 1964.
[3] *Jewish Journal of Sociology*, 1962, Vol. IV, No. 1.

Topics and Methods of Future Research: Sociological

first point to be made clear is that sociology in this country is underdeveloped. It is starved of money both for the training of research workers and for research. This has a direct impact on the study of Jewish questions—as on most other fields of study. At some time or other every Jewish sociologist and anthropologist in Britain must have had the experience of being consulted by a well-meaning young man or woman about the chances of conducting research into an aspect of Jewish life. The aspirant may have had no education in the social sciences; he will have needed to be told what training he must undergo before being able to do something useful; he will almost certainly have departed stunned. He may have been a student of sociology or anthropology; he will then have been warned about the slender opportunities open to him and then either gone out into the world to earn his bread or turned to some aspect of sociological research for which money was available. In this way talent, trained and untrained, is lost to us. It is important to underline the fact that, unlike history, which is taught universally in the schools and widely in the universities, sociology can hardly be done by amateurs. Sociologists are sociologists *de carrière*. It follows that people who are concerned with developing a sociology of Anglo-Jewry must face up squarely to the problem of recruiting, training, and providing continuous employment for the men and women who are to do the work.[1] That issue cannot be shirked.

A further practical question arises. Research into Jewish matters calls not only for sociological training but also for some sort of education in Jewish subjects. Let us not beat about the bush. The young people who offer themselves to 'Jewish sociology' are not likely to know enough about Jewish religion and history. We are, in fact, confronted by the same educational problem as faces scholars interested in the development of what our American colleagues call 'area studies'. How do we combine a thorough sociological training with an adequate training in the background of the subjects to be investigated? What institution of higher Jewish learning in this country is capable of providing this sort of education in conjunction with sociology? And if it is capable, is it willing?

We have so far dealt with problems of recruitment and training. There is also the question of demand. This conference has been sponsored by an Israeli body. Does Anglo-Jewry itself want

[1] It is worth pointing out that sociological study of Anglo-Jewry need not (and, for scientific reasons, should not) be deemed a preserve for *Jewish* social scientists. Obviously it would be for Jewish scholars that the field would have the strongest appeal. But in the United States (where both the Jewish and the general cultural background is different in scale and quality from our own) some non-Jewish scholars have made significant contributions—and others are likely to make still more.

sociology? Our impression is that there is some indifference to it and, in places, resistance. The indifference is partly to be ascribed to a general un-intellectualism in organized Anglo-Jewry. The resistance comes to some extent from the feeling that a minority needs to be careful about what it exposes to the public view; if anything is to be said it must be flattering; sociology sounds like muck-raking. Moreover, some people want to maintain intact the image of a homogeneous and unified community and fear lest impartial inquiry reveal a very different state of affairs.

It is not for us to plead a case. We can limit ourselves to three simple points. First, sociological knowledge, like all knowledge, is good in itself. If there survives in organized Anglo-Jewry a love of learning and reasoning for their own sake then let it consider the case of sociology. Second, sociology includes techniques for discovering and organizing facts which are relevant to the shaping and carrying out of social policy; and it implies a mode of systematic thinking about society which is equally germane to the process of formulating and executing plans. Many different kinds of bodies within Anglo-Jewry (synagogues, school boards, welfare organizations, and so on) need to understand the properties and dimensions of the social groups they cater for, and the likely results of the provisions they make; to this sort of realism sociology can contribute. Third, sociological understanding is a way of giving perspective to one's problems. To study Jewish society in Britain is to put it into the context of its wider contemporary setting, to see it in relation to its past, to measure it against Jewish and other minorities elsewhere in the world—in short, to inhibit the parochialism which flows from the legitimate concern with the affairs of one's own community.

Little knowledge, small resources, modest initial objectives—these are the points from which we start. We cannot hope to undertake a massive inquiry which would locate every Jew in the country. Nor is it possible, given the lack of basic data on numbers and distribution, to mount a statistically satisfactory sample inquiry for Britain as a whole. Instead, it is better to begin by stating the problems which seem to merit high priority and then to consider how best these problems may be tackled as field tasks. (Thus in Part II below we deal with certain demographic questions of direct sociological concern, socio-economic structure, family, kinship, and youth, leadership, organization and the roles and functions of the religious ministry.)

Each problem dictates its own methods, but there is a broad distinction in types of method which applies to all, or nearly all, the problems to be tackled. Some kinds of information can be gathered by questionnaire inquiries. One decides precisely what one wants to find out, one designs a form listing the questions, and one administers the questionnaire to a scientifically selected group or 'sample' of people. The information sought may be questions of fact (e.g. what people do for a living) or questions of belief, value and attitude (e.g. whether people view with favour a proposed innovation). If the questionnaire is carefully thought out and properly used it can yield an abundance of useful data. This method has several advantages. A large number of people can be brought within the scope of the inquiry, because each interview is relatively short. The sociological sophistication called for by the inquiry can be concentrated in a director who leaves the administration of the questionnaire to people who, while they are skilled interviewers, are not necessarily fully trained sociologists.

But there is a limit to the usefulness of this method, for in so far as matters of fact are concerned one is forced to rely on the informant's perception of reality. If, for example, a man makes a statement about what he does (the amount of pocket money he gives his children, the number of times a year he goes to the synagogue, the help he gives his neighbours, and so on) he may, in all honesty, be substituting an ideal for a reality or amplifying memory by guesswork. There comes a point where data must be collected by observation. In a highly urbanized and industrialized society such as ours it is no easy matter to apply the methods of 'participant observation' (living in a community and taking part in its everyday life) as they have been developed for the study of small-scale rural communities. But, depending on the problem and the situation, one can often go very far towards building up close continuous relations with informants and seeing them behave in a variety of social contexts.

One advantage of this method is that it allows the observer to inquire into many things at once. Imagine a man who has established himself in a Jewish neighbourhood in a provincial town. In the course of his everyday life he will be able to see people going about their business, talking informally to one another, making their way to the synagogue, or going to a 'function', and, in the case of those to whose houses he has access, behaving in a family situation. The more formal associations of local life and the associations in which people participate beyond local life will take on greater meaning for the observer when they are measured against what he knows of the intimate life of the neighbourhood. So that on the basis of this sort of method a sociologist might have something important to say about a variety of matters: family life, religious life, class relations, friendship patterns, leadership, youth organization, and so on. The great disadvantage in the method is that it calls for a highly trained field worker and a considerable expenditure of time. But we have only to consider how much further forward we should be if we had, say, three or four such pictures of local communities to recognize the magnitude of the profit in relation to the investment of a few thousand pounds.

The further one moves from the study of a local community towards the study of wide-based organizations the narrower becomes the range of observation and the more important the interview. But it does not follow that informality and free and easy rapport with informants must disappear. Not everybody is potentially a good interviewer (or any other kind of field worker), but the trained sociologist who has the confidence of his teachers can be relied upon to practise techniques which by now have a long history.

The ultimate aim of a strategy for research into Jewish society in Britain is to document and analyse both the community as a whole (that is to say, as a network of 'political' relations from the centre to regional centres and thence to locally defined communities) and as a collection of groupings and institutions (families, local communities, synagogues, youth organizations, economic associations, and the like). The list of points we touch on below is not complete enough for the construction of such a picture of Anglo-Jewry; it is a list merely of those things which seem to us important enough to merit early attention. If we begin—and succeed—with these few things we can then consider how to move a step further along the road to a sociology of Anglo-Jewry.

II

As we have said, it is not our intention here to set out the full range of topics over which sociological study of Anglo-Jewry might range. Elsewhere one of us has discussed in some detail the complex problems which, in general, face the student of diaspora Jewry—problems which the techniques of demographic study, social psychology and sociology can collectively explore.[1] In what follows our aim is to specify and comment briefly upon five areas of study which, in our view, should command some measure of 'priority' consideration.

(a) Demographic and Statistical Data

Demographic information is obviously of the greatest importance. In Great Britain Jewish vital statistics are slender in quantity and most inadequate for wider research purposes. All too often they represent tentative inferences based upon other and yet more tentative inferences.[2] If the social patterns of Anglo-Jewry are to be intelligently

[1] See J. Gould. 'American Jewry—Some Social Trends', *The Jewish Journal of Sociology*, Vol. III, No. 1, June 1961, pp. 55–56.

[2] See H. Neustatter's contribution to the symposium *A Minority in Britain* for a detailed discussion of the extent of our knowledge and of some of the conclusions which it permits.

Topics and Methods of Future Research: Sociologica

mapped, we need a far firmer and more coherent statistical basis upon which to work. We do not feel that either the subject matter or present-day circumstances permit of an unofficial 'national Jewish census'. Such a census, were it possible, would be of the greatest value: but it is not the only way of securing more reliable demographic data. Indeed it may be argued that present needs lie not in the direction of a global estimate of the total Jewish population but in that of realistic assessment, based upon painstaking local inquiry, of the distribution (and changes in the distribution) of the Jews in Britain. Especial importance attaches not only to the major urban areas in which the bulk of Anglo-Jewry has been traditionally located but also to the newer, more scattered areas of Jewish settlement that have not been carefully studied. So far as the major urban areas are concerned a good deal could be learned if the demographic and statistical techniques employed, for example, by Mr. E. Krausz in his study of Leeds Jewry could be applied to comparable communities. If this approach were combined with other recognized techniques of field research, a most useful picture of such urban areas could be constructed. Our view is that we must now move, in the study of provincial communities, away from the simple chronologies which sometimes are presented as 'local history'—and that we must now study population growth and movements in such communities alongside wider institutional issues. All that is known of contemporary Jewish trends in industrial societies confirms the need for this dual approach. A related if more pioneering task confronts the researcher in the newer areas of Jewish settlement. The numbers who have moved are quite unknown; and the institutions which cater for their needs (as and when these needs are articulated) are less organized and active. If the development of these new areas is a portent of Anglo-Jewry's future, the study of its beginnings and growth to date is a matter not only of scientific but also of practical importance.

Two other areas of inquiry are mentioned here by way of illustration. (i) Systematic study of Jewish family life (see below) must rest upon specialized demographic data of a kind not now available. For example we would need to have in systematic and cumulative form elementary data drawn from an adequate sample concerning, e.g. the age of marriage of Jewish women, fertility experience, spacing of births, etc., and to analyse such data with regard, e.g. to the occupation of their husbands. Only thus, incidentally, can scientific estimates of future Jewish population growth be intelligently derived. (ii) The problem of intermarriage has been frequently discussed by communal leaders; but the discussion has often conveyed more heat than light. Sample studies designed to illuminate both the extent and motivations of intermarriage could be devised; the results would provide a rational basis for the continuing discussion of this central issue in Jewish family life.

(b) Socio-Economic Structure

The problems in this area relate to the occupational patterns of the Jews; the changes in such patterns: and the comparison of such patterns and changes with what is known of the general British scene. In this area Jewish trends are, at present, more conspicuous than the evidence upon which the trends may be judged. Here too we would welcome much more systematic inquiry into the situation. Thus, for example, systematic study of the entry of Jews into the professions could become part of the much wider research concern with Jewish youth. Synagogue records could be systematized so as to make available elementary data upon the occupation of synagogue members: such data would be a most helpful foundation for subsequent, and more extensive, inquiries by sociologists. A special line of inquiry which has never, to our knowledge, been pursued, would focus on the extent to which Jews in business or professional life predominantly have dealings with other Jews: the aim of such an inquiry would be to see how much of an occupational community Jews can and do form in modern society.

If it is true that the bulk of Anglo-Jewry is 'middle class', then a good deal of attention should be given to mapping the contours of the 'middle class'—and indeed to conducting 'attitude' studies of the different strata of middle-class Jewish society. But it should not be forgotten that there is, and has long been, a Jewish 'upper class' and that members of this 'upper class' are to be found in the top echelons of many Jewish organizations and charitable bodies—especially in London. It would be most useful if the nature of this *élite* could be examined: its influence and functions recorded and other information set out. Here too we might come to focus research effort into selected topics. What, for example, are the facts about the extent to which this *élite* is 'reproduced' through marriages within its own circles? And what is the amount of 'intermarriage' to be found among this important group of British Jews?

Nor should it be forgotten that the Jewish working class, though much shrunk, has not disappeared; it would be worth while to study it both qualitatively and quantitatively.

(c) The Jewish Family and Jewish Youth

Stereotypes about the Jewish family abound—especially 'favourable' ones. It would be good to test these stereotypes against current and changing reality. What are the contemporary roles of the Jewish father and mother?¹ What are the patterns of family discipline, moral surveillance, concern with education, both Jewish and secular? And what love-hate relationships bind the children to their parents? Such topics are far too important to be left solely to novelists or journalists. They ask questions which need to be broken down into manageable form and directed to specific geographical areas, occupational groups, age-groups, etc. The answers to such questions would shed light upon the community's aspirations and future: they would indicate whether we are encountering in Anglo-Jewry, as in other sections of contemporary Britain, the phenomena to which the term 'youth culture' has been increasingly given.[2] The flavour of this Anglo-Jewish 'youth culture' will not *determine* the community's future: but it will be one of several important factors which call for analysis and interpretation.

Although analytically distinct, the family cannot in practice be studied in complete abstraction from the kinship relations within which it is embedded. And it might be well worth considering a fairly ambitious attempt to work out what significance extra-familial kinship relations have at the present time for Jews in this country. One may look both outwards from the family (to see the extent to which people implement and make use of their kinship relations—in ritual, economic, and 'social' life) and inwards to the family (to measure the degree to which these relationships have a bearing on the operations of the family). Fortunately for anybody interested in this kind of study, a good deal of work has been done in Britain in recent years on topics belonging to this class, and it should be easy to apply the concepts and methods devised for the study of kinship in the general population to the study of Jews.[3]

(d) Leadership and Organization

Anglo-Jewry is not 'corporatively organized',[4] but, for so small a community, it abounds in organizations of various kinds, each with their distinct, if overlapping, catchment areas. The links which

[1] For American data drawn from child guidance case material, see 'Two Types of Jewish Mothers' by M. Wolfenstein in *The Jews*, ed. M. Sklare (1958), pp. 520, et seq.

[2] For comparative insights see the article 'Jewish Teen-Age Culture' by David Boroff in *The Annals of the American Academy of Political and Social Science*, Vol. 338: November, 1961.

[3] See especially the papers by R. Firth, O. R. McGregor, L. Lancaster, and J. B. Loudon in *The British Journal of Sociology*, Vol. XII, No. 4, December, 1961. An example of the interest which lies in the study of Jewish kinship is to be found in W. E. Mitchell, 'Descent Groups among New York City Jews', *The Jewish Journal of Sociology*, Vol. III, No. 1, June 1961.

[4] See M. Freedman, *The Structure of Jewish Minorities* (World Jewish Congress), 1957, p. 19.

families form with such organizations present some of the 'hardest' evidence of continuous Jewish identification. And leadership, both lay and professional, within such bodies is a most overt and conspicuous form of identification. The main 'overarching' bodies, claiming as they do to represent the community, do in fact offer Anglo-Jewry's most public face; they display, as we all know, problems of leadership which should be sociologically studied. It is not enough that, at times of celebration, they should commission good historical studies of their distinguished past;[1] they should be prepared to offer their present operations to responsible scrutiny. Neither they nor the community would lose thereby. For at a time of obvious transition an organization needs to know its own structure and problems no less than the changing society which it is there to serve. It would be equally wise to assess what benchmarks for Jewish identification organized Jewish life, at various levels, provides for the community. For how many does it provide a vital and meaningful link, for how many a habitual, routinized kind of attachment? And how many people are just indifferent? We do not know. Evidence, of course, suggests that Anglo-Jewish organized life evokes less vital attachments than is often the case with organized Jewish life in the U.S.A. How much, we might inquire, are the differences the result of broader differences in culture and social structure? And how much are they the consequence of organizational poverty, or of snobberies and inertia in the workings of the organizations or of their public image?

(e) The Ministry

The functions of the ministry in Anglo-Jewry can become a field for lively, controversial discussion. Yet it is possible to be lively without being partisan, and to be controversial without being offensive. The subject is not one which the sociologist can evade. The ministry in the open diaspora also acts as a focus of identification—most obviously at times of crisis and celebration. But there are grounds for the view that the ministry, in its Anglo-Jewish forms, has entered on a time of crisis: and it would be wise to survey its structure, its personnel, and the wide variety of the roles which it is called upon to play. What do people expect from their Minister? Do they get it? How many and what kinds of Jews have opinions on such matters? And if they have no views on such matters, why not? Careful study of the place of the minister in his congregational setting would shed invaluable light upon the realities of the contemporary scene—realities which are now more talked of than understood. There is no field in which Jewish self-knowledge could be more profitably extended. It need hardly be added that such a study of the ministry

[1] And not all of them do even this.

and its roles can only be fruitfully carried through if the ministry itself co-operates in the survey work which it would entail. Some ministers may, of course, feel threatened by the kind of question which we have sketched. They may feel, for example, that the laity should 'expect' from their minister just what the minister has to give or chooses to give. But not all Jewish ministers will approach the matter with such admirable composure: many already sense the uncertainties and pressures which surround their roles. With their co-operation their multiple and genuine problems could be clarified —to the advantage of ministers, laity, and, may we add, social science.

III

This paper is programmatic. Different sociologists will have different ideas about what ought to go into the programme and about the order of priority among items on which all might be agreed. But we think that certain points made in the paper are likely to command very general assent from the profession.

First, we should like to underline the need to keep the sociology of Anglo-Jewry unparochial. Jews are legitimate material of study for non-Jews, and a non-Jew wanting to conduct an inquiry into a Jewish topic should be encouraged and helped. In some respects the outsider sees more of the game; because they seem obvious to us certain things tend to remain unanalysed; a non-Jewish sociologist would not take them for granted. We need a broad perspective on our problems, and we should be foolish to reject what aid we can get from outside the ranks of the community.

Second, sociological investigations are highly technical. They require people who are trained. There is no large reservoir of personnel in the country on whom Anglo-Jewry may call whenever it feels that a particular subject needs to be looked into. It follows that a successful attempt to launch a sociology of Anglo-Jewry will depend directly on the investment made and the foresight exercised in planning to create a cadre of men and women capable of doing the work. Research costs money: money for training and money to be spent in the field. It would be useless to begin a discussion on planning unless this premise were granted.

A third point follows from the second. To be useful research ought to be co-ordinated. It is rational to decide where priority lies (in terms both of the requirements of basic research and of the community's needs) and to take steps to avoid duplication of work. How can this co-ordination be achieved? The answer is for debate; here, we need only say that whatever type of co-ordination may be devised it ought to be associated with some permanent body in the community to ensure stability and long-term planning.

Discussion

DR. HIGHET opening the discussion asked whether they felt that 'what we might call rank and file Jews would co-operate in sociological investigations? Would this co-operation be the more or less likely if it were made clear that the inquiries were being conducted under the auspices of the Board of Deputies? Further, would it be more or less likely to be extended to Jewish than to non-Jewish investigators?'

Professor Leonard Reissman, the American sociologist, said that his experience of studying the Jewish community in New Orleans had made him realistic about the research process. 'A basic feature of any kind of sociological research on the Jewish community involves the scientist with people and organizations and for that reason his activity is necessarily affected. He should be somewhat aware of what to expect. The point I want to make is at once obvious but germane: sociological research is a social process. It is not carried out in a laboratory but in a living community that involves people and organizations. The desperate need for research on Jews has been stressed here repeatedly and no one can dispute that fact. The need for basic statistics about the Jewish population in England is great, but even this presumably objective act involves the community. For, I would stress that even collecting statistics involves the scientist in a social process. It is not just a matter of getting figures, for we must recognize that people and organizations must willingly give such information. Another aspect of this matter arises because priority among the problems to be studied must be established. Clearly there are not enough researchers to study everything. The need for choice, then, involves a relationship between social scientists and the leaders of the Jewish community to decide what needs to be studied and what can be studied. Sometimes these answers cannot be given in advance and some research may be needed to make the problems themselves clearer. Ask yourself the question "What is a Jew?" and you might appreciate the difficulties I point to. Two other related points must be stressed: the unequivocal need to rely upon skilled people to do this research and the need to allow them a high degree of autonomy in performing it. Science must proceed by its own rules. It cannot be compromised by anyone who would like only pleasant answers or answers that fit his impressions. This may very well mean getting answers which do not always please us, but this is a cost for research we must pay.'

The next speaker was Miss S. Strizower. 'We are told that sociological

Discussion

understanding is a way of giving perspective to one's problems. It seems to me that we ought to give perspective to the problem of esteem.

'Jews belong simultaneously to two esteem systems, that of their own society and that of the host society—esteem systems which are not, however, of equal importance.

'In England Jews frequently rate themselves according to the rating they receive in the host society. And if the host society does not rate them highly (or Jews think that the host society does not rate them highly), this carries over into Jewry and Judaism. As a result, Jews may even be unaware of what they have given to the Gentile world, and, indeed, believe that Jewish contributions to the Gentile world are Gentile contributions to the Jewish world. (For example, I asked a number of children and adults, from the Liberal to the Orthodox camps, about the origin of the Hebrew alphabet. I asked the Liberals first, and they promptly replied, "It comes from the Greek—of course!" I jumped to the conclusion that this type of reply was peculiar to Liberal Jews. However, members of the United Synagogue and the Federation of Synagogues gave the same reply. Some even explain, "Aleph, Bet—Alpha, Beta; it must come from the Greek." It did not occur to any of them that it might be the other way round.)

'On the other hand, while among coloured people "passing" is permissible (and those too dark-skinned to attempt it will nevertheless assist their more fair-skinned kinsfolk where possible), we tend to regard the "passing" Jew as a social renegade, as someone betraying an ennobling impulse. What are the values which make Jews (who have a conception of the price paid and the loss incurred) feel that the game is worth the candle?

'Surely, esteem in a minority group, especially one which lacks "racial" characteristics differentiating it from the host society, is vitally important for survival—and the factors which tend to inhibit it or encourage it ought, therefore, to be studied.'

Mr. Emanuel de Kadt referred to the previous day's discussion on education.

'Education can be roughly defined as transmission of culture. We have had a contribution which deals exclusively with religious education. As it seems in fact to be the case that the only formal Jewish education of Jewish children is *religious*, we should at least ask why it is that only this part of a very differentiated culture is formally transmitted to the next generation—a part which apparently plays a minor role in the lives of the majority of adults and which the children themselves will so often want to discard at an early opportunity. It is a problem which merits investigation. I have a strong hunch that the causes of this one-sidedness will be found to lie in the power—and influence—structures within the community.

'Now I should like to make two practical suggestions. The first is that it might be very valuable to use survey materials which have been collected for other purposes, in which certain questions have been asked enabling us to identify the Jews in the study. Secondary analysis of general surveys in the community not specifically directed at Jews could thus yield valuable information. I myself am at the moment trying to do a secondary analysis of this kind of a sample survey amongst British university students, which included a question on the religion into which one was born. A number of further questions were asked and I suspect that one can identify almost 100 per cent of the Jewish students, "active" or "not active", as virtually all will have declared themselves to be born Jewish. It has been suggested that those people who do not normally identify themselves as Jews are "lost" and of no interest; I would hold, to the contrary, that precisely these people are of particular interest to us. The second point I should like to make is that it is not only important to see our Jewish studies in the context of the problems of the surrounding community—as Professor Ginsberg has pointed out, it is also important to link up the sociological studies of the Jews with sociological studies in general. Many problems in general sociology can be approached very advantageously if we take a Jewish group as our empirical case. This consideration ought to be stressed repeatedly—only via this avenue can we hope to induce scholars to work on specifically Jewish topics.

'There has been a great deal of talk about about "who is a Jew". But let us not forget that they are other things as well (businessmen, Conservatives, CND-ers, Rotarians, etc.). We hardly know anything about the circumstances under which people "become Jews" in the sense that their being Jews effectively influences their behaviour. I suggest that we might find something like a life-cycle of Jewishness: there are certain periods in a person's life during which being a Jew is important to him and other periods during which it completely fades away. Research into this problem may well be both interesting and of practical importance for the Jewish community.'

Dr. P. S. Cohen was concerned about the dangers of parochialism: a tendency to discuss the institutions, organizations, values and beliefs of Anglo-Jewry in isolation. 'Dr. Freedman has argued that it is of primary importance at present to study the community as such, and to veer away from too much emphasis on anti-Semitism. But why must a study of race relations or inter-ethnic relations necessarily over-emphasize hostility? Is there no cordiality and friendship in the relations between Jews and the wider society? In fact the study of Jewish communal organizations must be a study of the inter-action between Jewish organizations, practices, moral and other standards and beliefs, and those of the wider society.

'Anglo-Jewry is not the same as American, French or Israeli Jewry, since it is very much the product of English society and culture. Jews are not subject to very much discrimination in Britain. But British society defines this kind of relationship very much in implicit terms. The whole fabric of the relationship is complex and fragile in its ambiguities. Is this the reason why there is an unwillingness to discuss this matter except in terms of the occasional blatant expressions of anti-Semitism? Is there at work some conscious or unconscious act of repression in the neglect of this important topic? Amongst American Jewry the whole thing is much more open and blatant. Does the difference reflect a difference between the two societies? America is a much more heterogeneous and plural society. It is not simply a question of anti-Semitism. The structure of Anglo-Jewish

Discussion

social and cultural life is a function of its relations with the wider society. To neglect this is parochial.'

Dr. Levenberg argued that 'if we are to make a sociological inquiry, there must be one principle that I should like to put to you by quoting the famous maxim: "Facts are sacred—comment is free." If we are to make an inquiry we should not worry about the results with regard to the Jews—there must be no fear as to the results of an inquiry, even if they are quite different from what we may expect. This principle must be established from the beginning.

'The question was raised as to whether the Jews here are just part of the general society or something else. You cannot limit an inquiry into Jewish life by just saying that the Jews are a part of the general society. Of course the Jews here are a part of the British community. It is clear that a study of Anglo-Jewry must take into consideration the general conditions in this country. But there are other factors, too, which have to be taken into account. The large majority of the Jews here are immigrants, sons of immigrants or grandchildren of immigrants. Jews here are linked by many ties with Jews in other countries and in Israel. In other words, a study of Anglo-Jewry cannot be confined to one factor; it must be an inquiry which takes into account all factors which shape Jewish life.

'The main problem is, I think, that we are discussing the question in a vacuum. Mr. Gould and Dr. Freedman raised the question; they said you cannot get proper research unless you know who is going to do the research. These discussions have surely justified themselves. But there will have to be an independent research unit. Unless something tangible is done there is a danger of the Conference being an interesting episode without any practical results.

'There are certain definite things to be done. We should encourage students, Jewish and non-Jewish, to study Jewish life in this country. We should urge individuals and organizations to give scholarships to these students. We can try to form a proper climate of opinion for research in this country—in London and the provinces. Work should begin in the smaller centres but in order to do this we need the complete goodwill of the provincial communities and their leaders, because there is a danger of people resenting an inquiry and refusing information. There is a danger of people taking a reactionary point of view by considering that an inquiry is against the interests of the community.

The final point is that when we come to real sociological work the decisive factor will be the question of priorities. We have no means of discussing everything; we do not have the funds or the men. There could be fifty headings for an inquiry, but the question is, what are the priorities? We must choose priorities carefully. There must be agreement between political leaders and the scholars. What is essential? What is important for the understanding of Jewish life? Certain fields are more or less known. The communal life is known, more or less, too. But there are certain fields where we are almost blind. The question of priorities for research must receive the most serious consideration.'

Mr. Gould and Dr. Freedman then replied.

Topics and Methods of Future Research: Sociological

Mr. Gould said that the discussion had been very valuable. 'Very little has been said in the way of destructive criticism and I think a number of the points made help in the understanding of the kind of thing we have tried to say. I will not answer in detail all the points raised, though we have noted them carefully. Let me single out three things. Firstly, despite some of Dr. Cohen's anxieties about this, I do not think we ignore the importance of the wider society. We are not interested in continuing parochial inquiries which are not set within the wider context of contemporary British life. Secondly, both Professor Reissman and Dr. Highet raised important questions about the autonomy of science. There is, as we know, and as Professor Reissman and Dr. Levenberg both reminded us, a key problem in the enforcing and laying down of priorities. These must be worked out between researchers and community leaders; none can say what resistances might be encountered in such a dialogue and in the consequential attempts to get at data. We are certainly encouraged by the atmosphere at this meeting. Thirdly there was the point which was stressed by Dr. Levenberg—how important it is not only to know what you are doing but to do it in a tactful, diplomatic and firm way. That is again something which cannot be arranged in advance.'

Dr. Maurice Freedman said: 'Mr. Gould has really dealt with the points which I thought were particularly of interest. I should just like to reply to Dr. Cohen if I may. There is so much common ground between us that the slight difference in approach is really highlighted by that large area of agreement. I would say that the point of my remark was to forestall any encouragement which might be given to us to waffle on endlessly about points we have been discussing for years. I think a lot has been said on the point he raised and the time has come when we must get down to fact grubbing. There is not enough fact grubbing. I am not myself just a fact grubber and I have always attached great importance to the study of Jews as a phenomenon of the society of which they are members. I think we ought to get out a list of priorities for the next two or three years, as we should be striving towards the discovery of basic data which we know to be strikingly deficient.'

Oral History and its Potential Application

SHAUL ESH and GEOFFREY WIGODER

THE systematic application of Oral History to research in contemporary Jewish affairs is an innovation of the Hebrew University's Institute of Contemporary Jewry. Indeed the method remains comparatively revolutionary and is still little known outside the United States. When a book appeared recently containing conversations with Justice Frankfurter recorded within the framework of a parallel American project,[1] a distinguished British historian stated in a review that it was regrettable that no Oral History project had as yet been undertaken in Britain. And although we are still unaware of any overall scheme in Britain, we believe that there is room to apply this method within the framework of future research on Jewish topics in Britain and in other communities. However, before proceeding further, we should first answer the question 'What is Oral History?'

Oral History is an instrument of contemporary historical research made possible by the availability of the tape-recorder. The collection of written testimonies, of course, is no recent innovation although its systematization is comparatively recent. But useful as is the collection of written testimony—either by encouraging the persons interviewed to note down their evidence or by having it noted by the interviewer —there are inevitable shortcomings. If noting verbally, the interviewer can seldom keep up with the rate of speech, with the result that either material and nuances are lost or else the rate of speech has to be slowed down or interrupted so that the interview becomes dragged and unnatural, losing the requisite flow and concentration.

[1] *Felix Frankfurter Reminisces.* Recorded in talks with Dr. Harlan B. Phillips. New York, 1960.

Shaul Esh and Geoffrey Wigoder

The noted American historian, Professor Allan Nevins, some dozen years ago put forward his proposal to found an American Oral History Centre. He claimed that many men or women who have made important contributions to society or who have been in a position to observe significant developments die without leaving a memoir, diary or record of substantial value. We would like to quote from a paper by Professor Gerhard L. Weinberg on 'Nazi Party and Military Records' read in December, 1958 at the American Historical Association Convention.

'... We must also be aware of the great gaps in the sources. Certain types of records, invaluable to the historian of nineteenth-century Europe, are nowadays rarely created in the first place. Officials seldom write periodic detailed letters; they dictate innumerable inconsequential notes to their secretaries; or, worse still, they resort to that calamitous invention, the telephone. Even in the rare cases where we do find a telephone log, such as Himmler's for part of the war years, there is still no record of what was said. But even of the created record, much is lost. Vast quantities were destroyed during and after the war, and often only fragments of important files survive.'

Professor Nevins concluded that the failure to record first-hand experiences results in a waste of human knowledge and experience and the loss of vital source material. He advocated the establishment of an organization which would make a systematic attempt to obtain from the lips and papers of distinguished Americans a fuller record of their participation in the public life of the country, according to their various spheres of activity. The objective was therefore the collection of living testimonies using the significant technical innovation—the tape-recorder. Feeling that this would add a new dimension to historical research, he established an Oral History Centre at Columbia University which is still the parent project for similar institutions established elsewhere.

The basic method of working is as follows. The interviewer must be thoroughly familiar with research methods. After the determination of the subject of the interview—either the personal experiences of an individual or the exploration of a subject through linked interviews with a series of individuals—the interviewer must first familiarize himself with all the available written sources and documentation on the topic. It is obviously pointless to duplicate material already to be found in writing; sometimes it happens that the examination of the written sources will lead to the decision that the subject is not worth pursuing by oral means. However, generally the researcher can discover those aspects in which documentation is deficient and where the gaps can be filled by recorded interviews.

Oral History and its Potential Application

After a preliminary consultation with the person to be interviewed, the interviewer prepares his questionnaire. The extent to which this questionnaire should be detailed may differ in accordance with various factors. Its preparation enables the interviewer to clarify to himself exactly what he wishes to elucidate while its presentation to the person to be interviewed maps out for him the course of the interview and enables him to prepare in advance his recollections together with any documentation to which he might have access. At the same time it is clear that—unlike in sociology—the questionnaire is not rigid and the interviewer must be prepared to add and improvise questions and even to enter new channels of thought as he goes along. In some instances prior presentation of the questionnaire throws off the person to be interviewed. The practice at Columbia is not to prepare detailed point-by-point questionnaires and not to submit questions in advance. Among our interviewers in Jerusalem there is still a difference of opinion as to the advisability of presenting questionnaires to the persons to be interviewed prior to the actual recording. Further experience is still required before we can determine whether or not a unified policy should be adopted in this respect. If a topic is to be covered chronologically, for example, the person to be interviewed is only told in advance what period is to be covered with an indication of the topics to be considered.

The actual interview period generally lasts between one and two hours and the number of sessions with each individual will depend on the amount of relevant material to be elicited; some persons are recorded for one session, others for ten or twelve. After the recording a transcript is prepared of the interview and passed to the interviewer who notes down any further questions or points requiring clarification. It is then sent to the person interviewed who answers any further points in writing, corrects any facts or wrong impressions conveyed by the recording. However, he is not encouraged to polish up the material and make it more literary; the interview is captive conversation, not polished prose. The final version is entered into the archives as a new source of contemporary historical documentation. In view of the delicacy of certain topics, the persons interviewed are allowed to designate the interviews or sections thereof as classified matter, unavailable to consultation until some future date. This may prove irksome to scholars today but the eventual availability of this material will prove a major boon to historians of the future.

Already the method of oral history is being increasingly used in various parts of the world, including Universities in America, Asia and Europe, and a growing number of books and works of research published in recent years is based on this method. For example, the Institute of Contemporary History at Munich has been engaged in the systematic collection of testimonies in recent years and is already applying them in its researches in modern European history.

This process has been taken up and applied to contemporary Jewish historiography by the Oral History Section of the Institute for Contemporary Jewry at the Hebrew University, at the instigation of the head of the Institute, Professor Moshe Davis. No people has undergone such fundamental changes in this century as the Jews and it was felt desirous that these should be thoroughly and carefully documented. Certain institutions have been gathering material of this nature—thus Yad Washem in Jerusalem has been collecting testimonies of the Nazi period.

In this connection we would like to cite one of the pioneer applications of the method in Israel by Zve A. Brown and Dov Levin in connection with their researches into the history of the Kovno Ghetto and partisan activity in the Kovno area during the Second World War, a book which has just been published in Israel by Yad Washem.[1] For this work the authors recorded over one hundred survivors of the Kovno Ghetto and Lithuanian partisans and questioned them according to a carefully constructed questionnaire.

The Haganah archives and the Israel Military Archives have collected important testimonies dealing with the fight for Israel's independence and the preceding struggle. It should be mentioned that even in the midst of the tragic years of persecution and extermination there were some Jewish historians who understood the importance of oral documentation. For example, Dr. Emmanuel Ringelblum incorporated in his famed clandestine archives in the Warsaw Ghetto eyewitness testimonies built around specific subjects. The method was also used in post-war Poland and Germany by the various Jewish Historical Commissions while here in London a noteworthy collection of such testimonies is housed in the Wiener Library. But these are individual instances and there has been no global application of this method to contemporary Jewish problems—most archives are content with the existing written material they manage to collect and all too seldom set out systematically to initiate documentation covering lacunae. Written documentation, however, is fortuitous; in some spheres it can be ample, in others woefully inadequate. Very seldom does the survival of documents depend on a properly planned programme.

There are various reasons for the inadequacies in written documentation. For one thing, technical innovations have resulted in less material being committed to writing than hitherto, partly as a result of what Professor Weinberg called 'that calamitous invention the

[1] *The Story of an Underground.* Jerusalem, 1962. 422 pp. Hebrew and xvii pp. English (Introduction and Summary).

Oral History and its Potential Application

telephone'. Even advances in communications and transport have resulted in the facilitating of personal encounter and many negotiations which in the past would have laboriously been conducted in writing are now conducted by personal meetings even when this involves the getting together of people from different continents which no longer presents any problems. Another factor operating against written material is the nature of modern dictatorial and totalitarian régimes under which the amount of useful written material is often minimal. This applies both to official documentation which is obviously more sparse than under a democratic and parliamentary régime, and to records concerning opposition forces which are obviously wary of committing anything to paper. A third element that must be taken into consideration is the absence of written material concerning Jewish communities living under unfriendly régimes. The relationship between Jews living in an unfriendly atmosphere with those in free countries is such that documentation is almost completely—and sometimes entirely—absent. In this respect one only has to think of the situation in Europe a generation ago and even today in those various groups of countries where Jews among others are denied free communication and expression.

The work being carried out in Jerusalem is still only in its infancy and is far from reaching the global proportions to which we aspire, but we realize that this must be a gradual process dependent on the development of resources—notably trained scholars to undertake the interviews—in Israel and in other countries. After getting to know our instrument, we have begun to direct our interests to different aspects of Jewish life—politics, sociology, education, culture, thought, economics and the life and thought—internal and external—of Jewish communities throughout the world. To some extent the direction of our work has been dictated by the availability of suitable supervisors and scholars, but where one or the other or both have been absent, we have tried to develop young scholars and encourage an interest in the subject. Consequently the personnel problem must be seen within the framework of the Institute of Contemporary Jewry and its challenge in building up a corps of scholars expert in the problems of the Jewish world today.

The type of work undertaken by the Oral History Section can be classified under two categories; there have been the interviews with outstanding individuals who have themselves played a significant part in the development of some aspects of Jewish life and there have been interviews within the framework of research projects in which a topic has been investigated by means of a series of interlinked interviews. Among the more outstanding figures, Oral

History is potentially more applicable in the case of the man of action rather than the thinker or writer. The latter in any event tends to commit his more original thinking to writing, although there are occasionally spheres here too where the person can be usefully interviewed—public activity, the tracing of his spiritual development, summing up his life and work in retrospect and so on. But, by and large, a more obvious and fruitful source can be found in the public figures and men of action whose experiences have never been committed to a permanent form.

One of the important advantages of this method is the participation of a trained interviewer who has familiarized himself with the background and the available factual material. The human memory, as we all know, is notoriously fallible and it is therefore essential to confront the person being interviewed with facts and documents. We can claim to provide a more valuable source than the plain writer of reminiscences by virtue of the participation of the trained interviewer who can control the interview and, on the basis of his knowledge of the subject, prevent the speaker from building up idealized material or launching into unwanted self-defence. Moreover there is the additional opportunity—one that we have used—of checking the facts and viewpoints of the person interviewed through supplementary and complementary interviews with other individuals who participated in the same historical process. We do not assess the material gathered (except in so far as it is collected within the framework of a recognized research project); but we do in effect take the first step towards such an assessment by the presence of our interviewer who, as it were, provides an on-the-spot sifting of the evidence without interposing a personal evaluation.

Some of the Oral History projects have created documentation in fields that have been almost devoid of written sources. For instance, a series of interviews on the position of Polish Jewry in the area of Poland under Soviet rule 1939–41 concerned a subject of which all too little is known. A scholar approaching the topic in half a century's time would find himself faced with almost a blank. But these interviews now form the groundwork for any investigation of the subject. A similar difficulty has been recorded by Meir Korzen in his article, 'Problems arising out of research into the history of Jewish refugees in the U.S.S.R. during the Second World War', (Yad Washem Studies III. 1959). Mr. Korzen writes of the difficulties of getting written material (pp. 120, 122 f.).

'It may be presumed that the various archives of the Soviet Government in the Ministries of Interior and Defence contain documentary data on the refugees in question—their number, backgrounds, education, schools of thought, etc. However, it is

Oral History and its Potential Application

difficult to conjecture whether any scholar will ever have access to these sources.'

'... It is clear that no particular importance should be attached to the documentary material in the Soviet archives as a historical source for research into the annals and experiences of the Jewish refugee community in Soviet Russia.... The non-Soviet documentary material is not completely objective either, nor does it lack superficial conclusions, haphazardly coined generalizations, etc., so that it must be considered as offering a far from reliable guide to the history of the Jewish refugees in the Soviet Union. The recording of evidence and eyewitness accounts may, therefore, be useful here as a means of checking the authenticity of the documentary evidence available or of complementing it wherever it seems deficient.'

These remarks sound rather similar to those made by the Master of St. Catherine's that 'not only is oral evidence an invaluable supplement to documents and written memoirs but it is also of the greatest value in teaching the historian to be critical of written records'. From his talks with witnesses and participants in events he explores, the historian will learn 'that the written account may often be drawn up to conceal as much as to record what was said and decided'. Taking down oral evidence is therefore 'an invaluable training for any historian'.[1]

Another extensive project undertaken by the Institute for Contemporary Jewry was devoted to the rescue of Jews from Western Europe during the war, via Spain and Portugal. This involved the recording of dozens of interviews—with members of the underground in France and other Western European countries, with Jews who escaped across the borders into Spain and with representatives of Jewish organizations working in the Iberian peninsula. Other subjects which have been the subject of research within the framework of Oral History include the Jewish partisan movement in Slovakia, problems of Jewish education throughout the world, the Lithuanian Division, etc.

The interviews with the individuals have covered a wide scope and touched on many aspects of Jewish life. They have included the recording of material of historic interest as well as the conversation of outstanding thinkers on general or specific problems, as we have recorded with personalities such as Professor Mordecai M. Kaplan, Professor N. H. Tur-Sinai and Mr. Philip Klutznick. But generally when we have recorded interviews the object has been to elicit specific information. For instance a series of interviews (lasting

[1] Alan Bullock: 'Is it possible to write Contemporary History'? *On the Track of Tyranny* (ed. by Max Beloff), London 1960, p. 69. Also cf. ibid. p. 199 (Dr. Eva G. Reichmann).

some twenty to twenty-four hours) were recorded with the present Director-General of the Israel Foreign Ministry, Dr. Hayyim Yahil, on his experiences as Jewish Agency representative in Germany in the immediate post-war years. We have recorded such varied individuals and topics as Dr. Nahum Goldmann on the reparations negotiations with Germany, Mr. Baruch Zuckerman on the Jewish labour movement in the U.S. before the First World War, Rabbi Dr. Mordecai Nurok on various aspects of his long public activity, and Mr. Gus Saron on his experiences as General Secretary of the South African Jewish Board of Deputies.

On occasions we have found ourselves embarking on what was meant to be an individual interview but have discovered that it has branched out into a project. Of interest to this gathering in this connection is the series of interviews with Mr. Berl Locker on the work of the Jewish Agency in London in the crucial decade between 1938 and 1948 (incidentally of particular importance inasmuch as a great part of the Agency archives for that period were sent to Canada and still cannot be traced). After the interviews with Mr. Locker were concluded it was realized that these could be most usefully supplemented by his collaborators from that period and already a number of such supplementary interviews have been collected in Israel (e.g. with Mr. Moshe Rosette, Mr. Gershon Avner).

Whether the subject is a general or an individual project, Oral History can have equal validity. One of the essential pre-conditions to its success is the selection of the interviewer and his familiarity with the subject. Indeed his role is decisive and requires a number of qualities; these include a general background of contemporary Jewry and its problems; a thorough grounding in the sphere which he is investigating (we have encouraged our interviewers to specialize in particular branches); he must understand research methods; and in addition must possess a friendly personality which will prove sympathetic to the interviewee and sufficient common sense to guide the interview along the lines he wants and not along those where the person interviewed may wish to wander. It is therefore advisable to prepare long-term projects so that the interviewer can afford to acquire the broadest and deepest possible background to his researches. It is easy to adopt a dilettante approach and record the interviews only after a perfunctory and inadequate preparation; the result may well then be virtually useless. Preparation in depth is essential. Moreover in no instance is the ultimate direction of the interview left solely to the initiative of the interviewer; in each case, this direction is laid down by a member of the university's academic staff who has been asked by our Institute to supervise the work and guides the interviewer towards the requisite goals.

Oral History and its Potential Application

The potential application of this method to the Anglo-Jewish community is clear. There are various aspects of communal life over the past decades which will be lost if the initiative is not taken to record them. There are scholars and thinkers—and we are thinking first and foremost of some of our veterans—whose views and experiences should be preserved as a valuable guide to the research workers as well as to future generations. In the past few months we have lost a number of personalities whose views we would dearly have wished to record—such as Rev. J. K. Goldbloom, Sir Basil Henriques and Mr. Leonard G. Montefiore. If only we had got to them in time, what valuable material could have been saved. But more important than regretting the past, is to plan for the future so that the conscious effort will be made to forestall such losses.

The potential application in Britain can run along various lines. In the first place there is the possibility of the project. Thus Dr. Cecil Roth has suggested that the method could be applied to gather valuable information concerning immigration to England and initial integration problems going back to the period before the First World War. He would like to find out just why the average immigrant came here rather than to another country; why he chose one town rather than another (why Glasgow rather than Edinburgh, why Leeds rather than Sheffield, why Manchester rather than Birmingham); why he got into a particular trade; and similar questions concerning his absorption into British life. This is only one potential project—others could deal with such questions as the problems, varieties and experiences of Jewish education; the various religious expressions and the types of personal observance; Jewish cultural life and its manifestations; the connections between Jewish life in Britain and the British Commonwealth; developments in the provinces, etc.

Another very important aspect of Jewish community activity in Britain that has been inadequately documented is the tremendous response of Britain and British Jewry to the challenge posed in the 1930s by the Jewish refugees from Nazi Germany. There is a great deal of important material relating to the reception of German Jewry in Britain and the work of the Central British Fund which should be obtained from leading Jews who were active in these community activities in that period.

Secondly, apart from the broadly communal, there is a rich field of research in the Zionist world and in the history of the relationship between the British government and the Zionist movement as well as the Jewish community as a whole during the crucial years of the Mandate.

Thirdly there are the individuals whose experiences should be perpetuated. These include the 'old-timers' whose memory goes back a long way and can talk about the changes in the community over many decades; it includes many individuals who have played crucial parts in communal endeavour in all its manifestations; it includes leaders and thinkers whose views on specific issues would be of general value and interest.

The main problem is to find an appropriate framework. There are scholars who are interested in the possibility of applying the Oral History method in Britain but they so far lack cohesion. In Belgium there has been founded recently the Centre des Hautes Etudes Juives which has expressed its interest in sponsoring Oral History projects in Belgium. But there is no parallel group in Britain engaged in contemporary Jewish research. The Jerusalem Institute of Contemporary Jewry is anxious to stimulate and co-operate in such research but clearly this is a project which must primarily be directed in London and not by remote control from Jerusalem. We are very anxious to be partners in such a programme but we do not want the work to be haphazard. It must in effect come under proper academic supervision in this country in addition to the assistance and guidance we can proffer from Jerusalem.

In considering this instrument of research, we do not wish to make any exaggerated claims. From the scholarly viewpoint, it is largely an extension rather than an innovation. It extends the traditional form of scholarly research—the memoir, the written document, the minute—but it extends them in a facile, practical and efficient manner. There are still cases where evidence can be better collected in writing, for instance where the witness is overawed by the microphone. But these are the exceptions. Most people of the calibre whom we require to be interviewed are willing and able to talk freely and fluently, as long as they have the assurance that they will have the opportunity of checking the transcript and of designating all or part of the material as confidential, should they so desire.

The fields of potential application where the gaps in contemporary documentation can be filled by the vital experience are numerous. We would like to see a network of Oral History Centres throughout the Jewish world collecting material of the type we have outlined. England is in many ways a perfect pilot plant for such a Centre and we hope that the possibility will be realized of establishing a group willing and able to work with us and concerned with lacunae in the records of the community and in creating living sources.

Topics and Methods of Future Research in Contemporary Anglo-Jewish History[1]

VIVIAN D. LIPMAN

THE objects of this paper are to suggest a number of subject for study in contemporary Anglo-Jewish history, to indicate a few guiding principles in the treatment of material for publication, and to discuss some of the sources on which such study can be based. Anglo-Jewish historiography has with a few exceptions—admittedly outstanding exceptions—been a field for amateurs; and accordingly this paper is not directed primarily at professional historians or even at those amateurs with a body of published work behind them. It sets out to try to encourage the writing of Anglo-Jewish history either by those for whom it must be a spare-time pursuit or by those beginning serious historical research who could choose an Anglo-Jewish theme; it is hoped that both groups will be helped by a discussion of possible subjects and sources, including in the latter some suggestions for the compilation of bibliographical material that would be of service to others doing work in this field.

Definition of Period
For the purpose of this paper, contemporary Anglo-Jewish history is defined as beginning in 1840. So early a *terminus a quo* is bound to be subject to question: 1881, which saw the beginning of the mass immigration from Eastern Europe, would no doubt be generally accepted as a suitable starting point for the contemporary period in Anglo-Jewish history, or even 1870, since the flow of Eastern European immigration is now recognized to have begun some years

[1] The following abbreviations are used in footnotes: B.P.P., *British Parliamentary Papers*; J.H.S.E., *Jewish Historical Society of England*; Trans., *Transactions*. For books published in London, the name of the publisher is given, for books published elsewhere, the place of publication.

Vivian D. Lipman

before 1880. The case for the earlier date (apart from the advisability of giving the bowler a good run-up before delivery) is threefold. First, 1840 marks the beginning of a new age in British history: the start of the Victorian age, the period of middle-class political control, the spread of the railways, the introduction of the telegraph. Second, it coincides with a new era in Anglo-Jewish life: the battle for political emancipation, the organization of the community on a national basis with the development of the Chief Rabbinate and the Board of Deputies, the introduction of religious reform. Third, from just after 1840 there is available a continuous contemporary record of the Anglo-Jewish community in the Anglo-Jewish Press; and from about the same date there is material available for statistical study and analysis of the community, including the censuses of 1841 and 1851 (the only national censuses for which the original enumerators' returns are open to inspection).

SUBJECTS FOR STUDY

What then are the themes that specially call for attention in the period from 1840 onwards? The initial point to make is that there is no definitive work covering Anglo-Jewish history during the period as a whole. The standard work (Cecil Roth, *A History of the Jews in England*, 2nd edition, Oxford, 1949) deals with the period after 1858 only in a brief epilogue. Dr. L. P. Gartner's *The Jewish Immigrant in England 1870–1914* (Allen and Unwin, 1960) covers a much wider field than its title would imply and is to a considerable extent a history of Anglo-Jewry within its period, but that period is limited. The present writer's *Social History of the Jews in England 1850–1950* (Watts, 1954) covers practically the whole period but is admittedly only an introductory study, and its treatment of the period after 1914 is only summary.[1]

One cannot therefore turn to a general history to see at a glance what gaps remain to be filled by the writing of specialized monographs. On the contrary, the general and definitive history, when it comes to be written, will be based on the monographs, most of which still await an author. One can therefore only suggest a number of topics to which monographs might be devoted, selecting those fields in which relatively little of value has been done so far and where further study can make the most significant contribution to the appraisal of Anglo-Jewish history in the last century.

[1] Mention should also be made of the relevant essays in *Three Centuries of Anglo-Jewish History* (J.H.S.E., 1961) and, for their respective congregations, Cecil Roth, *History of the Great Synagogue* (Goldston, 1950) and A. M. Hyamson, *The Sephardim of England* (Methuen, 1951).

Future Research in Contemporary Anglo-Jewish History

Provincial Communities

First, Anglo-Jewish historiography has tended to concentrate on London for understandable reasons—the material available and the size of the community. There is as yet no full-length study[1] of an Anglo-Jewish provincial community in the modern period comparable with those on American Jewish communities, among which one may mention in particular that by Selig Adler and Thomas E. Connolly on the Jews of Buffalo, since it is a city comparable with Leeds in the size of both its Jewish and general populations and in the length of Jewish settlement there.

Provincial communities are suggested for study for two reasons. First, they often show developments different from those in London. For instance, the proportion of recent immigrants at the beginning of the present century engaged in factory work in Leeds, and possibly other provincial centres, was very different from that in London. There are also special types of provincial community: the resort (e.g. Brighton, Bournemouth, Southport), overlapping with the dormitory (Brighton, Southend); the fortresses of orthodoxy (Sunderland, Gateshead, Letchworth); the purely industrial towns (e.g. Blackburn); and the settlements in the mining areas in South Wales and the North. The second reason is that a relatively small community can often be much more easily studied in depth; and there will be old residents, who will be able to fill in the gaps in the written record by personal reminiscence; indeed, even statistical problems can be solved in the small community where someone can literally count all the local Jews and distinguish the doubtful cases.

Communities in the London Area

The history of London Jewry as a whole during this period would be a major work but there are more limited aspects which can be treated like monographs on provincial communities. The most important single subject is probably that of East London Jewry in the age of mass immigration but, in view of Dr. Gartner's work, studies in this field no longer claim priority, although the history of the East End since 1914—including the dispersal during the war of 1939-45 and the limited return subsequently—would repay study. Of even greater significance, however, is the study of the great middle-class suburban areas: first North London, then North-West London, and the settlement of Jews in widely dispersed areas of North-East London, especially since 1945. There are a number of brief records of individual congregations but no one has yet tried to compose a rounded portrait of one of these great suburban communities. A full study,

[1] But see E. Kransz's book *Leeds Jewry* published by the Jewish Historical Society: Heffer 1964.

with statistical, demographic and sociological data, would be particularly valuable because the life in North London Jewry, especially between 1880 and 1914, and in North West London after 1914, presents a characteristic picture of the Anglo-Jewish bourgeoisie—religiously conforming, even orthodox, and yet significantly anglicized.

These two groups of subjects—provincial and London communal studies—are geographical but there are a number of 'functional' subjects needing attention; and four groups of them are suggested.

Economic History

First come studies in economic history. Perhaps the most interesting period for this is the eighteenth century—outside the terms of reference of this paper—but there is also much ground to be covered after 1840. There are the usual subjects of 'business history'—the history of individual enterprises founded by Jews, the contribution of Jewish *entrepreneurs* and the study of the types of business in which Jews have been prominently engaged;[1] and, parallel with these, the identification and study of Jewish occupations. In all these studies, there are various questions to pursue: the influence of previous countries of origin upon immigrant workers, the choice of occupation, the Jew as a worker compared with other workers, differences between London and the provinces, changes in occupational distribution and recent trends as measured by, e.g. apprenticeship and vocational training.

Working-class Organizations

Another range of subjects can be loosely grouped as working-class organizations and left-wing movements. This includes the early benefit and the friendly societies; the *landsmannschaft* groups; Jewish trade unions and Jewish participation in general trade unions; and the radical, socialist and anarchist groups. On the latter, the contemporary sources for the later nineteenth and early twentieth centuries are often silent or determinedly hostile; but, with the passage of time, the historian can review dispassionately what, at the time, he might not necessarily have approved. The working-class and left-wing movements have produced a literature, and possibly an impact on the community, disproportionately smaller than their

---

[1] The following possible topics have been suggested for investigation in studies of Jewish business history in the United States: (*a*) the role of Jewish businessmen in the general economy; (*b*) influence of family ties on business development; (*c*) attitudes to business expansion and to delegation of management authority, and to the introduction of new practices and skills. See Thomas C. Cochran, 'Business History in the Social Sciences', in *The Writing of American Jewish History*, ed. M. Davis and I. S. Meyer (Philadelphia, 1957) pp. 210 ff.

opposite numbers in the U.S.A. Study of the American material should suggest analogous studies, if only to explain the differences. But it must be emphasized that there is danger of what original material there is on trade unions and friendly societies being seriously diminished unless action is taken for its conservation.[1]

Institutions and Organizations
Institutional history forms another group—the histories of synagogues, educational bodies, welfare institutions and the like. So far most histories of Anglo-Jewish communal institutions have tended to be rather blinkered chronologies, which do not put the institution within its setting either in the Anglo-Jewish community or within the wider community; they record lists of office-bearers and extracts from minute-books but rarely try to show the problems with which the organization was faced at each period and how it set about dealing with them.[2] This is particularly true of synagogal histories. Admittedly these often have only a limited field, but they could at least attempt a picture of the local Jewish community of which the synagogue is the focus, and relate it to its environment.

This defect in institutional histories is a pity because the centenary or other anniversary of an institution often provides the occasion and the funds for the publication of a history. Looking ahead one can see suitable occasions for institutional history coming—notably the centenary in 1970 of the United Synagogue, one of Anglo-Jewry's most important and characteristic institutions. Apart from the general aims of an institutional history mentioned in the preceding paragraph, one may suggest three points: first, the importance of preparation a long way ahead; second, the use of expert advice in suggesting the method by which the history should be written and the angle from which the institution can most usefully be studied; third, the advisability, if it is not possible to get an author who can deal reasonably expertly as a professional with all the aspects of an important institution's history, of dividing the work between a team, or possibly of finding a young research worker who could, under supervision, make the writing of this history his work for a research degree.

Religious and Intellectual History
A final group of topics might be the intellectual and religious history

[1] It is understood that a volume on the Jewish Labour Movement in England is under preparation and will shortly be issued by the Yivo, New York.

[2] One must however recognize that, in dealing with the most recent history, the author can hardly avoid limiting himself to facts and general trends and cannot, for instance, deal with the influence of particular personalities on policy.

of the community. Very little, for instance, has been written so far on the development of religious thought. It is true that controversy over the fundamentals of religious belief, as distinct from the details of ritual practice, has in the past been relatively rare in Anglo-Jewry, at least compared with the preoccupation with questions of doctrine that seems by contrast so marked in the history of American Judaism.[1] The reasons for this difference in what are Jewries of similar origin would be illuminating for an understanding of the essential character of Jewish life. There is also scope for study in the movements for alteration of ritual in the United Synagogue in the latter part of the nineteenth century, and in the changing pattern of orthodoxy in the present century (for instance, in the relationship between the influences of the Lithuanian-born rabbis of the earlier immigration, the traditions of Frankfurt, and the more recently arrived *Chassidim*).

The Jew as a character in English literature has received attention[2] but there is little in the way of historical discussion of whether one can define an Anglo-Jewish intellectual tradition and the relationship between intellectuals and the community as a whole.[3]

In selecting topics for study, a number have not been mentioned because important work has already been done on them in recent years and they accordingly present less of a priority case for attention: for instance, the early history of Zionism has been illumined by Mr. Leonard Stein's book on *The Balfour Declaration* (Vallentine, Mitchell, 1961) and the most important period of immigration has been covered by Dr. L. P. Gartner's book. But in listing topics, an attempt has been made to select those that will particularly serve to throw light on the essential character of the community—if one may adapt Pevsner's phrase—the Anglo-Jewishness of Anglo-Jewish life. This can the more easily be appreciated if the writer is able to contrast Jewish experience in England with that in a comparable community abroad, comparison with American Jewry probably being generally the most significant. Thus the writer of Anglo-Jewish history, even though he may be an amateur, spare-time historian, should try not to be a student of Anglo-Jewish history alone. He might, indeed, be given three guiding principles.

[1] There is, for instance, no study remotely comparable with those by Prof. Moshe Davis on the development of Jewish religious thought in the U.S.A.

[2] See for instance M. F. Modder, *The Jew in The Literature of England* (Philadelphia) 1939, reprinted as a paperback by Meridian Books, 1960; and Harold Pollins, 'Sociological Aspects of Anglo-Jewish Literature', *Jewish Journal of Sociology*, II, 25.

[3] For Hebrew scholarship, see the paper by Raphael Loewe in *Three Centuries of Anglo-Jewish History* (J.H.S.E., 1961) and the bibliography listed there.

Future Research in Contemporary Anglo-Jewish History

GENERAL APPROACH

Limitations of Antiquarianism

First, he should be a historian, and not an antiquarian. He should be concerned not merely to collect facts, but to use them to find the answers to problems. That Jewish local historiography is too often not the writing of real history is a complaint often levelled against the studies of this kind. American Jewish history, for instance, has been described as 'mostly steeped in amateurism, filiopietism and apologetics. . . . It is for the most part a collection of biographical material about those who "contributed" to America'.[1] Anglo-Jewish history can be regarded as a branch of English local history and is subject to the same dangers, since the latter has been described as 'preoccupied with facts and correspondingly unaware of problems. . . . Enormous collections of facts, the raw materials for history and not history itself. Many local historians are working in this tradition, without perceiving the fundamental questions they should be answering . . . wandering blindly among the multitudinous facts, unable to distinguish between the significant and the trivial, between those facts that raise problems calling for an answer and those that are isolated pieces of information about the past and no more.'[2] The same authority, however, points to a remedy which can serve also for Anglo-Jewish history. 'The central theme is the origin, growth and (often) the decay of the local society. If the local historian keeps this firmly in mind, he will find that he can discard a multitude of miscellaneous and quite insignificant facts and concentrate upon those that really throw light upon the basic problems of local history.' The history of a Jewish community can appropriately be regarded as that of a local society, distinguished from its local surroundings by distinctiveness of origin, by membership of particular organizations, by adherence to a particular faith, often by employment in particular occupations. The extent to which it ceases to be distinct by assimilation to its environment is also properly part of the story. But the local community as a society must be studied in its relationship to both Jewry as a whole and to its local setting.

World Jewish History

Thus the second principle is to bear in mind always the relationship of Anglo-Jewish to general Jewish history. It is not only that Anglo-Jewry has grown by immigration and is entirely an immigrant community, though of varying strata according to length of residence, but also that Anglo-Jewry has been caught up in general movements affecting world Jewry and has, to some extent, exercised an

[1] B. Weinryb in *The Writing of American Jewish History*, p. 373.
[2] W. G. Hoskins, *Local History in England* (Longmans, 1959) p. 23.

influence on those movements. Thus anti-semitism in Europe and elsewhere in the 1930s had its reflection in the anti-Jewish fascism in this country; the events in Palestine from 1944 to the founding of the State of Israel also had their repercussions on the relations between Anglo-Jewry and its non-Jewish neighbours. In the other direction, one need refer only to the part played by Anglo-Jewish institutions and individuals in the fight for political emancipation of Jewish minorities in Europe and Asia, or their contribution to the realization of Zionism.[1]

The Local Setting
But if Anglo-Jewish history must be viewed as part of world history, it is also part of English history. On the national scale, for instance, the development of public-supported Jewish day schools needs for its understanding an appreciation of the legislative history of English education; Jewish social welfare organizations need to be studied against the background of English social history and conditions, the English voluntary tradition in philanthropy and the growth of the Welfare State. Where possible a non-Jewish organization of analogous purpose should be selected for use as a 'control' so that the progress of the Jewish organization can be measured against it.[2] On the local level, the life of an Anglo-Jewish local community needs to be related to the life of the surrounding town or district. This may provide the answers to the questions why Jews were attracted to a particular area at a given time, why they were able to build up a particular kind of business, why they settled first in one area and then moved on to another, and how their numerical and economic growth as a community compared with the growth of the town as a whole. Unless the history of the local Jewish community is set within the framework of the development of its town or region, it appears unreal, set in an unnatural vacuum.[3]

[1] For a general reference book of Jewish history in the period see Ismar Elbogen, *A Century of Jewish Life* (Philadelphia, 1944). A more recent book is Howard M. Sachar, *The Course of Modern Jewish History* (Weidenfeld & Nicolson, 1958), though this is not always accurate on the details of Anglo-Jewish history.

[2] In his study of the London Jewish Board of Guardians, *A Century of Social Service* (Routledge & Kegan Paul, 1959), the present writer used the Charity Organization Society (later the Family Welfare Association) as such a 'control'. The book contains information on trade, fluctuations, wage-rates, changes in the value of money, social welfare payment rates, a bibliography, etc., that may be useful for students of Anglo-Jewish social history.

[3] The present writer's appreciation of the otherwise outstanding work on the Jews of Buffalo, Selig Adler and Thomas E. Connolly, *From Ararat to Suburbia* (Philadelphia, 1960) was sadly marred by its lack of maps showing the topography of Buffalo and its relation to neighbouring towns such as Rochester, and of a statistical table comparing the growth of the Jewish community with that of the city.

Future Research in Contemporary Anglo-Jewish History

It follows from these three principles—that Anglo-Jewish history should not be merely the collection of unrelated facts, and that it should be related to world Jewish history and also to local English history—that the range of sources to be drawn on will be very wide, although under any one class of source the amount of material may be small. In the hope that they may be of assistance to those beginning Anglo-Jewish historical writing, the following notes are appended on some of the main sources, including suggestions for action needed to improve their availability.[1]

SOURCES

Archives

In discussing sources, archives come logically first. Archives have been defined as 'pieces of writing of all kinds, from formal registers to small notes, which accumulate naturally in the course of the conduct of affairs of any kind, at any time, and are preserved by the person or body concerned or their successors.'[2]

For the purpose of this paper, one need not adhere too strictly to this definition. One may include also the collections of historical materials assembled by individual scholars;[3] and one can be thankful also that many institutions have bound up with their minute-books and similar records pamphlets and other documents, not produced by the institutions themselves, but which are relevant to the Jewish life of the period. Broadly, modern Anglo-Jewish archives fall into two classes—archives of synagogues, schools, charities, friendly societies and organizations of all kinds; and private family and business or professional archives.

Archives need to be located, listed, and, where necessary, transferred to a central repository for safe keeping. While the archives of certain important communal bodies—notably the United Synagogue[4] and the Spanish and Portuguese congregation—are in safe custody and have been listed, this is not true of a substantial number of Anglo-Jewish archives. Many of these are not listed; others are in

[1] Since Anglo-Jewish history is often part of English local history, reference should be made to the discussion of methods and sources, together with the bibliography, in W. G. Hoskins, *Local History in England* (Longmans, 1959).

[2] Sir Hilary Jenkinson, 'Jewish History and Archives', *Trans. J.H.S.E.*, XVIII, 54.

[3] Examples are the Lucien Wolf archives now in the Mocatta Library, University College, London; the papers of the late Mr. Wilfred Samuel; Dr. Cecil Roth's collection; and Mr. A. R. Rollin's archives of the Jewish labour and socialist movement (much of which is now at the Yivo Institute, New York).

[4] See C. Roth, *Archives of the United Synagogue, Report and Catalogue*, 1930. These include the archives of the Ashkenazi congregations which founded the United Synagogue in 1870.

danger of being lost, especially as congregations, friendly societies or other bodies like trade unions come to an end; and other collections of archives have disappeared, though possibly not beyond all hope of recovery. The Anglo-Jewish community needs an organization like the American Jewish Archives to locate, list and, where necessary, to safeguard archives, including the private archives, for which practically nothing has been done so far and yet which, as the collections in the American Jewish Archives show, often contain essential material on social history.[1]

Mention should also be made of Anglo-Jewish material in archives not specifically devoted to Anglo-Jewish history. There is a good deal of material in the YIVO archives in New York and in the Central Zionist Archives in Jerusalem. The Wiener Library in London has both books and a Press file, more especially on anti-Semitism in Britain. It includes the material on Anglo-Jewry commissioned by the Nazis, including the book *Das Judentum in England*, by Peter Aldag (F. P. Krüger) and the publications of the Nazi Institute for the study of the Jewish Question. Although prepared for an anti-Semitic purpose, these publications include factual material compiled from diverse sources with German thoroughness.[2]

Statistics

Statistical material on Anglo-Jewish history has, generally speaking, been listed by members of the Jewish Statistical Society of Great Britain.[3] But there is little in the way of ready-made surveys or demographic studies. The historian of a community or of an area in the metropolis may therefore have to begin by setting his study in its statistical framework and this may involve forming estimates of the Jewish population of the area concerned for a number of dates in the past. The historian has, as it were, to conduct a synthetic survey by the use of contemporary materials and draw deductions from them about the size of the Jewish population which contemporaries did not draw.[4]

[1] An instance of one result of the lack of an archive organization is shown by the fact that very few memoirs of English Jews in the period 1775–1865 have survived. Yet American Jewry, with a population originally smaller, and even at the end of the period not so much larger than Anglo-Jewry, produced enough to fill three volumes of Prof. J. R. Marcus' *Memoirs of American Jews*. The explanation cannot be the greater illiteracy of Anglo-Jewry but rather the fact that American Jewry have an adequate organization for locating this material.

[2] Dr. S. Levenberg and Mr. C. C. Aronsfeld have kindly drawn attention to these sources of Anglo-Jewish material.

[3] S. J. Prais, 'Statistical Publications on the Jewish Population of Great Britain: A Bibliography', *Jewish Journal of Sociology*, I, 136.

[4] This is what the present writer tried to do for Anglo-Jewry as a whole in the year 1851 in the paper published in *Trans. J.H.S.E.* XVII, 171–88.

Future Research in Contemporary Anglo-Jewish History

It is worth while to draw attention to one source of statistical information that has not been systematically used and which can provide an essential starting point for study of the contemporary period. The official Censuses in Great Britain[1] do not discriminate according to religious belief. But the original enumerators' returns of the 1841 and 1851 Censuses are open to inspection at the Public Record Office and anyone with a working knowledge of Anglo-Jewish nomenclature of the period, together with an idea of the likely places of origin and occupations of contemporary Anglo-Jewry, can be reasonably confident of being able to pick out virtually all the Jewish entries.

Of the two censuses, the 1841 one has the advantage of being at a more interesting date in social evolution—the beginning of the Victorian age, the coming of the railways and telegraph and so on. But it records only name, address, sex, age-group of 5 years (apart from children, whose exact year of age is given), occupation and whether the person was born locally, in the British Isles, or abroad. The 1851 census gives in addition relationship to the head of household (which can usually be guessed in the 1841 returns), the age in years and the country (sometimes the town) of origin.[2] These enumerators' returns can be made to yield evidence on the social, demographic and occupational structure of Anglo-Jewry at the beginning of the period of contemporary history. But their use needs careful planning to pick out the areas where Jews were concentrated, so as to avoid endless search through literally millions of entries with virtually no Jewish names.[3] Even so, the number of enumerators' books is so great that to use them really thoroughly some co-operative effort between a team of research workers would be required.[4]

[1] The Irish Censuses do contain information about religious denominations though for Jews only totals are given. Even so, some points of interest emerge. For instance, among Jews in 1901 there was a preponderance of males (2,036 males, 1,862 females, with corresponding figures for Leinster and Dublin) whereas in the general population females predominated.

[2] As regards legibility, the 1851 returns, which are written in ink (though scored through), have the advantage over those of 1841, which are written in pencil and often very faint and sometimes quite indecipherable.

[3] The district and street indexes to the London returns, and the street indexes for many provincial towns, on the reference shelves of the Long Room in the Public Record Office, make it possible to select books of returns with known Jewish addresses, and the City of London contains some small parishes which then had considerable Jewish populations.

[4] The present writer has analysed the returns for St. James's, Duke's Place, a City of London parish with less than a thousand residents, about half of whom were Jews. This contains a reasonable sample of the middle and lower classes (though with perhaps too few of the upper-middle class). This can be seen in the number of servants per household and the findings have been checked by

Vivian D. Lipman

Bibliographies

The Anglo-Jewish historian is fortunate in having the comprehensive *Magna Bibliotheca Anglo-Judaica* (compiled by Dr. Cecil Roth) which in Part I lists historical works (i.e. books about Anglo-Jewish history) published up to 1937 and in Part II lists historical materials (i.e. original books, pamphlets, orders of service, etc.) up to 1837. The *Magna Bibliotheca* has now been supplemented, so far as Part I is concerned, by the *Nova Bibliotheca Anglo-Judaica* (compiled by Miss R. P. Lehmann) which brings Part I up to 1961 and also lists certain classes of material, corresponding to Part II of the *Magna Bibliotheca*, for the 1937–61 period. An obvious gap therefore is the absence of a list of historical material (Part II of the *Magna Bibliotheca*) for the period from 1837 to 1937. The amount of material is so vast, and much of it so ephemeral, that a complete list would be neither necessary nor possible but it might be possible and useful to extend Part II of the *Magna Bibliotheca* to 1850, or even 1870 or 1880 in respect of certain classes of material (e.g. B.8, liturgy; B.18, contemporary Jewish life and customs; B.19, the Jew in English literature; B.22, School Books; and some aspects of B.7—communal organization—such as constitutions and reports).

Maps and Illustrations

No history which purports to describe the relationship of a community to its geographical or topographical setting should be without a map or, better still, a series of maps showing the growth of the community in stages. If the relationship of the community to others in neighbouring towns is significant, then there should be a map of the region as well. It is strange how often this simple provision is omitted; the English reader cannot be expected to know the topography of Philadelphia or Chicago, or the relationship of Buffalo to Rochester, N.Y., nor the American to know the topography of Manchester or the position of the Welsh valley settlements in relation to Cardiff. Yet from the eighteenth century at least onwards there should be no difficulty in obtaining town plans for English towns or districts since, if the local histories or guides or directories have no suitable maps or street plans (which is unlikely), the local reference library or, failing that, the map collection at the British Museum is bound to produce something suitable. Maps or sketch diagrams which can be reproduced as line drawings are inexpensive

---

reference on the one hand to known lower-class Jewish neighbourhoods (e.g. near Houndsditch) and, on the other hand, upper middle-class areas such as the Finsbury Square area. Preliminary findings appeared in an article 'The Year is 1841' in the *Jewish Chronicle*, 3rd November, 1961.

to print and a series of sketch-maps can be fairly easily drawn to show the spread of a local community.

Illustrations are useful, not only for enlivening what may inevitably be an unexciting subject, but for recreating visually the atmosphere of the period described. For this purpose of evoking 'period', pictures of buildings, street scenes, views of streets in which Jews lived or had businesses, or group portraits are often more effective than pictures of individuals; indeed, the latter might be restricted unless they suggest the character of a person who played an important part in the story; and there could be a very severe rationing of illustrations of documents, the well-upholstered exteriors of minute-books, and tombstone inscriptions.

For the period covered by this paper there is no comprehensive catalogue of illustrations—indeed, the material is too vast to make it feasible. Mr. Alfred Rubens' *Anglo-Jewish Portraits* and *A Jewish Iconography* are directed to the period before 1840 but include (especially in the appendices) some material (topographical, cartoons, etc.) after that date. The catalogue of the 1956 Tercentenary Exhibition at the Victoria and Albert Museum (and also that of 1887 Anglo-Jewish Exhibition) contains a good deal of material and indicates its whereabouts. Illustrations in the *Jewish Chronicle* do not occur earlier than about 1900 but the files of the *Illustrated London News* and the *Graphic* (to mention only two) contain much of Anglo-Jewish interest; a list of such material would be a useful addition to Anglo-Jewish bibliography and one pleasant to compile.[1] For local topographical illustrations, the local public library's reference department will usually have a file of prints, photographs, newspaper cuttings, etc.[2]

Official Publications
Under this heading are included the Reports, Minutes of Evidence and Appendices to Reports (including memoranda and statistics) of Royal Commissions, Parliamentary Select Committees, Departmental Committees and similar bodies, as well as reports produced by Government Departments. An idea of what is available can be seen from the bibliography of such material relating to immigration

[1] The Stepney Public Libraries Reference Collection includes material illustrating Jewish life in East London, especially in the 1880–1914 period. Mention should be made also of the Jews' College Library collection of Press cuttings of pictures of Jewish notabilities, mainly of the 1890–1920 period. The private collections of Mr. Alfred Rubens and Dr. Cecil Roth are, of course, extremely rich in illustrations of all kinds.

[2] G. W. A. Nunn, *British Sources of Photographs and Pictures* (London, 1952) has lists of museums, libraries, photographers and photographic agencies with an indication of the kind of illustrative material available at each.

from 1870 to 1914 on pp. 286–8 of Dr. L. P. Gartner's *The Jewish Immigrant in England*. The value of this material, particularly of minutes of evidence, varies and has been contested, notably by Beatrice Webb. Certainly minutes of evidence contain a good deal of repetitious and incoherent dialogue. On the other hand, the question and answer form does bring some vividness to the narrative —it is interesting, for example, to be able to read Theodor Herzl under cross-examination by the Royal Commission on Aliens; and when a man is giving evidence to an outside body he may, for their benefit, crystallize in a few phrases ideas which in his own circle are taken for granted (e.g. Samuel Montagu explaining to the same Commission why he founded the Federation of Synagogues).

Much else of Anglo-Jewish interest can be disinterred from Parliamentary Papers: for instance, the evidence of Dr. Nathan Marcus Adler and Moses Angel to the Newcastle Commission on Education (1858–61),[1] or the returns to the Charity Commission on Endowed Schools of 1903, which contains information about Jewish educational foundations.[2] The material mentioned so far has been printed[3] but relatively little use has yet been made (other than by those doing research on foreign affairs or Zionist history) of departmental archives now in the Public Record Office; for instance, the files dealing with aliens in the Home Office archives are now open for inspection for the period up to 1878,[4] and these, including the lists of aliens arriving at the ports, should provide material for further research on nineteenth century immigration up to 1870.

Biographical Details
Studies of the kind envisaged in the earlier part of this paper are less likely to be concerned with the biographical or genealogical details of individuals than with communities or groups, but such details will be important for, e.g. establishing the origins of a provincial community. The student is therefore reminded of Wilfred S. Samuel, *Sources of Anglo-Jewish Genealogy*;[5] the list of wills and letters of administration at Somerset House up to 1848 compiled by Arthur P. Arnold and included in *Anglo-Jewish Notabilities* (J.H.S.E., 1949);

[1] B.P.P. 1861, XXI, Pt. V.

[2] See also B.P.P. 1902, VI for reports on other Jewish charities.

[3] A reader new to the printed publications might begin by consulting P. and G. Ford, *A Guide to Parliamentary Papers* (Blackwell, 1955); the same writers have also compiled *Select Lists of British Parliamentary Papers* for 1833–99, 1900, 1917 and 1917–39. A list of those containing material of Anglo-Jewish interest could usefully be compiled.

[4] 1844–71, H.O.1; 1872–8, H.O. 45.

[5] This appeared originally in the *Journal of the Society of Genealogists* for December, 1932, and has been reprinted as Jewish Museum Publication No. 2.

and, also in the same volume, A. M. Hyamson, *Plan of a Dictionary of Anglo-Jewish Biography*, up to 1st January, 1949, which lists references to obituaries and similar sources for all names cited. Alphabetical indexes of certificates of naturalization (including details of country or place of origin, as well as place of naturalization) have been printed for the years 1844–1900, 1901–10 and 1911–14. These can be consulted, together with typescript indexes of denizations and naturalizations up to 1844 and from 1915 to 1924, in the Long Room of the Public Record Office.

Directories and Year Books

The complete run of the *Jewish Year Book* from 1896 onwards is invaluable for data on the organization and structure of the community, nationally and locally, communal biographies, summaries of events and so on. Mention should be made also of the earlier Jewish directories within this period: Asher I. Myers, *Jewish Directory* for 1874; Mrs. Rachel Myers, *The Jewish Calendar, Manual and Diary*, 1888–9; and G. L. Harfield, *The Commercial Directory of the Jews of the United Kingdom*, 1889. Membership lists, with addresses, of synagogues can be used to plot the topographical distribution of a community; such lists were printed for London congregations of the United Synagogue up to 1939 and volumes containing all the lists for a year can be found (there is a set in the offices of the United Synagogue). Local directories make it possible to chart the origins and development of provincial communities, with details of occupations and, for the earlier period where this sort of antiquarian research is relevant, it may be possible to use rate books.[1]

Periodicals

As was explained at the beginning of this paper, one reason for defining the contemporary period as beginning in 1840 was that it practically coincides with the appearance of a regular Anglo-Jewish Press. From the autumn of 1841, the *Jewish Chronicle* (with a short break from 1842–4) provides a continuous record. In the first few years, the *Voice of Jacob* is generally fuller. Later, the *Jewish Chronicle* was supplemented by other important contemporaries, notably the *Jewish World* from 1873 to 1934.[2] A summary index of the *Jewish Chronicle* down to 1935 was compiled by A. M. Hyamson

---

[1] *A Guide to Directories (excluding London) published before 1856* was issued by the Royal Historical Society in 1950; and there is a collection of London directories in the Guildhall Library.

[2] See, for instance, the annotated list of periodicals for the 1870–1914 period in L. P. Gartner, *The Jewish Immigrant in England*, pp. 289–90. For a historical survey of the Anglo-Jewish Press, see the *Jewish Chronicle 1841–1941* (1949).

and a typescript copy is in the Mocatta Library, University College, London; Mr. J. M. Shaftesley is now compiling a detailed and cross-referenced index and it is to be hoped that this will be made available with perhaps a summary index printed, for students who will find it of first-class importance for research.

The ordinary national newspapers contain much Anglo-Jewish material and *The Times* Index is a useful key. The provincial Press is, of course, of vital importance for the history of local communities.[1]

SUMMARY

Contemporary Anglo-Jewish history must seek to answer questions and deal with problems, rather than merely list facts; it must be set equally within the framework of world Jewish history and in its local British environment. Topics suggested for study include the histories of provincial communities and of the growth of London suburban communities; economic history; communal institutions and organizations; working class and radical movements; and religious ideas and intellectual life.

Of the tasks that need to be undertaken to assist research, the most important is the location, listing and, where necessary, safeguarding of archives. Others include work on the 1841 and 1851 censuses, and the listing of some historical materials from 1837 onwards, of illustrations of Jewish interest (e.g. in the periodical Press), and of sources among Parliamentary Papers.

[1] See *The Times Handlist of England and Welsh Newspapers 1620–1900*. The British Museum collection of local newspapers is divided between the main building (pre-1800) and Colindale (post-1800).

Joint Discussions

AFTER these two papers had been presented by Dr. Esh and Dr. Lipman there followed a discussion opened by Dr. Richard D. Barnett. He drew attention to a paper he had published about a piece of 'oral history' that had come his way. It concerned a case of a lady over eighty who had some historical records of her great-grandfather, Isaac Leonini Azulay, a character of the eighteenth century of whom she preserved a most interesting series of oral and written records, including letters which are still preserved and could be traced. 'There is a tremendous amount of work involved in this field and we would have to deal with elderly people mostly. It is not people of my age who have most to tell, but aged people who have to be treated in a special way. We must have a great deal of patience to hear their endless repetitions, and it is not as easy as it sounds. There are also men, humble men, who can tell us what happened in the ghettos of Russia and Poland, or Persian Jews and Indian Jews in London, all of whom have probably extremely valuable information about their lost and destroyed past to give us—sometimes in the form of music, sometimes in the form of folk-lore, etc. If it has done nothing else, this Conference will have contributed something of great value in drawing attention to the possibilities of judicious application of oral history, and I very much hope it will be followed up.

'In the near future we hope to establish some kind of depository for archives in University College, London under the aegis of the Mocatta Library, and Mr. Scott, the Librarian, will I am sure be the first to welcome it. I would also say that one of the most useful tasks for the future is the compilation of a Dictionary of Anglo-Jewish biography and I hope everyone will co-operate in such a useful venture.'

Dr. Steinberg said that he was perturbed by the title of the paper, 'Oral History'. 'Dr. Freedman and Mr. Gould have made the point that field-workers in sociological research must be well trained—this applies also to historical research. Thought must be given to the question of whether field-workers, in collecting raw material to be put on record, should be trained in recording facts, especially attitudes towards facts. I wonder whether we could invite the Jewish Historical Society to take care of this work, perhaps to supervise it and advise the actual workers as to the generally accepted methods of inquiry. We have all participated in historical events. I myself went through two Russian Revolutions, two World Wars, and migration, etc. If I were used as a source of history, I would be very careful to do a lot of research before I would agree to being interviewed. I do not know whether those present know about the great work done by the British section of the New York YIVO Institute for Jewish Research. A lot of material which is regularly sent to New York is being collected here, and archives are being established, in particular, of data on emigrés from Poland.

'It would be of great value if our Historical Society were to take an interest in this subject. Furthermore, historical material is being found in the heritage of early immigrants from Eastern Europe. This is recorded mostly in Yiddish, and field-workers enlisted to do this work should at least be acquainted with and able to speak Yiddish.'

Dr. Levenberg, who followed, also questioned the terminology 'Oral History'. 'I am speaking from personal experience. When I was in Jerusalem about two months ago, Dr. Wigoder had a preliminary talk with me about the best way I could recall certain facts and certain chapters relating to Zionist history in this country. When I began to think I really did recall certain facts that I thought I had forgotten long ago. In the course of conversation memory came into play. People, impressions and facts came to mind, and from this point of view I believe that what is called "Oral History" is a very important method of getting results. However, this is not history. If I had to write what I told Dr. Wigoder, I would check it and counter-check it. I would do a great deal of reading and a great deal of thinking before I would commit myself even to certain impressions. Therefore I suggest it cannot be called "Oral History". It is evidence and as such it is extremely useful, but you cannot call it history.

'The second point I would like to make is this. I know that it is very difficult to get various people together because the factor of distance. But I would suggest an exploration of the method of what I would call "Round Table Evidence". Call together three or four contemporaries, people who have lived through a certain chapter of history, sit them around a table with an interviewer who is conversant with the facts. The results would be much more useful than if the interviewer spoke just to one man.

'I would like to say one word about archives. I was interested in what Dr. Barnett said about the advisability of having some kind of archives at University College. It is vital to take the task seriously and open Anglo-Jewish archives. There are valuable sources. A lot of material on Anglo-Jewish history was sent to the Central Zionist Archives in Jerusalem. The YIVO Archives in New York also contain an enormous amount of material about the Jewish Labour Movement in this country. Hansard is invaluable. By studying the questions and answers in the Parliamentary Debates one can obtain information on matters relating to Anglo-Jewish history—for example the controversy on alien immigration at the beginning of the century and during the Nazi period. Study of the back numbers of *The Times* would prove important in the study of Anglo-Jewish history. In other words, if we speak about history, I think we should also pay particular attention to the problem of Anglo-Jewish archives in this country.'

Joint Discussions

Mr. De Kadt pointed out that 'oral history seems to use methods which are basically similar and which have been developed and studied at length and in depth in other fields, particularly in social anthropology. I was rather surprised that these methods were presented as altogether novel, and that there was no discussion of the problems which they pose. Thus we should at least ask under what circumstances a tape-recorder can (or cannot) be profitably employed. Experience in sociological field-work has shown that in many cases it would be better merely to take notes; in other cases we might use a tape-recorder and make notes (rather than a complete transcription) when we listen back to the tape'.

Mr. M. Richardson observed that there were two particular aspects that he had come across in his work. 'One is the treatment Jews received a generation ago in Anglo-Jewish circles which has had a profound influence on their attitude to life. The second is that the Dutch Jewry seems to have been assimilated more into the British working class than any other immigrants to this country. Even today, a large proportion of the electors of the City of London are people almost entirely Jews of Dutch origin who are not merely English but essentially Cockney. We might well investigate the "Cockneyness" of Jews in London. This could be a particularly fascinating field of research. In this connection some of us may have heard a broadcast of a group of actors and writers on the English stage all of whom originated from East London, and all spoke of the influence this had had on them—such things as a street-market scene which was essentially a combination of Jewish and Cockney influences. One way of investigating by means of "oral history" could be the commentaries of people who left this country in 1917 to join the Russian Army and then returned after the war. This is a fascinating group and must be investigated quickly as they are dying off.'

Mr. C. C. Aronsfeld pointed out that 'in the Wiener Library where we have a section on each national Jewish community, you will find specialized material, both books and a Press file, on Anglo-Jewry, more particularly on the subject of anti-Semitism in Britain. Many of the writings are by British authors, but a very considerable number also by German Nazis who went to great lengths in exploring Anglo-Jewish history (or rather exploiting it for the purposes of anti-British propaganda). In fact one of the most remarkable works which no student of Anglo-Jewish history will be able to ignore, was written by a German who was expressly commissioned by the Nazi government to compile the book in the British Museum. Its title is *Das Judentum in England*, a volume in two parts, "Juden erobern England" (Jews Conquer England) and "Juden beherrschen England" (Jews Rule England), (Berlin 1940, 562 pp.), with a scientific apparatus reflected in more than 1,500 footnotes. (The author, Dr. Peter Aldag—a pseudonym of Dr. F. P. Krüger—is, so far as we know, now practising as a barrister in Hamburg.)

'I would also mention the research undertaken by the Nazi Institute for the Study of the Jewish Question. The subjects (published in a series of nine volumes) include the life of Disraeli, Jews in English literature and, rather absurdly, the "British Israel Movement". Some of this material has been adopted by anti-Semites all over the world, but some of it will also be examined with profit by serious students. I extend a cordial invitation to all present at this Conference to visit the Wiener Library and see for themselves.'

Mr. Levi Gertner argued that 'Jewish historians should give us a history of the development of Jewish youth—their desire to organize themselves into various groups, the problems that interest them—the important Jewish problems that are presented to them. I would like to say that in a community like ours there is always such a vast difference between generations. The father generation does not pass on the values in the proper way to the coming generation. The academic youth looks for its own ways, and as they are a very important section of the community, it would be of interest and importance to find out what are their problems.'

Mr. D. Kessler said that he had often urged 'that some form of Institute for Contemporary Jewish History should be founded in this country. About ten years ago, after a meeting with Mr. Leonard Montefiore and Dr. Alfred Wiener when we discussed this matter, I wrote a piece on the subject, but without effect. So if this Conference is likely to result in the furtherance of the study of contemporary Jewish history, then it may indeed attain considerable importance.'

He then drew attention to the fact that the *Jewish Chronicle* has in hand the micro-filming of its volumes since 1841. 'This task is nearly completed and copies of the whole set of the paper will be available within a very short time for libraries throughout the world.'

Dr. Esh and Dr. Lipman then replied to the discussion in the following terms:

Dr. Shaul Esh: 'It seems that there has been some misunderstanding in regard to some of the points treated in the paper. For instance I would not stress the term "Oral History" too much. In Hebrew we call this method by an expression which means, translated literally: "Oral Documentation". We did not intend to say that the material collected in this way is any more than source material with which the historian will be able to work. It is not history in itself.

'The interviewers who are engaged in the Oral History Section of our Institute are mainly graduate students from the departments of History and Sociology. As regards the subjects, there is a great variety of subjects on which we are collecting material. There is a possibility of what is called mass documentation, but I am not sure if this really gives us what we are looking for. The Jewish Agency, in a rather dilettante way, immediately after the war in 1945/6 collected such material from 3,000 children in Budapest. As far as I know, no one has up to now used it. What I said before about the nature of sources refers also to the remarks made about falsifying history. Of course we only ask witnesses about the things we are interested in and which are covered by the subject.

'Dr. Levenberg suggested what he called "Round Table Evidence". I may add, that we already have started to use this method. Some time ago there was held such a meeting on the rescue activities of the Youth

Joint Discussion

Aliya during the Second World War. It was quite a success and we intend indeed to follow up in this way.[1]

Regarding the remarks on the need for a thorough and detailed preparation of the interviews, I refer to my earlier comments,[2] where it will be seen that we have explicitly stated the need for the interviewer first of all to make a serious study about the subject he intends to deal with.'

Dr. V. D. Lipman said: 'The point about education in Jewish schools and attitude to life is extremely important. It is interesting to see how keen was the desire of the parent and the child fifty to sixty years ago to get the English atmosphere and I think this greatly influenced the attitude of Jews to assimilation plus the fact that you could get an English education in what was religiously a Jewish school.

'On the point about Dutch Jewry, they form an interesting cluster among the Jews in the East End, mostly associated with the cigar and tobacco trade. I would welcome more information from Mr. Richardson on this and possibly he might be prepared to write a paper on the specifically Dutch Jewish settlement in the East End.

'On archives I feel rather strongly myself and I was extremely glad to have the support of Dr. Barnett, Dr. Levenberg and Dr. Steinberg.

'Finally I would like to thank Mr. Aronsfeld for referring to the collection in the Wiener Library and in particular for pinpointing the parts of the Library's collection which are of particular interest to people working on Anglo-Jewish history. We in the Jewish Historical Society are very conscious of the works on anti-Semitism he mentioned, and Peter Aldag's books are listed in the recently published *Nova Bibliotheca Anglo-Judaica.*'

[1] During 1963, for example extended meetings were held with people active in Slovakian Jewish institutions and organizations during the same period.

[2] p. 156.

Future Research Studies

Discussion

THE final discussion was devoted to the subject of lines of future research studies. It was opened by Professor Ginsberg, who said:

'In considering the bearing of the contributions to this Conference and the discussions following them on future studies, we may usefully distinguish two areas of investigation, those in which the primary need is for fuller knowledge of facts and those which call for reflection on values and principles of social policy. Among the latter I should like to lay particular stress on the problems of Jewish education. Dr. Fishman and Mr. Harold Levy have given us the essential facts. No doubt further factual study is needed, but even more urgent is the need for reflection on the goals or aims at which Jewish education should be directed and for an examination of the limits within which these aims are attainable under modern conditions. These are problems which call not so much for elaborate research as for an analysis, from the religious and philosophical point of view, of the fundamental principles involved.

'In coming to the second group of problems the need for further research is perhaps greatest in the field of population studies. The survey made by Dr. Neustatter (included in the book edited by Dr. M. Freedman *A Minority in Britain*), and Dr. Prais' paper for this Conference indicate that the Jewish birth-rate and the average size of the Jewish family are lower than those of the population as a whole and this, together with the uncertainty of the extent of inter-marriage, raises the question whether, if existing trends continue, Anglo-Jewry may not be biologically on the decline. The basic facts, however, are inadequately known and the inferences based on present data uncertain. It is therefore of the greatest importance that a sustained effort should be made to obtain fuller and more reliable data, so that long-range trends may be estimated with greater accuracy.

'Closely related to the collection of demographic data is the qualitative study of Jewish family life. Considering the importance traditionally attached by Jews to family life the absence of really systematic studies in this field is remarkable. Is there, as ordinary observation suggests, a weakening of family and kinship ties? Are there significant changes in the nature of parental authority and the patterns of family relationships? To what

Discussion

extent are distinctively Jewish values fostered within the family? What social roles are now played by women in Jewish society? These are questions which urgently call for a systematic exploration and interpreation.

'From the papers devoted to the wider aspects of communal structure it is clear that the synagogues are now, as they always have been, the central institutions, the nuclei around which other associations and institutions cluster. Upon their vitality depends the survival of the Jewish community as a distinctive unit.

'Dr. Lipman has rightly stressed the importance of the historical study of synagogal organization and has himself made valuable contributions to this study. But equally important are sociological and psychological investigations into the actual working of the synagogues today and into the way in which they meet the religious and ethical needs of their members. For investigations of this kind, as in the study of the family, an unusual equipment is required, combining training in sociology and social psychology with a knowledge of the fundamental principles of Judaism and of the impact of modern science and philosophy. This Conference will have served a really useful purpose if it leads to further discussion of the best ways of attracting research workers of suitable calibre to this field of studies and of giving them the opportunity of acquiring the necessary equipment.

'On the economic side we have dwelt, among other things, on the distribution of occupations among Jews compared with that of the rest of the population. The data suggest that the age-long peculiarities of Jewish occupational structure are being steadily reduced. But here again the facts are imperfectly known. In particular, the effects of the diversification of occupation upon the relations between Jews and non-Jews require to be carefully investigated. Furthermore, occupational distribution has to be related to the wider problem of class stratification and especially to social mobility, or interchange between classes. In this context, as in others, there are peculiarities in the Jewish situation which call for investigation, such as the prestige attached to economic and social status and the effects of social mobility on cultural assimilation and on the unity and cohesion of the family.

'The methods now available for the study of the problems I have singled out and of others related to them have been admirably set out by various hands. I should like, in conclusion, to lay particular stress on the importance of not treating Jewish problems as a thing apart but in relation to the wider context in which they originate. To give a few examples. The problem of religious apathy or indifference is not peculiar to Jews and has to be studied in the setting of similar developments in secularized, urbanized and industrialized societies of the modern world. The changes in Jewish occupational distribution have to be examined in relation to the general changes in economic and social structure. What happens to the Jewish family cannot be understood without considering the general effects of urbanization and industrialization on society.

'Finally, it has to be borne in mind that Jewish societies lend themselves

Future Research Studies

admirably to comparative study. The comparative method has frequently been considered as the method *par excellence* of sociology. However this may be, its importance for Jewish sociology is plain. From this point of view, the establishment at the Hebrew University of an Institute for the study of contemporary Jewry is especially to be welcomed. In stimulating investigations in several areas of the world, the Institute may well facilitate the adoption of similar methods of investigation and the statement of the results in comparable forms. In this way it may make an important contribution not only to the study of Jewish societies but to the wider field of comparative sociology.'

Professor Bachi spoke next, on behalf of himself, Dr. Prais and Mr. Hajnal—all of whom had spoken on the need for statistical and demographic data.

'It seems to us that there is a general consensus on some basic points.

(1) In regard to *aims*:

A minimum knowledge, at least, the size, structure and movements of the Jewish population of Great Britain is highly desirable, both for practical and scientific reasons;

(2) The most urgent *tasks* seem to be:

(*a*) to obtain at least some rough estimates on the size of population, its age and sex structure, its changing geographical distribution over the country and topographical distribution over the largest towns, and its distribution by occupations;

(*b*) to obtain some hints at least on nuptiality, fertility, mortality and natural increase or decrease;

(*c*) to obtain some hints at least on the distribution of the Jewish population by its manner of affiliation, or lack of affiliation, to various Jewish bodies.

3) In regard to *means* for attaining these aims, it seems to be agreed that any permanent register of British Jews, or a complete census of them, is not feasible. It is necessary therefore to utilize largely indirect demographic methods. Possible suggestions are:

(*a*) The systematization and centralization of current statistical data arising from the activities of various Jewish organizations such as circumcisions, bar mitzvahs, marriages and burials, synagogue membership, etc.

(*b*) A detailed survey of a medium-sized community, which may help in evaluating coverage and meaning of currently available data in addition to its own sociological interest.

(*c*) Special tabulation of census and other material available at the Registrar General's Office.

(*d*) Special surveys, using sampling, which will yield the greatest possible coverage of the Jewish community. Inter-generation changes could be studied on this basis.

'It would be highly desirable that the surveys should be sponsored by an independent body, acceptable for its authority and objectivity, which might guarantee that individual records are kept secret and used only for statistical purposes.'

Discussion

Mr. Gould raised the problems of research training and organization. 'It is necessary to say again here that the number of trained research workers in the social sciences is very small. The question therefore arises and I think the conference should face this point clearly, as to how and in what ways and through what institutions, we should achieve the objective of securing some trained social scientists to deal with the kind of priorities that we have been discussing. Where are they to come from? I would submit that as far as Great Britain is concerned there is only one place they can come from and that is the universities. Training in this sort of field cannot be directly undertaken by public agencies or community organizations. Only the universities have facilities for this training. Social anthropologists, sociologists and statisticians in the universities would have to shoulder the tasks of organization and planning, and of guiding young people. But when the young researchers have been trained in Jewish subjects within the social sciences, what are their career prospects likely to be? In the U.S.A. a good deal of "applied sociology" on the Jewish question has taken place: there are *some* places for the trained sociologists within Jewish community agencies. This is not yet the case here: far from it.'

Dr. Max Gottschalk spoke next. 'I am very interested by the papers which have been read. It is very inspiring for the meeting which our *Centre National des Hautes Etudes Juives* intend to hold in Brussels with the Institute of Contemporary Jewry. If I am permitted, as a guest, to make some comments, I would like to make three short remarks. From listening to some of the papers I came to the conclusion that a great deal could be done by young researchers during their studies if their professors would agree to select topics of Jewish history, sociology or social sciences for their university work. I intend myself to organize a group of professors, and if we could get professors of history, sociology or social science to ask their students to undertake this kind of research I think some excellent results could be attained. I think it is an easy way to get some valuable contributions.

'The point has been raised about the co-operation of non-Jews in the Jewish studies. I just want to say that in our Centre, in Brussels, studies are being made by non-Jews on the proposal of their non-Jewish professors. One will be on the history of the Jews in Antwerp and the second on Jewish folk-lore in Flemish and Walloon literature. There was no difficulty in finding young researchers to do this work. The third point is about the ways of looking for statistics. The need for social and demographic surveys was mentioned yesterday. I was told yesterday that it is a question of money mainly as these studies are very expensive. I agree. We are intending to start one of the Jewish community in Brussels. We will aim at a survey of about 1,500 out of 6,000 heads of families and this will cost between £3 to £4 per head. But if you are determined and you have all the elements—the agreement of the community and the necessary people to conduct the survey—I think the money will be available and what has proved possible for our relatively small Jewish population will I am quite sure be possible in some other countries as well.'

Future Research Studies

Dr. James Parkes hoped that the Institute of Contemporary Jewry, in its general statement on the various Jewries of the world, would include a fairly detailed statement of the necessity for studying Jewish communities in their relationship to their non-Jewish environment. 'What is the attitude of the different political parties; of the churches and mosques; of the business community? What is the attitude of trade unions and educational authorities?

'To be a realist in the middle of the twentieth century one has to tackle the problem of anti-Semitism. To what extent are the Arab Offices a medium in which Nazism is being pushed out to the present-day world?

'To deal with these problems I did, some years ago, turn myself into an educational charity and formed the Parkes Library. It is, I hope, a beginning of a non-Jewish effort to co-operate with institutions like that of the Institute in Jerusalem. I trust it will always be able to draw on both Christian and Jewish scholars, and include Moslems in due course. In so far as the Library continues to exist I am sure it will always be ready to collaborate in the fullest sense.

Mr. Myer Domnitz raised the possibility that Jewish officials, the community's 'civil service', trained, for example in history and education, might contribute towards research studies. When the Board was celebrating its bi-centenary in 1960 its officials carried out investigations from the Board's records and discovered valuable information.'

Dr. Richard Barnett spoke of the historical role that University College, the scene of the Conference, had long played in relation to Jewish studies. 'Here the Jewish Historical Society meets regularly, and together with the college keeps up the Mocatta Library. We also welcome the Institute of Jewish Studies, which meets here.

'The Historical Society is recommending that certain small libraries of Judaica should be added here to the Mocatta Library on indefinite loan, to help in the gradual building up of an Institute of Jewish Studies with all this material. The establishment of a centre of archives, not only of the past, but of the present, should be part of such an Institute. With such a basis already in existence, any further studies could be done in such a way that our feet would be on the ground and we would have something positive to start with. I am sure both the University of London and University College would welcome any suggestions from the Jewish community as to the development of such an Institute of Jewish Studies here.'

Mr. Emanuel De Kadt raised the question of a possible research seminar in the field of the Conference's interests. 'People engaged in empirical research could test out their ideas and pass on their results as they go along. As material becomes available they could send out working papers which can be discussed with other scholars in their own fields and other fields. The organizers of the present meeting should try to get this sort of thing going.'

Professor Davis then made the following statement:

'This Conference is part of the programme of the Institute of Contemporary Jewry. The Institute recognizes that it cannot undertake work

Discussion

in the Diaspora on its own, since it does not have the personnel and, in fact, it would be incorrect if it attempted country-wide studies without reference to the local interest and existing bodies. It is therefore necessary to find a *modus operandi*, whereby the Institute in Israel can enter into full academic partnership with learned bodies in the Diaspora.

'This we have attempted to do in England with the co-operation of the Scholars' Group specifically organized for this purpose. Conferences are conducted in different ways and under different auspices because Jewish life varies with each locale. For example, when we planned this Conference, we did not know how it would turn out nor that it would obtain such a remarkable reception among the scholarly community. For the Institute, this is of prime importance, for a university is an academic institution which functions mainly through scholars. Therefore, the crucial problem for the Institute when we embarked upon the programme in England was to find the group of scholars who would associate themselves in this enterprise. Fortunately, you already have a group of historians and sociologists who are dedicated to this work. When I discussed this matter with Professor Ginsberg, with Dr. Freedman and with Mr. Gould, it was clear that they would take an active part.

'What was true for this conference, holds for the future. Moreover, just as the Institute cannot assume the continuity of the task, neither can the groups in the various countries continue by themselves. The obvious conclusion is that the effort must be co-operative. For our work we require several things: (1) materials; (2) direct contact with scholars throughout the world; and (3) we must see Jewish life with two eyes, one eye on Jerusalem and one on the Diaspora. The problem of continuity is a natural problem which concerns everyone.

'We waited until now to take the first step; it may take another year or so before we undertake the kind of projects which Professor Ginsberg presented to us. First we must have careful planning; then we must concentrate on the training of people who combine the qualities of specialization in the field and a deep Jewish knowledge. Therefore we propose to continue humbly, with a great deal of meditation in order not to rush into a mistake. Knowing our needs and lacks, I would rather work slowly, and not repent in leisure.

As regards our future relationship, I can state unequivocally that I, for one, look forward to the new kind of partnership between Jerusalem and the Diaspora, and I stand committed to do all I can to promote this relationship, both personally and through the Institute. However, in a more concrete way, you will understand that I have no authority to go further at this time. I have to return and together with my colleagues, report to the Dean and to the Rector. I do feel certain, however, that once we have reported this Conference back to Jerusalem, some action will be taken through the appropriate channels set up by the Hebrew University for this purpose.'

He ended by expressing the thanks of the participants to the staff of the Board of Deputies, led by Mr. Brotman, for their invaluable help in organizing the meetings.

Future Research Studies

The Conference was then closed by Lady Janner, who said:

'I too want to join in the thanks given to the staff of the Board and also to the scholars who served on the Committee and worked so hard to make this Conference the success it has evidently been. I also want to take this opportunity of saying how very happy we are to have with us Professor Davis, Professor Bachi and Dr. Esh. They have added colour and interest to this Conference which we have all appreciated.

'Listening to the discussions during the past two days, it has been evident that there is an unlimited field of research. Every idea that has been put forward has brought with it a new trend of thought, and the realization of how little we know about these subjects.

'I want to assure you all that while at this stage it is naturally not possible for me or the Board of Deputies to give any undertaking, I can assure you that the Board will consider all the suggestions made at this Conference. I personally feel sure, however, that with the help of the Scholars Committee, work on some of the lines suggested will be carried out under the auspices of the Board of Deputies.'

Progress and Prospects: A Postscript

JULIUS GOULD

THE main concern of this book has been with the inner structure of the Jewish community in Britain and with the need for a clearer, more informed view of that structure. This concern now enjoys a very widespread support. In 1963 the Board of Deputies set up a Special Committee on Research and Studies on Contemporary Anglo-Jewry: and a Research Officer, within the Board's framework, will, it is hoped, begin to collect basic quantitative data (the absence of which many contributors to this book deplored) and assist in the planning of special studies. And this will be done in consultation with the distinguished academic figures now interested in these matters but who are quite independent of any 'official' Jewish organizations.[1] On the current research front Mr. Ernest Krausz's book on *Leeds Jewry* has shown what an independent scholar, working without any elaborate research team, can achieve in this field.[2] His more complex study of Jewish suburban life in North London, which I have helped to direct, has been well-supported and is near completion. From this, and other research

---

[1] S. M. Lipset once commented upon the complex reasons why American sociologists of Jewish origin had, until recent times, 'shied away from dealing with their own ethnic and religious group'. He noted that 'one reason ... lies in the fact that for many of them becoming sociologists or anthropologists has been one way of escaping from their Jewishness'. ('Jewish Sociologists and Sociologists of the Jews' in *Jewish Social Studies*, 1955, Vol. XVII, No. 3). No doubt an analogous problem exists in Great Britain—but it is no longer a serious obstacle.

[2] Some of the criticisms that were hastily made of his book have shown something else as well—that scientific work which does not confirm every cherished belief about Jews will be regarded as 'controversial'. The extent of such 'controversies' has a scientific interest of its own: it may tell us as much about Jewish life in an area as any strictly statistical survey.

studies,[1] a research tradition, as well as a group of trained researchers, has gradually emerged. How fast and how far it will develop depends upon the aid (not least the financial aid) that the Jewish community will provide. There is a straightforward case for the empirical study of 'problem' topics—distribution of the Jewish population and their synagogue attendance, their educational and welfare services, and the controversial issue of 'intermarriage'. To know the 'facts' in these areas would obviously be useful to those who are planning costly educational and other services in many Jewish communities: and one can safely predict a growing *internal* demand for data on the social composition of the Jews. What, however, will such data 'mean'? They will certainly not 'speak for themselves'. They will require interpretation: and 'controversy' may follow. For if the interpretations clash with current myths, they will be accepted grudgingly and with suspicion—if, indeed, they are accepted at all. This strengthens the case not simply for the study of the social *composition* of British Jewry (that is, its numbers and distribution) but also for the scientific study of its social *structure*. For the idea of social structure involves more than facts and figures—however cogently assembled. It stresses the values and beliefs, the rules and ideals which bind a population together. Acceptance of these values is seldom total: there are always stresses and strains. One of the most subtle aspects of the sociology of the Jews stems from the variations in these stresses: the Jewish 'identification' of those who have rejected both Judaism and many Jewish *cultural* connections remains a source of teasing questions and insights. For even when a social group—or part of one—rejects 'its' values or, in a changed situation, singles some of them out for emphasis in preference to others, it may do so in a distinctive way: and this distinctive, selective pattern gives the group concerned its own new strengths and weaknesses. It is a very thin line which divides questions of structure from those of culture. Nearly ten years ago Dr. Freedman stressed the difficulty and importance of these frontier zones. It is here that we ask 'what precisely is meant by Jewish culture, what minimum amount of Jewish culture will guarantee the kind of security sought . . .'[2] Dr. Freedman went on to discuss in rational terms the key concepts of acculturation and assimilation. For, as he observed, it is important to widen the analysis, to link the study of a minority's values with what is known about the values of the 'host' society. It is, of course, regrettable that general sociology can tell us often so little about the

[1] These include a project on Jewish youth: a study of Jewish political preferences: a secondary analysis of data on Jewish university students: and a planned study of Jewish life in a Scottish city.

[2] *A Minority in Britain*, ed. by M. Freedman. Vallentine, Mitchell, 1955, p. 239.

values, over a specific range, of British society.[1] But it is vital for 'minority' studies to establish such links. Otherwise they will produce worthwhile but parochial inquiries, fruitful at best in 'applied' results but divorced from the concerns of general sociology. In no country can the religious or the secular life of 'the Jews' (however defined) be studied sensibly by 'inward-looking' research: it must be seen as part of the wider society—influencing it and, often tragically, influenced by it.

How a 'host' society treats or regards its Jews can tell us much about that society, about its strains and operative ideals. Some of this, of course, emerges from any study of Jewish relations with non-Jews—of the actual incidence of 'tolerance' and 'hostility'. And I have some sympathy with those contributors to this volume who felt that the main papers had sidestepped these questions. There was, of course, no intention or desire to do so: or to exclude them from future research. On the contrary they are of profound importance—and much devoted work, not least by Christians, has gone into their study. It remains true, however, that these studies, too, can suffer from a routine parochialism—geared as they tend to be to past preoccupations and established themes. And even when they proceed on a more sophisticated level they have yet to be related to the more immediate concern of these essays—the detailed study of British Jewry's composition.

No two societies 'tolerate' their Jews in exactly the same way —and even within one society 'toleration' at one end of the social ladder will be rather different from that seen at the other. There are, indeed, national styles in such matters—and within each of them there will be regional and social diversity. Such styles are, of course the product of history: they reflect past patterns of bigotry and migration. Of especial importance to European Jewry have been, as Dr. Cecil Roth has insisted, the specific contexts of 'emancipation' —the historical circumstances in which Jews were accorded civil rights. These have been, quite literally, 'determining' factors—in that they set the 'limits' within which Jewish life was to develop. Equally important has been the variation, from one society to another, in respect for the rule of law.[2] Indeed the fate of the Jews is closely bound up with the rule of law. If a society's rulers show a *general*

---

[1] Part of the reason for this is the rather narrow bias still sometimes encountered in British sociology which has given low priority to the study (as distinct from the assertion) of values. There has also been the pathetic assumption among some social scientists that their own values and preferences are paramount in 'society' at large. Happily all this is changing in many ways.

[2] This was brought out in a brilliant article by Max Beloff, 'From The Other Side', written for the *Jewish Chronicle Supplement* on the Tercentenary of British Jewry, 27th January, 1956, p. 28.

contempt for the rule of law, they will hardly make a *specific* exception for the benefit of strangers. And respect for the rule of law is the outcome of Britain's century-old continuity, of the framework of legitimacy within which constitutional *and* social changes have occurred. The contrast that may be drawn with the U.S.A. will underline this point. Certainly the rule of law is an operative ideal within American society: but it is conjoined with other ideals that, in their differing ways, reflect the special experience of the U.S.A. and its physical extent—e.g. those of egalitarianism, of recurrent populism and of a moving geographical frontier. In the British case the rule of law has been an operative ideal within a very different social system—one in which, to cite the words of Dr. Howard Brotz, an American observer of British Jewry, there has been a 'relatively firm' aristocratic component and a remarkable, almost unique, diffusion of 'the gentlemanly ideal'.[1] This ideal has had a powerful influence not only on how Jews have been 'tolerated' in these islands: it has also moulded the behaviour of the Jews themselves—especially of educated Jews who have moved into the non-Jewish world. Brotz commented upon what one might call the 'hospitality' extended to Jews within the nuances of the British class-structure. The barriers within that structure, he argued, can be crossed by upwardly-mobile Jews provided that they acquire the 'gentlemanly' education appropriate to their new milieux. The *élites* in the 'host' society, the argument continued, had not felt threatened by the trickle of mobility (and because of the small size of British Jewry it will remain a trickle): as self-confident gentlemen they are proof against the grosser forms of status panic. Brotz went on to claim that in its own pursuit of the 'gentlemanly' ideal British Jewry had lost a sense of 'attachment to a tradition that is something of its own'[2] and to link this pursuit with the 'low' intellectual vigour of British as compared with American Jewry.

Brotz's case may, in places, be overdrawn: and the patterns, within Britain and within British Jewry, are more intricate than he suggests. Yet it is not without force. The 'gentleman ideal' *has* been operative. Its components—good 'manners', self-restraint, amateurism—have been widely respected: and respect for this ideal has lowered the temperature on many potentially burning issues. Today this ideal is in disrepair and disrepute. It is widely held that its defects are stronger than its virtues: that it can inhibit, that it takes the passion and excitement out of things, that it can lapse into incom-

[1] See H. Brotz, 'The Position of the Jews in English Society.' *Jewish Journal of Sociology*, 1959, Vol. I, No. 1, p. 99.

[2] Brotz, op. cit., p. 111.

Progress and Prospects: A Postscript

petence and indifferentism. The social hierarchy that it legitimized is, notoriously, under challenge, if not under notice to quit. That deep changes in British social structure are now under way is more than a cliché. Will Jewish life, geared to the 'premodern' norms now eroding, be equally affected? The pace of overall change may—and I believe it is—be somewhat exaggerated in current discussion. The symbols of the 'premodern' society are deeply respected still—and they will not vanish on request. All the same it seems likely that the continuing 'acculturation' of Jews to the 'host' society in Britain may take new and unexpected forms.[1]

How the Jew sees himself, and how he is acculturated, depends in part on how he is seen by others. Over the last decade Jews and Jewish themes have come to be of growing interest in many countries of Continental Europe.[2] Who can tell what feelings of guilt or curiosity have brought this about? In Britain—which has so much less cause for guilt—the same trend has been observed. Some diffusion of Jewish themes has resulted from the work of young Jewish novelists and dramatists. It would be wrong, of course, to exaggerate either the quality of their work or the extent of their cultural influence. But they have contributed to, and engendered, what has been called 'cultural philosemitism'.[3] It is too soon to 'explain' it. Part of an explanation was recently suggested by Jonathan Miller, himself Jewish and a creative innovator in the world of satire. Writing in an American journal[4] he claimed that the British interest in things Jewish, stimulated by some of the writers of the Jewish 'new wave', had been part of a 'revolt against modernism', of the romantic search for the simple and the folksy

---

[1] Brotz, in the article under review here, may have underplayed the role of the Jew as a commercial innovator in the post-war period. Since 1945 the centre of gravity of the Jewish community has moved further in the direction of business: and the 'new' millionaires have reached some of the highest positions not only in Jewish philanthropy but in the religious structure too. (See Norman Cohen, above, page 47). The path from Sir Robert Waley Cohen's Presidency of the United Synagogue to that of Sir Isaac Wolfson may seem quite short: but in the intervening years there have been important changes both in the tempo of British business and in the place of the Jews therein. That there are risks for British Jewry in this position was certainly obvious to Brotz in 1959—and is clearer still today. Caught between the tough ghost of the 'gentleman ideal' and the thrusting pace of business enterprise, neither Jewish scholars nor Jewish scholarship find it easy to flourish.

[2] See, for example, the discussion in H. Boas, 'Jewish Figures in Post-War Jewish Literature.' *Jewish Journal of Sociology*, 1963, Vol. V, No. 1.

[3] T. R. Fyvel, 'The Jewish New Wave.' *Jewish Chronicle*, 13th September, 1963, p. 37

[4] *Commentary*, November, 1963, p. 404–5.

which has preoccupied vocal sections of the literary *avant garde*. Miller believes—and he is correct—that this image of the Jew is a spurious one: but neither he nor anyone else has traced out its consequences. It would be difficult to do: for many other forces have been at work. Television drama[1], for example, has brought Jewish characters into many an unlikely, or uncomprehending home. Satire programmes and documentaries on television have treated Jewish problems—and on the whole in a sympathetic style. Serious and humorous periodicals[2] have come up with articles on the Jewish scene. In the quality Press the tensions within Jewish religious life have been compared to the crisis of 'modernization' within the Church of England.[3] Both the Eichmann trial and the play 'The Representative' led to widespread, and largely sympathetic, comment on the Jewish catastrophe. Similarly, favourable coverage was given, in 1963, to the resignation of Lord Mancroft from the board of the Norwich Union. And, by way of contrast, the debate in the same year over Rachman and 'rachmanism' at no time came to centre on his Jewish origins. Indeed, for some time, the Press referred to him not as a Jew but as a Pole. One can think of few other countries where, at a time of political trauma and noisy populism, such restraint would have been shown.

No 'total' or magisterial interpretation of all this is possible—or, at this stage, necessary. The need continues to examine Jewish life, not only itself as a changing field but in the wider setting—cultural and political—of British society.

[1] Recent titles have included 'My Son the Doctor' and 'The Price of Smoked Salmon'.

[2] See, for example, the articles in *New Society* on 30th January and 6th February, 1964, and the article by Elspeth Huxley, 'Settlers in Britain' in *Punch*, 15th January, 1964.

[3] Since the above was written, the crisis at the West End Synagogue (April—May 1964) has had widespread attention in the Press and on T.V.

List of Participants

MR. C. C. ARONSFELD, Director of the Wiener Library.
PROF. R. BACHI, Professor of Statistics, Hebrew University, Jerusalem.
DR. RICHARD DAVID BARNETT, Keeper, Dept. of Western Asiatic Antiquities, British Museum; Elder, Spanish and Portuguese Synagogue; Vice-Pres. Jewish Historical Society.
MISS B. J. BARWELL, President, National Union of Hebrew Teachers and Editor of its journal; Member of the Board's Education and Youth Committee.
DR. J. BRAUDE, Chairman of Mizrachi Federation; Member of Board's Executive Committee.
MR. A. G. BROTMAN, Secretary, Board of Deputies of British Jews.
MR. R. N. CARVALHO, President of Anglo-Jewish Association 1954–1963; Hon. Sec. Jewish Memorial Council.
MR. NORMAN COHEN, Author and Writer.
MR. PERCY COHEN, C.B.E., Jt. Director of Conservative Research Dept. 1948–1959; Member of Board's Executive Committee.
MR. SOL COHEN, Chairman, Central Council for Jewish Religious Education; Secretary/Curator of Jewish Museum; Jt. Hon. Sec. Jewish Book Council.
PROF. M. DAVIS, Director, Institute of Contemporary Jewry, Hebrew University Jerusalem.
MR. JOHN DIGHT, Chairman of Board's Jewish Defence Committee, and member of Board's Executive Committee.
PROF. CYRIL DOMB, Professor of Theoretical Physics, University of London.
RABBI DR. LESLIE EDGAR, Vice-President of World Union for Progressive Judaism; Minister Emeritus, formerly Senior Minister Liberal Jewish Synagogue, now President, Union of Liberal and Progressive Synagogues.
DR. SHAUL ESH, Institute of Contemporary Jewry, Hebrew University of Jerusalem.
DR. I. FISHMAN, Director of Education, London Board of Jewish Religious Education.
DR. MAURICE FREEDMAN, Reader in Anthropology, University of London; Managing Editor *Jewish Journal of Sociology*.
DR. SALOMON GAON, Haham of the Spanish and Portuguese Synagogue.

List of Participants

MR. LEVI GERTNER, Education Officer Zionist Federation; Director Dept. for Education and Culture of the Jewish Agency (British Branch).
PROF. MORRIS GINSBERG, Emeritus Professor of Sociology, University of London.
PROF. H. GOITEIN, Professor of Law, University of Birmingham.
MR. JULIUS GOULD, Reader in Social Institutions, University of London.
MR. J. HAJNAL, Reader in Demography, University of London.
DR. JOHN HIGHET, Lecturer in Applied Sociology, University of Glasgow.
DR. BERNARD HOMA, Chairman, Board's Shechita Committee, Member of Board's Executive Committee.
SIR BARNETT JANNER, M.P., President, Board of Deputies.
LADY JANNER, J.P., Chairman of Board's Education and Youth Committee; Member of Board's Executive Committee.
MR. E. J. DE KADT, Lecturer in Sociology, London School of Economics.
PROF. R. F. KAHN, Professor of Economics, University of Cambridge.
MR. A. M. KAIZER, Journalist, Chairman of Association of Jewish Journalists.
DR. C. KAPRALIK, Jt. Secretary, Central British Fund for Jewish Relief and Rehabilitation.
DR. LIONEL KOCHAN, Lecturer in History, University of Edinburgh.
MR. JON KIMCHE, Editor, *Jewish Observer & Middle East Review*.
MR. ARMIN KRAUSZ, Member of Board of Deputies.
MR. E. KRAUSZ, Nuffield Scholar in Sociology at London School of Economics and Political Science.
MR. H. LANDY, Treasurer, Board of Deputies; Vice-Chairman, Mizrachi Federation.
MR. JOSEPH LEFTWICH, Director, Federation of Jewish Relief Organizations; European Representative Yiddish P.E.N.
DR. S. LEVENBERG, Jewish Agency Representative in Great Britain.
MR. S. S. LEVIN, Chairman, London Board of Jewish Religious Education.
MR. HAROLD LEVY, Inspector, Central Council for Jewish Religious Education; Hon. Warden at Jews' College.
MR. R. LIEBERMAN, Chairman of Board's Law, Parliamentary & General Purposes Committee, Member of Board's Executive Committee.
DR. V. D. LIPMAN, Civil Servant and Historian.
REV. I. LIVINGSTONE, Chairman, Central Jewish Lecture Committee of the Board of Deputies; Minister Emeritus, Golders Green Synagogue.
MR. RAPHAEL J. LOEWE, Visiting Professor, Brown University, R.I., U.S.A. Member of Council of the Society for Jewish Study; and on the Committee, and London Society of Jews and Christians.
PROF. D. G. MACRAE, Professor of Sociology, University of London.
MISS MIRIAM MOSES, O.B.E., J.P., Vice-President and former Warden, Brady Club and Settlement.
ALD. A. MOSS J.P., Senior Vice-President, Board of Deputies.
DR. JAMES PARKES, Author and Director, The Parkes Library.
DR. S. J. PRAIS, Statistician.

List of Participants

PROF. LEONARD REISSMAN, Professor of Human Relations, Tulane University, New Orleans.
MR. M. RICHARDSON, Welfare and Youth Officer of the United Synagogue.
DR. CECIL ROTH, Reader in Jewish Studies, University of Oxford; Historian.
DR. S. ROTH, General Secretary of the World Jewish Congress, British Section; Member of Board of Deputies' Foreign Affairs Committee.
MISS RUTH SALZBERGER, Graduate Student in Anthropology, University of Oxford.
MR. W. M. SCHWAB, Editor of Publications, Jewish Historical Society.
MR. HENRY SHAW, Director, Hillel Foundation.
REV. W. W. SIMPSON, General Secretary of the Council of Christians and Jews.
MR. LEONARD STEIN, O.B.E., Vice-President and former President of Anglo-Jewish Association.
DR. SIEGFRIED STEIN, Reader in Hebrew, University of London.
DR. AARON STEINBERG, Member of Executive of the World Jewish Congress, Director of its Cultural Department.
MISS SHIFRA STRIZOWER, Graduate Student in Anthropology at School of Oriental and African Studies.
MR. S. TEFF, Vice-President of Board of Deputies; Chairman of the Board's Erets Israel Committee.
DR. J. L. TEICHER, Lecturer in Rabbinics, University of Cambridge.
RABBI DR. VAN DER ZYL, Director of Jewish Studies Leo Baeck College; Vice-President World Union for Progressive Judaism.
DR. GEORGE WEBBER, Reader in English Law, University of London. Chairman, Jewish Memorial Council; President of First Lodge of England B'nai B'rith (1935–36); Member of Executive of District Grand Lodge; Chairman Jewish Book Council.
DR. J. G. WEISS, Reader in Hebrew, University of London.

Glossary

[If not otherwise stated, all terms are Hebrew]

Agudath Hashochetim	Union of Shochetim.
Alef-Bet	The first two letters of the Hebrew Alphabet and, by extension, the Alphabet itself.
Aliyah	Immigration to Israel.
Ashkenazi (plural: Ashkenazim)	Descendant from European Jews, whose medieval predecessors lived at one time in Germany ('Ashkenaz'—*see* Genesis x, 3—being its traditional Hebrew name). The descendants of Spanish Jews are called 'Sepharadim', since 'Sepharad'—*see* Obadiah xx—was identified in Jewish tradition with Spain. The Ashkenazi rite is the commoner in Britain.
Barmitzvah	'One who is obliged to fulfil the commandments.' A boy becomes Barmitzvah and bound to fulfil the commandments on the day after his 13th birthday.
Beth Din (plural: Batei Din)	Jewish Ecclesiastical Court.
Beth Hamidrash	House of Study.
Binyan Ha'aretz	Building of the Land (of Israel).
Brith Mila	Covenant of Circumcision.
Chevra Kadisha	Burial Society.
Chumash	*See* Humash.
Dayyan (plural: Dayyanim)	A rabbi who is a member of the Beth Din.
Din	Ecclesiastical decision.
Eretz Israel	Land of Israel.
Froom	Pious, observant (from German 'fromm').
Golah	Diaspora.
Halacha(h)	Either the whole body of Jewish law or a specific ordinance.
Hazzan	A cantor in the synagogue.

Glossary

Hazzanuth	Theory and practice of the cantor's art.
Humash	Literally 'a fifth', one of the five books of Moses: also the Pentateuch as a whole.
Ivrit	Hebrew language.
Kashruth	Dietary Laws prescribed for Jews.
Kehilla	Jewish community.
K'lal Yisrael	The whole of world Jewry of all generations.
Kol Nidrei	The service on the Eve of the Day of Atonement, called after the opening words of the first prayer.
Koppel	Head covering (Yiddish term).
Kosher (Ashkenazi pronunciation for 'kasher')	Term describing food conforming with the Dietary Laws.
Limmudei Chol	General Studies.
Limmudei Kodesh	Religious Studies.
Magbit	Literally: Collection, Drive. In general usage connotes the central Israel appeal in a country.
Mahamad	The Wardens and Treasurer of the Sephardic Synagogue.
Matza (plural: Matzot)	Unleavened bread eaten on Passover.
Mikve	Ritual Bath.
Minyan (plural: Minyanim)	Ten males over 13 years of age—the quorum for holding a religious service.
Mishnah	The authoritative collection of the Halachah, compiled about 200 C.E. The Mishnah serves as the nucleus of the Talmud.
Mitzwa (plural: Mitzwot)	Religious duty.
Mohel (plural: Mohalim)	Person qualified to perform circumcision in accordance with Jewish religious ordinances.
Rashi	Abbreviation for Rabbi Shlomo Yitaki (1040–1105), author of the most famous and studied commentaries on the Bible and on the Talmud.
Sepharadi (plural: Sepharadim)	*See* Ashkenazi.
Sephardi	*See* Sepharadi.
Sha'atnez	A mixture of wool and flax which Jewish law forbids in any one garment (*see* Leviticus xix, 19; Deuteronomy xxii, 11).
Shabbat (plural: Shabbatot)	Sabbath.

Glossary

Shechita	The slaughter of animals or poultry for food in accordance with Jewish ritual prescription.
Shiur	A lesson.
Shiva	Seven days of mourning for the dead.
Shochet (plural: Shochetim)	Slaughterer of animals or poultry for food (*see* Shechita).
Shomer (plural: Shomerim)	Literally: 'Guardian'. In the religious usage: Person who supervises the selling, manufacture or cooking of kosher food.
Talmud	The classic collection of Rabbinic Law and Commentaries recording legal decisions and discussions from about 200 B.C.E. to 450 C.E.
Talmud Torah	The study of Torah; in a more limited connotation, a school of Jewish studies.
Tanach	Abbreviation for *T*orah (Pentateuch) *Nev*i'im (Prophets), and *Ch* (or K) etuvim (Hagiographa), which are the three divisions of the Hebrew Bible.
Tephillin	Phylacteries worn by men at the morning service.
Torah in Derech Eretz	'Learning and Right Conduct'.
Yeshiva (plural: Yeshivot)	Academy of higher Jewish learning.
Yishuv	Collective term for the Jews settled in Israel.
Yom Kippur	Day of Atonement.

Index

(Page numbers in italics indicate references to participation in discussions.)

Abenaes, Solomon, 94
Aberdeen, 71
Abraham ibn Ezra, 94
Abramski, Dayan, 44
Adath Yisroel, 3
Adler, Nathan Marcus, 178
Adler, Selig, 167, 172 n.
Adler House, 2
Africa, North, 105
Agudath Israel, 57
Agudath Hashochetim, 15
Aldag, Peter, 174, 183
Algeria, 107
Aliens Immigration, Royal Comsion on (1903), 99, 178
Alliance Israélite, 101
alphabet, origins, 150
Alsace, 108
America, Latin, 103
American Jewish Archives, 174
American Joint Jewish Distribution Committee, 8
Amsterdam, 104
Angel, Moses, 178
Anglo-Jewish Preachers, Union of, 24
anti-semitism, 99, 172
Antwerp, 94
archives, use of, 173 f., 182
Argentina, Jewish community, xi
Aronsfeld, C. C., *183*
Ashkenazi synagogues, London, 2f.
assimilation, 62, 195
Association for Jewish Youth, 13
Association of Jewish Friendly Societies, 12 f.
Association of Jewish Journalists, 15
Association of Jewish Refugees, 13
Association of Ministers of Great Britain, 15
Association of Non-Provided Schools, 67
Association of Synagogues of Great Britain, 70
Avner, Gershon, 162
Azulay, Isaac Leonini, 181

Bachi, R., *60*, 117, *127* f., *189*
Balfour Declaration, 102
banking, Jews and, 27
Bar Ilan, 13
barmitzvah, 42 f., 51, 56
Barnett, Richard D., *181*, *191*
Barwell, Beatrice, *22*
batmitzvah classes, 76
Bearsted Hospital, 8
Bedford, 108
Belfast, 71
Belgium, 164
Belloc, Hilaire, 99
Beloff, M., x n., 161 n., 196 n.
Bene Israel, 108
Bensusan, S. L., 108
Ben Uri Gallery, 15
Berlin, 108, 122
Beth Din, 5, 43, 44, 46 f., 65; rigidity in, 48

Index

Beth Din Zedek, 51
Beth Ya'akov Seminary, 79
Bevis Marks synagogue, 3
bibliographies, of Anglo-Jewish history, 176
bibliography, demographic, 131
biography, sources for, 178
Birmingham, 2, 11, 16; birth-rate, 118 f.; education, 71
birth-rate, 117 ff.
Blackburn, 167
B'nai B'rith, 23
B'nei Akivah, 14, 44, 77
Board of Deputies of British Jews, 9 ff., 22 ff., 100; Committees of, 10; constitution, 11
Board of Orthodox Jewish Education, 69
Boas, H., 199 n.
Booth, C., 116 n.
Bournemouth, 3, 167
Bowley, A. L., 36
Bradford, 3, 61, 71
Braude, J., 76, *90*, *134*
'Bridge' in Britain, 13
Brighton, 3, 167
Bristol, 71
Britain, Jews, in number, 2; *see also* Population
Brodie, Israel, 49
Brotz, Howard M., 138, 198
Brown, Zve A., 158
Büchler, Dr, 43
Budapest, 122
Buenos Aires, xi
Buffalo, 167, 172 n.
Bullock, Alan, x, 161 n.
Bureau für Statistik der Juden, 129
Burial grounds/societies, 6
Burton (Montague), 27, 28

Canada, 114; marriage rate, 120; schoolchildren, 123
Canterbury, 108
Cardiff, 3, 71
Carmel College, 7, 44, 76
census(es): Jewish, 143; and religious affiliation, 114; and statistical data, 129, 130, 133, 175
Central Board for Hebrew Education (Manchester), 71
Central British Fund for Relief, 8
Central Committee for Jewish Education, 67
Central Council for Jewish Religious Education, 6, 68, 70 ff.
Central Examining Board, 75; examination syllabus, 83 ff.
Centre National des Hautes Études Juives, 164
Channel Isles, 110
charitable organizations, 7 f.
Chassidim, 170
Chatham, 2
Chesterton, G. K., 99
Chief Rabbi/Rabbinate, 4 f., 43, 64, 65
child population, 71 f., 123
Christianity, social aspects, 56
Church of England, 54
Churchill, Winston, 99
circumcision, prevalence of, 132
cities, Jewish congregation in, 103, 108
City (of London): attitude to Jews, 99 f.; Jewish influence, decline, 27, 39
City Centre Properties, 28
Civil servants, Jewish, 39
class, definition of, 35 f.
class structure, 144, 188
clothing industry, 29
Cochran, Thomas C., 168 n.
Cockney influence, 183
Cohen, P. S., *151*
Cole, G. D. H., 36
colonialism, 105 f.
Columbia University, Oral History Centre, 156
community: local, reason for location, 172; size of viable, 109

210

Index

Connolly, Thomas E., 167, 172 n.
Consistories, 100
consumption patterns, change in, 32
'controls', in history writing, 172
conversionism, 43
Council of Christians and Jews, 15
Council of the Four Lands, 100
cousins, first, marriage of, 121
Coventry, 71
Crawley, 3
cremations, 122
Cromwell, Oliver, 96
cultural organizations, 14 f.
culture; Jewish, and English-speaking world, 103; non-religious, transmission of, 150

Damascus Mission, 100
Davis, Moshe, *58*, 158, 168 n., 191 ff.
death statistics, 122; and population estimate, 116
definition, of Jew, 113 f., 132, 135, 151
demographic data, importance of, 127 f., 142 ff.; difficulties in collecting, 129, 189; methods for collecting, 189; processes, Jewish, special character of, 128
dietary laws, observance, 41; *see also* kashrus
directions, 179
disabilities, Jewish, in England, 97
dispersal about large towns, of community, 117
Disraeli, Benjamin, 98
divorced persons, marriage of, 121
documentation, written, inadequacy of, 158
Domnitz, Myer, *191*
Dutch Jewry, 183

Edgar, Leslie I., 60
Edinburgh, 2, 71
education: adult, 53; further, 77 f.; goals of, 187; length of

Education (*cont.*)
tuition period, 74; Reform movement and, 51; religious, 6 f., 45; secular, Jewish, 87; standards of, 75 ff.; statistics, 122 ff.; textbooks, 80
El Arish, 102
élite, 36 f.
emigration from Britain, 23
England, history of Jewry in, 93 ff.
English language, use by Jews, 102
entrepreneurs, Jews as, 27 f., 37
Esh, Shaul, *55* ff., *87* f.
esteem systems, 150
examinations, educational, 75; syllabuses, 80 ff.
Exeter, 2, 108
expulsion (1290), 94
Ezra, 77

Falmouth, 2, 108
family life, study of, 143, 144 f., 187 f.
Far East, 105
Farjeon family, 178
fascism, British, 172
Federation of Jewish Relief Organizations, 9
Federation of Jewish Youth Societies, 14
Federation of Synagogues, London, 2, 178
Federation of Women Zionists, 13, 14
Finland, 110
Finn, James, 101
Firth, R., 145 n.
Fishman, Dr, 62
Ford, P. and G., 178 n.
Frankfort-on-Main, 44, 170
Frankfurter, Felix, 155
Freedman, M., 195
friendly societies, 12 f., 168
Friends of the Art Museums of Israel, 13
Friends of the Hebrew University, 13

Index

Friends of the Midrashia, 13
furniture-making, 30, 31
Fyvel, T. R., 199 n.

Gartner, L. P., 166, 167, 170, 179 n.
Gateshead, 3, 6, 78, 79, 167; Seminary for Training of Teachers, 79
Gemeinden, Central European, 1
G.C.E. examination, 75 f.
Gertner, Levi, *91*, *184*
'ghettos', 32; 'Gilded', 103
Ginsberg, Morris, ix, *19*, *35* f., *187* f.
girls, classes for, 76
Glasgow, 3, 6, 11, 16, 32, 37 f., 63, 134; education in, 71, 76, 78 n.
Gloucester, 108
Glückel von Hameln, 94
Goitein, H., *61*
Goldbloom, J. K., 163
Golders Green, Beth Hamidrash, 62
Goldmann, Nahum, 162
Goldsmid, Col., 101
Gompertz, Lewis, 99
Gottschalk, Max, *190*
Gould, Julius, *57* f., *190*
Great Synagogue, London, 1 f.
Great Universal Stores, 27, 28
Guedalla, Philip, 108

Habonim, 14, 42, 77
Haham, 5
Hajnal, J., *131* f.
Harris, I., 111
Harrogate, 71
Hebrew, teaching methods, 88
Henriques, Sir Basil, 163
Henson, Bishop Hensley, 20
Hertz, Dr, 44, 50
Herzl, Theodor, 101, 178
Highet, J., *37* f., *58* f., *134* f., 149
Hillel Foundation, 77
Hirsch, Samson Raphael, 48, 53, 57, 63

histories, institutional, 169
history: Anglo-Jewish and English, 172; Anglo-Jewish and general Jewish, 171 f.; local, approach to, 171
Homa, Bernard, 44, *65*
Home for Aged Jews, 8
Hore Belisha, Leslie, 108
Horowitz, C. M., 115
Hoskins, W. G., 171 n., 173 n.
hospitals, 8
Hoveve Torah, 77
Hull, 2, 11
Huxley, E., 200 n.
Hyamson, A. M., 166 n.

illness, incidence of, 122
immigration, 4, 9, 13, 44, 47, 59, 62, 97, 171; from Russia, 95; reason for immigrants' choice of goal, 163; seventeenth-century, 94
India, 105, 106, 108
indifference, religious, growth of, 19 f., 42 f.
Initiation Society, 5, 118
Institute of Contemporary Jewry, 155, 189; and demography, 131; Oral History Section, 158 ff., 164; tasks, x
Institute of Jewish Studies, 14
Institute for the Study of the Jewish Question (Nazi), 183
institutions, history of, 169
integration, 23
intermarriage, 50 f., 64, 121 f., 143 f.
interrelations, business and professional, 144
Inter-University Jewish Federation, 14, 77, 90
interviewer, for oral history, selection, 162
Ireland, 115; census information, 175 n.
Israel, State of, 104; demography in, 129 f.; effect on British

Index

Israel, State of, (*cont.*)
  Jewry, 23 f.; formation of, 102 ff.; marriage rate, 120; religious orientation in, 55
Italy, 98, 108, 109; demographic records, 130; marriage statistics, 131

Jacobs, Joseph, 93, 95, 111, 121
Jacobs, Louis, 49
Jehovah's Witnesses, 59
Jenkinson, Sir H., 173 n.
Jerusalem, British Consulate, 101
Jerusalem Baby Home, 13
Jewish Agency (London), 162; Department for Education and Culture, 77
Jewish Board of Guardians, 7, 172 n.
Jewish Chronicle, 15, 21 f., 47, 49, 179, 184
Jewish Health Organization, 112
Jewish Historical Society, 14, 181
Jewish Lads' Brigade, 14
Jewish Memorial Council, 70; Library, 14
Jewish Museum, 15
Jewish Observer, 15
Jewish Orphanage, London, 8
Jewish Religious Education Board, 67
Jewish Religious Union, 3
Jewish Review, 15
Jewish Statistical Society of Great Britain, 174
Jewish Welfare Board, 7 n.
Jewish World, 179
Jewishness, non-religious, 104 f.
Jews, identification of, 24
Jews' College, 6 f., 43, 44, 62, 77; Institute for Training of Teachers, 79; Library, 14; Principalship, 49
Jews' Temporary Shelter, 9, 107
J. F. S. school, 69
Joint Palestine Appeal, 13
Journal of Jewish Studies, 14

Judith Lady Montefiore College, 78

Kadt, Emanuel de, *150, 183, 19*
Kaizer, A., *24*
Kantorowitsch, M., 112, 116
Kaplan, Mordecai M., 161
Kashrus/kashrut(h), 5 f., 48
Kashrus Commission, 5 f.
Keble, John, 53 f.
Kedassia, 6
Kessler, D., *184*
Kimche, Jon, *22, 38*
King's Lynn, 108
kinship relations, 145
Klutznick, Philip, 161
Kochan, Dr, *63*
Kol Nidrei, 52
Korzen, Meir, 160
Kosher butchers, registrations with, 115 n.
kosher meat, taxation of, 6
Kosher School Meals Service, 22
Kovno, 158
Krausz, Armin, *21, 65*
Krausz, Ernest, 138, 143, 194
Krüger, F. P., *see* Aldag, Peter

Ladino, 103
Lancaster, L., 145 n.
leadership, religious, calibre of, 52 ff.
League of Jewish Women, 14
Leeds, 3, 11, 32, 63, 99, 113, 138, 167; education in, 71, 78 n. 92; United Hebrew Congregation, 3
Leicester, 3
Leo Baeck College, 78
Leo Baeck Institute, 14
Lestschinsky, 35
Letchworth, 167
Levenberg, Dr, *23, 38* f., *64* f., *152, 182*
Levin, Dov, 158
Levin, S. S., *39* f., *61* f., *91*
Levy, Harold, 62, 123, *133* f.
'Liberal', meaning, 4

Index

Liberal Congregation, London, 3
Liberal movement, 51
libraries, 14 f.
Limerick boycott, 99
Lipset, S. M., 195
literature, Jew in, 170
Liverpool, 2, 3, 6, 11, 16, 63; education in, 71, 76, 78 n.
Livingstone, I., *24, 61*
Locker, Berl, 162
Loewe, H., 52
Loewe, Raphael, *90*
Loi Crémieux, 107
London: areas of settlement, 167; child population, 72; East End, 64, 167; history of community, 167; Jewish population, 33 n., 62, 67, 108; synagogues, 2 ff.
London Board for Jewish Religious Education, 6, 68 ff., 115; examination syllabus, 80 ff.
London Jewish Hospital, 8
Loudon, J. B., 145 n.
loyalties, conflict of, 107
Lubavitch Foundation, 70, 76
Lyons, J., & Co. Ltd., 27, 28

Magen David Adom, 13
Mahamad, 100
Maidenhead, 3
Manchester, 2, 3, 6, 11, 16, 32; education in, 71, 76, 78
Mancroft, Lord, 200
maps, 176
Marble Arch Synagogue, 47
Marcus, J. R., 174 n.
Marks & Spencer, 28
Marrano period, 94, 106
marriage: age at, 121; consanguineous, 121; statistics, 119 ff.; *see also* intermarriage
Mattuck, Israel, 61
McGregor, O. R., 145 n.
meals, Sabbath, 47
Menasseh ben Israel, 94, 96
Meyer, I. S., 168 n.

middle-class: definition of, 35; growth of Jewish, 31 f.; 'new' and 'old', 36
'middle of the road' Jews, 47 f., 65
migration, town/country, 4, 109
mikve, 60
Milan, 108
Miller, J., 198
millionaires, Jewish, 39, 43
ministers: qualifications, 44 f.; shortage of, 53; *see also* rabbis
ministry: as profession, 52 f.; study of role, 146 f.; training for, 77 f.
Mitchell, W. E., 145 n.
Mizrachi, 13, 65
Mocatta Library, 14, 191
Mohalim, and birth registration, 118
Montagu, Hon. Ewen, 47
Montagu, Samuel, 178
Montefiore, C. G., 51
Montefiore, Sir Francis, 101
Montefiore, Leonard G., 163
Montefiore, Sir Moses, 100, 101
Moslem world, Jews and, 102

Nasi, Joseph, 94
National Union of Hebrew Teachers, 15
Neustatter, H., 19, 112, 113 n., 116, 125, 138, 142 n.
Nevins, Allan, 156
Newcastle, 11, 16, 71
New Zealand, 115
Norwich, 71
Nottingham, 11, 71, 134
Nunn, G. W. A., 177 n.
Nurok, Mordecai, 162

observance, religious, trends in, 16, 41 ff.
observation, participant, 141
occupation, choice of, 30, 40
occupational distribution, 29, 124, 144, 188
old age homes, 8

Index

oral history, 155 ff.; objections to name, 182, 184
organizations: intercommunal, 100; leadership in, 145 f.; *see also* women's organizations; working-class organizations
O.R.T., 9
orthodoxy; changing pattern, 170; meaning in Britain, 57; two types, 45
O.S.E., 9
Oxford, 4; Education conference (1941), 68
Oxford Movement, 53 f.

Parkes, James, 138, *191*
Parkes Library, 14, 191
Parliament, Board of Deputies and, 10 f.
Parliamentary Papers, 178
parochialism, 151
'passing', 150
Pentecostalists, 59
Penzance, 2, 108
periodicals, 179 f.
Pevsner, N., 170
Pioneer Women of Great Britain, 14
Plymouth, 2
Poland, 104, 160
population: estimation of, 114 ff.; indications of decline, 125; Jewish, in United Kingdom, 2, 67, 120 f.; need for research, 187; *see also* child population; London
Portsmouth, 4, 71
Portugal, 110
Prague, expulsion of Jews from, 101
Prais, S., *37, 89* f.
Press: Jewish, 15 f., *see also* periodicals; Yiddish, 24
professions, Jews in, 29
progressive Judaism, development, 50 ff.; and orthodox, 51 ff.; *see also* Liberal; Reform

proletariat, Jewish, disappearance, 103
provinces, synagogues, 2, 3 f.
Public Record Office, 178

questionnaires, 140; for oral history recording, 157

Rabbinical Diploma class, 44
rabbis; change in character, 46; *see also* ministers
Rachman, P., 200
Ramsgate, 3
rate books, 179
'Reform', meaning, 4
Reform Congregation, London, 3
Reform movement, 51
Reform Synagogues of Great Britain, 3
refugees: British response to, 163; *see also* immigration
Reinhart, Rabbi, 43
Reissman, Leonard, *149*
relief, organizations, 8 f.
religious thought, history, 169 f.
Representative Councils, provincial, 11
research: co-ordination in sociological, 147
research workers, training, 190
Richardson, M., *64, 183*
Ringelblum, Emmanuel, 158
Riverton study, 58
Rollin, A. R., 173 n.
Roman Catholics, 42, 59
Rome, 108
Rosenbaum (Rowson), S., 111, 116
Rosenberg, L., 120
Rosette, Moshe, 162
Roth, Cecil, *24, 37, 59* f., 138, 166, 197 f.
Roth, S. J., *24, 134*
Rothschild, 1st Baron, 101
Rothschild, Lionel de, 100
Rubens, A., 177 n.
Ruppin, A., 112, 120, 122

Index

Russia, 95, 104; material in archives, 161; secularization of Jews in, 102

Sabbath Observance Employment Bureau, 30
St James',s Duke's Place, London, 175 n.
Salford, 3
Samuel, 1st Viscount, 98
Saron, Gus, 162
Schechter, Solomon, 53 and n.
Schonfeld, Dr, 44
school attendances, and population, 115
School Certificate Examination, 75; syllabus, 83 ff.
schools, 7, 44, 45, 63, 67 ff.; day, 76, 88; London, 69; population, 68; secondary, 76, 91; ultra-orthodox, 46; *see also* education
Scotland, 38
Sears Holdings, 27, 28
secularization, trend towards, 105
self-employment, 28 f., 36
Sephardi synagogues, 3, 5
Sephardim, change in position of, 106
sex ratio, at birth, 118
Shaw, Henry, *40*, *63* f.
Shechita, 5
Shechita Boards, National Council of, 5
Sheffield, 11; education, 71
Shochetim, licensing of, 5
Shomerim, 6
Simpson, W. W., *40*
Sinclair, Sir John, 38
Sklare M., 58 n.
Slater, E., 121
Slaughter of Animals Act (1933), 5
slavery, England and, 99
Slovakia, partisan movement, 161
'small town' communities, 108, 109
Smith, Goldwin, 99

Smith, H. Llewellyn, 116
socialism, 95
Society for the Demography and Statistics of the Jews, 131
Society for Jewish Statistics, 111
sociology: methods of inquiry, 140 ff.; resistance to, 140; state of, 138 f.
sources, historical, 173 ff.
Southend, 3, 71, 167
Southport, 3, 167
South Wales riots (1903, 1911), 99
Spain, refugees in, 161
Spanish and Portuguese Congregation, London, 1, 3
Spengler, Oswald, 105
statistics: for Anglo-Jewry, history, 174 f.; need of, 66, 112, 142 ff.; unsatisfactory character, 127
Stein, Leonard, *23*, 170
Steinberg, Dr, *89*, *181*
Strasbourg, 108
Strizower, Miss S., *62* f., *149* f.
students: courses for, 77; university, 90
suburbs: move to, 31 f., 37 f.; need of community study, 167
Sunderland, 3, 6, 71, 78, 167
Swansea, 2
Sweden, 110
Switzerland, 110, 134
synagogues: average membership, 124; British, 1 ff.; function of, 20 f.; growth in number, 19; histories of, 169; importance of, 19, 188; membership, statistics, 61; number registered, 124; 'return to', 20

tailoring, *see* clothing industry
Talmud Torahs, fall in enrolments, 124 n.
Talmud Torah Trust, 67
taxation, special, absence in England, 96

216

Index

teachers, number, 78; training, 77, 79
Teachers' College, need of, 79
Teicher, Dr, *184*
textbooks, educational, 80
theology, 60
Trachtenberg, H. L., 112, 116, 117
trade unions, Jews and, 31, 40, 95, 168
Trieste, 122
Troyes, 109
Turin, 108
Tur-Sinai, N. H., 161

Uganda scheme, 102
Union of Hebrew and Religion Classes, 67
Union of Jewish Women, 14
Union of Liberal and Progressive Synagogues, 3, 70
Union of Maccabi Associations, 14
Union of Orthodox Hebrew Congregations, 2, 3, 62
U.S.S.R., *see* Russia
Unitarianism, 98
United Kingdom, Jewish population, 67; *see also* population
United States: collection of demographic data, 130; Jewish history in, 171; position of Jews in, 97; religion and census, 115; 'return to synagogues', 20; schoolchildren, 123; surveys on religious behaviour, 58
United Synagogue, London, 2, 47 n., 169, 170
Universitas Judeorum Anglie, 100
universities, Hebrew studies, 78
university students: accommodation for, 21; conversionism among, 43

Van der Zyl, Dr, *64*
Voice of Jacob, The, 179
Vosk, M., 58 n.

Waley Cohen, Sir Robert, 44, 199
Ward, Wilfred, 53 f.
Webb, Beatrice (Lady Passfield), 178
Webber, George, *59*
Weinberg, Gerhard L., 156
Weinryb, B., 171 n.
West London Synagogue of British Jews, 3
White, Arnold, 99
Whitehall Conference, 96
Wiener Library, 14, 158, 174, 187
Wigram, Lionel, 99
Wigram, Maurice, 99
withdrawal classes, 75
Wolf, Lucien, 94
Wolfe, Humbert, 61
Wolfson, Sir Isaac, 47, 199
women, employment of, 29
Women's Mizrachi Organization, 14
women's organizations, 14
working class, Jewish, 30 f., 37, 39
working-class organizations, 168 f.
written material, reduction in, 159

Yad Washem, 158
Yarmouth, 108
Yavneh, 77
Yeshivot(h), 6, 44, 62 f.; number of students, 78
Yesodey Hatorah, 76
Yiddish, 23, 76; decline of, 102
YIVO institute, 174, 182
'Yom Kippur Method', 115, 123
York, 71
youth, religious trends among, 63
'youth culture', 145
youth movements, 13 f., 44
youth organizations, 90 f.
youth study groups, 77

Zangwill, Israel, 46, 101
Zionism, 13, 14, 22, 52, 64 f., 77, 170; Britain and, 101 f., 163
Zionist Federation, 13, 44
Zuckerman, Baruch, 162

For Product Safety Concerns and Information please contact our EU representative GPSR@taylorandfrancis.com
Taylor & Francis Verlag GmbH, Kaufingerstraße 24, 80331 München, Germany

www.ingramcontent.com/pod-product-compliance
Lightning Source LLC
Chambersburg PA
CBHW052106300426
44116CB00010B/1557